T0083498

VĚRA SOKOLOVÁ

QUEER ENCOUNTERS WITH COMMUNIST POWER:
Non-Heterosexual Lives
and the State
in Czechoslovakia, 1948–1989

CHARLES UNIVERSITY
KAROLINUM PRESS 2021

KAROLINUM PRESS
Karolinum Press is a publishing department of Charles University
Ovocný trh 560/5, 116 36 Prague 1, Czech Republic
www.karolinum.cz

Cover and graphic design by Jan Šerých
Set and printed in the Czech Republic by Karolinum Press
First edition

This publication was supported by the Czech Ministry of Education,
Youth and Sports — Institutional Support for Longterm Development
of Research Organizations (2021) — Charles University, Faculty of Humanities,
Programme Progres Q20 "Culture and Society."

Cataloguing-in-Publication Data is available from the National Library
of the Czech Republic

ISBN 978-80-246-4266-6
ISBN 978-80-246-4322-9 (pdf)

CONTENTS

To Sebastian, Toby, and Kaisa —
Have the courage to live the life you desire.

CHAPTER 1
INTRODUCTION

PROLOGUE

Eva was born in 1952, during the dark years of Stalinism. Her family owned a modest house in the Motol neighbourhood of Prague, the capital city of then Communist Czechoslovakia, where she lived with her mother, father and an older brother. Despite the fact that she grew up in the height of the Cold War, she recalls her childhood as "happy and uneventful."[1] Since her early years, Eva "felt more like a boy" and was also "very strongly attracted to women." In 1963, when she was eleven, she went through, what she recalled, "a decisive moment of my life because I was visited by Jesus." Very young, and completely on her own, living in the most atheist country in Europe, enhanced by the recent destruction of all religious institutional life by order of the Czechoslovak Communist Party, Eva became, in her own words, "deeply religious." Neither her parents nor her brother believed in God, she could not join the church or attend any religious services. She practiced her faith alone in her own private way, believing that "God and Jesus are guiding all my steps — from that moment on, for the rest of my life."

Already as a small child, Eva exhibited great talent for the visual arts and spent a lot of time outside painting nature and animals. Later on, she enriched these themes with religious motifs and her painting became an interesting mixture of landscape art, Christianity, anatomy, and humanism. Despite this rather surrealist portfolio, she was accepted to the prestigious and highly competitive Hollar Art School in Prague. Or maybe, she was accepted because of that mix since she submitted her application during the rebellious and hopeful days of the Prague Spring of 1968. Eva loved her years at "Hollarka" where she "could get lost in my own world and no one cared how weird I was because all artists are fucked up." The careless and happy school days, however, had their somber side. After coming home from school, Eva would walk up to the attic of their house and lock herself up. "I stripped

---

[1] The list of biographical interviews and the dates when they were carried out is included in the bibliography section of this book. Names of all narrators were changed to retain their anonymity. The queer oral history project, which forms the foundation of this book is explained in detail in chapter two.

myself half naked and whipped myself bloody for being a lesbian." Under the watchful eye of the atheist, heteronormative and collectivist Communist state, during the early years of the tough Normalization era, in the privacy of her home and soul, young Eva fought her own highly individualized and secret battles of reconciling her belief in God with her homosexuality. Unlike most of my other narrators, who shared with me their lives from Communist Czechoslovakia, Eva had no problem identifying as a lesbian. On the other hand, most of her life she struggled with harmonizing her openly embraced lesbian identity with her secretly chosen religious identity. The collapse of communism in Eastern Europe in 1989 was a liberating moment for her not because of her homosexuality but because "for the first time in my life, I could openly admit I'm a believer."

In 1974, Eva was admitted to the prestigious Academy of Fine Arts in Prague, where she began to study painting. Young and vivacious, she lived openly and her sex life was quite wild. In college and in the social circles she moved around in the mid 1970s, "everyone knew that I was into women." At the same time, no one knew about her religiousness. She carefully separated her religious and sexual lives and guarded the secrecy of her religious beliefs because "faith was too fragile to talk about." Her inability to reconcile both aspects of her identity gradually led to a "strange schizophrenia"; on the one hand she became an alcoholic and enjoyed "wild anonymous sex in public toilets with other women" and, on the other hand, she "prayed to God for mercy." In 1980, when she graduated from the Art Academy, she had "such problems with drinking and mental stuff" that instead of becoming a respected painter she received a disability pension, which remained her only source of regular income through the rest of the Communist period. As will be clear later in the book, it is significant that the doctors who helped Eva receive the disability support were sexologists from the Sexological Institute in Prague, to whom she "came for help with my drinking" and that the reason why Eva went to this institute to solve her alcoholism was because "my queer friends told me that those guys will certainly help me."

At nights, Eva spent a lot of time in the (unofficial) gay bars monitored by the State Secret Police (StB), such as the *T-Club*, *U Petra Voka* or *Špejchar*. In the *T-Club* on Jungmann Square she even had her own table close to the band, where she would "sit and paint all night, walking home at 4am all the way to Motol. Those were magical nights and such great years." Eva remembers the last two decades of Czechoslovak communism during the 1970s and 1980s as "the best time of my life." During these years, she had numerous relationships with women, often "only for sex," but never engaged in a single relationship with a man. "Men repulsed me because I always felt like a guy myself. I always loved women." This, Eva recalled, was also the main reason why she never had any children. Even though she "now regrets a bit" this decision, she "never wanted to have children in [her] life" and "as a principle went out only with women who were childless." Eva found many of the women she dated through personal ads, which she regularly read, answered and placed in the officially sanctioned state newspapers.

Eva met her "most significant lover before 1989," a chemical engineer Helen, through a personal ad in the newspaper *Lidová demokracie*. Eva reminisced that Helen was her "femme fatale" and they had a wonderful, loving, beautiful relationship "full of love and sex." They lived together, "Helen looked all day long into a microscope and I painted." In their free time, they visited exhibitions, art shows and walked their two German shepherd dogs. The only problem in what seemed to be an idyllic relationship was that Helen was not religious. In 1984, Eva joined the Jehovah's Witnesses, who secretly met in home apartments and studied the Bible together. Longing "to find the Truth," Eva was soon "completely engulfed" in the Jehovah's Witnesses teachings. Since "the Witnesses preached that homosexuality was in direct contradiction with the teaching of Christ," Eva decided to leave Helen in order to "become closer to God." Retrospectively, she evaluated this decision as "the biggest mistake of my life." Her relationship with Jehovah's Witnesses did not last either. In 1987, she decided to leave their community because she could no longer stand Jehovah's Witnesses strict dress-code, requiring all women to wear only long skirts.

Miriam was born in June 1945, "christened by the Vltava river and joy from the war's end." Miriam's family lived harmoniously in a small apartment in Prague, which her father obtained with help from his boss during the war. In 1952 the time came to return the favor. Miriam's father helped his boss escape from Czechoslovakia to the West, for which he was sentenced to six and a half years in jail. Her father's imprisonment deeply affected Miriam because "it destroyed our family happiness. This guy [the boss] created a huge conspiracy around his escape. My dad's role was to go to Slovakia, travel around the Tatra Mountains and buy postcards there. He brought them back, the boss wrote them all up and when he was emigrating, he sent another person back to Slovakia to keep sending these postcards back as though he was on vacation. Twenty-nine people were involved in this scheme, including my dad. One day, dad went for some training to Kaplice and never came back. Seven guys came to our apartment instead. They destroyed the whole place because they were looking for the list of those twenty-nine people and unfortunately, they found it among our books... Because of such stupidity, because of one rich guy, my dad was jailed." Fortunately, Miriam continued, "President Zápotocký pardoned him so he came back in three and half years" but his health was broken and he died relatively young from lung cancer.

From these miserable times, Miriam recalled "one great memory of a wonderful StB officer" working in the prison, Hugo, who helped her mother and the girls to see their father more often and for much longer than officially allowed. Miriam didn't know why Hugo helped them but concluded that perhaps it was because he also had two children. Miriam recalled that "Hugo was even giving us Christmas presents from dad — of course dad had to pay for them but Hugo would make sure we got them." According to Miriam, her father and Hugo became life-long friends in the prison, visiting and writing to each other, and "Hugo even came to dad's funeral in 1981." It was because of all these "good deeds" from Hugo and Antonín Zápotocký (the second Communist president of Czechoslovakia), as well as due to assigning the blame for her father's imprisonment not to the Communist regime itself but to "the rich guy who emigrated," that Miriam had a paradoxically positive view of the Communist Party. She joined it in 1966, at the age of 22, and remained a loyal Communist Party member until 1989.

Already as a little girl, Miriam "dressed up like a tomboy and enjoyed boy's games." Her father's name was Pavel, but the whole family, including Miriam and her older sister, called him the female version of that name, "Pavla." Miriam insists that it had "absolutely no connection to being feminine even though it was a bit strange." Since she was "very little," Miriam "knew she was into girls" but she never discussed these feelings with anyone. Her platonic lovers were always girls, never boys, but she "had absolutely no idea that anything like 'that' [homosexuality] existed." During the interviews, Miriam resisted assigning any named identity to herself, claiming that she is "not into categories, then or now." Her aunt, her father's sister, however, "was a lesbian." Interestingly, Miriam explicitly talked about her aunt as being a 'lesbian' (*lesbička*), even though her aunt apparently never openly identified herself this way. Miriam said that she simply "connected the dots." Her aunt had been married a long time ago but then got divorced and "lived together with her girlfriend ever since." Miriam's family visited them occasionally in their apartment at Kampa but Miriam's mother "avoided inviting them over to our place as much as possible."

Because of her father's imprisonment, Miriam was prohibited from entering a regular high school and had to go to a two-year technical training school (*technické učiliště*). She was surrounded by boys, being one of only two girls in the entire school. Since Miriam felt like a boy herself, she concluded that "naturally, I was good at technical subjects." She excelled and after ending her first year with straight As, she was allowed to transfer to a better school. There Miriam joined a drama club and at one poetry competition she met her first husband, a waiter from the town of Písek. He was 15 years her senior, was "completely obviously gay" and according to Miriam they "immediately fell for each other because, you know, 'we' [homosexuals] recognize each other among other people." She married him four years later, in 1967, because he needed a visa to emigrate to West Germany and she, in turn, desperately wanted his apartment in Prague because she "was terribly in love with one beautiful woman, unfortunately a married one with a little child," and needed a place to meet with her. Because Miriam was already a member of the Communist Party, and because it was during the reformist late-1960s, her husband obtained a West German visa without a problem. His emigration came as a shock to her parents but Miriam explained to them that "it's totally fine because I got the apartment." She filed for divorce and started to secretly date her beloved married girlfriend with a child. None of Miriam's relationships with women, in fact, were ever openly admitted, neither before 1989 nor after. According to Miriam, it was "something that I think should stay hidden and private."

In 1972, Miriam married again. Her second husband and his large family were all active in water sports in the Prague neighborhood of Podolí. Miriam joined the group, had "a great time, really enjoyed the whole thing," became a coach for little kids and also worked as a referee for water slalom. She "especially liked his mom, my future mother-in-law." When Miriam was alone with her husband, "when we were together at holidays, he was great. I really loved him." But back at home, in a huge villa house in Podolí, where the whole extended family lived, "everything was decided by the mother in a big family meeting around a big round table." Gradually, Miriam started to resent not having any power over her personal life. She even became pregnant in her second marriage, but her husband and his mother "were not particularly crazy about a child" so she had an abortion. She shared that it's the only decision in her life that she regrets. In 1978, she got divorced for the second time and started to work in the Complaints Department of the State Gas company. She loved that job "because finally I could help somebody." Soon after, she met Vendulka with whom she spent "eleven wonderful years." They never lived together but it was "a great, exciting relationship." All her life, Miriam lived only in monogamous relationships, with both men and women. Before 1989 she never visited any 'gay' or 'homosexual' club or bar, nor looked for any community or "homosexual socializing," because as she said, it was not "her scene." Miriam never told her parents about Vendulka but she was "convinced that they both must have known. I was with Vendulka all those years. Vendulka was a nurse and so she also helped me with both of my parents in their old age."

Heda, the oldest narrator in this book, was born in 1929 in Brno. Her mother was a nurse and in 1935 got a decently-paid position and an apartment in the former "Masaryk Homes," today's Thomayer Hospital in Prague, where Heda moved with her mother and grandmother. Heda's father was a doctor but he did not move with the family, nor ever expressed any further interest in Heda. Heda went to an elite French high school, admired "Masaryk's democratic ideals," was well read in "Western philosophers," spoke fluently several foreign languages, and devoted her life to academic work at the Czechoslovak Academy of Sciences. Heda never joined the Communist party and was open about being a practicing Evangelical Christian.

Heda considered herself to be "transsexual from year zero" and felt that she was forced into the category of a woman "by social conventions." Her grandmother pressured her towards conventional women's behavior and dress, but fortunately her "mother was reasonable and let me be." In 1952, she was briefly married to her colleague, a mathematician, "to please her mom" but she did not consider the marriage a significant chapter of her life. She divorced rather quickly and for the rest of her life had short-term and long-term relationships only with women, adding that she was "always the man in the relationship." With quite a few of her girlfriends, however, she was not sure whether she was in a relationship or not because she "was not able to arrive at a stable definition of what constitutes a relationship." She experienced this difficulty, for example, while on a post-doc in Budapest in 1954. With her "girlfriend," she would often meet, talk, go for coffee; they would walk along the Danube hand in hand, study in the library together, "look each other in the eye for a long time. I think we both knew something was there but neither of us said it out loud. I really loved her. She was a beautiful, sharp, smart, redhead from Yugoslavia. We were on the same fellowship and spent two years together. Every day together, holding each other, kissing, cuddling. But we never had sex together... Hmm, too bad that it didn't work out. So I don't know, you tell me, does this count as a relationship or not?"

Heda came back to Prague in 1956, "just before the Hungarian uprising so that I could not even entertain the sinful thought of emigrating because I was no longer there." At a mandatory public meeting at the Academy of Sciences she refused to denounce the Hungarian Revolution. On the contrary, she stood up and openly supported it by saying that the "Hungarian working class was doing the right thing." She expected to get fired and imprisoned for that statement but she was "only taken out of the spotlight and moved to the archive of the Academy." But she was no longer allowed to travel, "not even to Poland. I could only visit Bulgaria so I concentrated [academically] on that [topic and context]." This event, in her own words, destroyed her professional and private life as she was "blacklisted forever." Heda evaluated the Communist past overall as "bad" but never felt "discriminated against for [her] sexuality." She did feel immensely persecuted before 1989 but "only for her political beliefs." Even when she was repeatedly harassed by StB agents for sitting on a park bench with a woman, she interpreted these confrontations as a consequence of her political blacklisting, "using alleged 'homosexuality' only as a pretense."

Heda's common explanation for a variety of situations in both biographical interviews I conducted with her was, "it was that Hungary again."

The two most important things in Heda's life were "work and faith." She led a quiet, modest and pious life, in her own words, "a boring life not worth mentioning." She never wanted to have children and did not attend bars or clubs. She loved technology and repair work and her only "extravagant pleasure" was ownership of a motorcycle, which she bought in 1963 and "rode for many years." She would usually meet her girlfriends in libraries or through same-sex ads placed in newspapers, which she "read with pleasure since the 1960s." Heda, however, never placed any ads herself. She only answered them because it felt "more natural that way." In our interviews she avoided any identification with the categories of 'lesbian' and 'homosexual.' But not because she would not have same-sex desires; in fact, she openly said several times that she "loves women" but she "was never sure whether I was a man or a woman." While Heda never officially challenged her sex-assignment as "female" nor felt any desires to surgically change her biological body, in the interview she firmly said that "I believe I am a transsexual. I have a female body but I feel like a man. I can't really explain this to anyone around me, but I think they wonder too." Heda died shortly after completing our second biographical interview at the age of 83. Close to three hundred people, both from the Czech Academy of Sciences and the Czech gay and lesbian community, attended her funeral held at an Evangelical Church in Prague.

ARGUMENT

Eva, Miriam, and Heda's biographical sketches serve as a fitting prologue to this book. Their complex self-understanding and unexpected trajectories reflect well the diversity of queer lives during the four decades of state socialism in Czechoslovakia and demonstrate why oral history is a valuable method for amending the dominant historiography of sexuality and state socialism. The recollections of queer people of their experiences and encounters with the Czechoslovak Socialist state, its employees and institutions at various contexts and levels of power, full of seeming contradictions, unanticipated empathy, and surprising decision making, provide remarkable opportunities for exploring and reconsidering the functionings of the Communist state and its approaches to homosexuality and non-heterosexual identities in the four decades of its existence.[2]

---

2   In this book, I use several different terms, such as 'queer,' 'non-heterosexual,' 'homosexual,' 'lesbian,' 'gay,' 'gay and lesbian.' The terminology is strictly historically contextual and is discussed at length in the end of the introduction.

This book, building on a wealth of archival sources and oral history, offers a new look at the history of sexuality in Communist Czechoslovakia. The life stories and experiences collected and analyzed in the following pages both supplement and challenge mainstream historical narratives about 'gays' and 'lesbians' during the Communist era. The book argues, in the first place, that queer people were themselves fundamentally diverse — in their discovery of their sexual identities, in their personal relationships, and in their relation to the state. During the Communist period, queer people did not use the terms 'lesbian,' 'gay,' 'transgender' or even 'homosexual' to describe themselves; they adopted these identity categories (or were attached to them) only after 1989. Rather than analyze a 'gay and lesbian history' that is readily identifiable from the categories of the present, this book aims to understand how Czechoslovak people, especially women, during the Communist period discovered that they were not heterosexual, how they described their experiences and passions in the terms they used in the past, and how the context of the Communist regime shaped their identities, choices and life strategies. Second, the book also argues that queer people were not necessarily 'victims' of the Communist regime. It is relatively commonplace to find historical narratives that treat queer people as victims of a regime that targeted them as sick and abberant. But narratives that divide historical agency into perpetration and victimhood often simplify how the exercise of power worked in practice and, above all, underestimate the agency of queer people to find their own ways to lead full and enriching lives. For example, the book challenges the predominant interpretation of Socialist sexological discourse as a heteronormative arm of the state, which worked to discriminate against homosexuals by defining them as 'deviant.' As will become apparent, the relationship between 'sexology' and the 'state' was never that of complete authoritarian power or ideological control, because sexologists exercised a great deal of agency in their descriptions and treatments of queer people that often served to empower and inspire them, not suppress them. By uncovering the dynamics between sexologists and queer people at the micro-level of everyday life, this book seeks to challenge both the myth that there was such a thing as a homogenous homosexual subjectivity and that queer people were victims of the authoritarian regime.

It may seem surprising that the Czechoslovak Communist regime, despite its brutality in many areas of life, never enacted a hateful or seditious campaign against homosexuality and queer people. Quite to the contrary, when we look at its laws on sexuality from a historical perspective, Communist legislation was not only more lenient in comparison to previous imperial, interwar, and Nazi legal codes, but the institutional discourse of sexuality in some ways provided an even more complex and emancipated context for non-heretosexual sexuality than what was legally possible in the democratic

West.[3] That certainly does not mean that homosexuality in Socialist Czecho-slovakia was accepted with open arms as a sexual orientation equal with heterosexuality. The Communist Party of Czechoslovakia of course did not support diversity and feared identities that questioned the ideological foun-dations of state socialism. In this sense, however, the repressive elements of the regime did not persecute homosexuals and transsexuals any more than, for example, hippies, rockers, or the religious. There is no inevitable logic in this reluctant behavior of the regime towards homosexual people and it is not entirely clear why the regime did not actively persecute gays and lesbians in similar ways it did some other groups. The regulation of sexuality in So-cialist Czechoslovakia also has to be placed in the context of the effort of the Communist Party to maintain the monopoly on power it gained in 1948 and which was manifested in the repression of private ownership and various civic and individual rights.[4] Historically rooted homophobic sentiments of mainstream society thus blended together with the systematic destruction of freedoms and individuality, affecting all people regardless of their sexual orientation.

In considering the degree to which queer people were repressed, it is important to ask, *who* or *what* actors and institutions are referred to by the terms 'state power' or 'Communist regime.' Despite only one ideological par-ty-line and the existence of a single party-state, there was never only one supreme or omnipotent 'power' in Communist Czechoslovakia. The 'regime' was a conglomerate of diverse institutions, expert discourses and individual actors that exercised their power and ideas about social discipline, political loyalty, need for repression or benevolence in quite different ways. In the context of the state approach to (homo)sexuality and queer people, other conditions were equally significant, such as laws regulating the criminaliza-tion and medicalization of homosexuality and transsexuality; attitudes of the

---

3   Jan Seidl, *Od žaláře k oltáři: homosexualita v českých zemích 1878–2006* (Praha: Academia, 2012); Roman Kuhar and Judit Takács, eds., *Beyond the Pink Curtain: Everyday Life of LGBT People in East-ern Europe* (Ljubljana: Mirovni Inštitut, 2007); Jiří Fanel, *Gay historie* (Praha: Dauphin, 2000); Leila Rupp, *A Desired Past: A Short History of Same-Sex Sexuality in America* (Chicago: University of Chicago Press, 1999); Margot Canaday, *The Straight State: Sexuality and Citizenship in Twenti-eth-Century America* (Princeton: Princeton University Press, 2011); Richard Green and Donald James West, eds., *Sociolegal Control of Homosexuality: A Multi-nation Comparison* (New York: Ple-num Press, 1997); John D'Emilio and Estelle B. Freedman, *Intimate Matters: A History of Sexual-ity in America* (New York: Harper and Row, 1988); Ann Snitow, Christine Stansell and Sharon Thompson, eds., *Powers of Desire: The Politics of Sexuality* (New York: Monthly Review Press, 1983); Josef Košela, *Homosexualita a její trestnost* (Diplomová práce. Brno: Univerzita Jana Evan-gelisty Purkyně, Právnická fakulta, 1981); Neil, Miller, *Out of the Past. Gay and Lesbian History from 1869 to the Present* (Boston: Alyson Books, 2006).

4   Libora Oates-Indruchová, "The Beauty and the Loser: Cultural Representations of Gender in Late State Socialism," *Signs* 37/2 (2012): 357–383; Karel Kaplan, *The Communist Party in Power: A Profile of Party Politics in Czechoslovakia* (Boulder and London: Westview Press, 1987).

police (both public and secret), educational and health institutions; the role of publishing houses; and at the end of the imaginary chain of power, the attitudes of supervisors and other superiors in a variety of jobs and offices. In all these contexts there were concrete people who, in spite of the censorship and single-party rule, had enough discursive space to understand the official approach to homosexuality and queer people in their own way. They often possessed the courage to apply their understanding of state directives in ways which they personally considered right, appropriate, or pragmatic in the given context. It is probably not surprising that such individualized attitudes and behavior dramatically differed from each other and sometimes were in direct opposition to official positions on homosexuality. In other words, even though an emphasis on the institutional dimension of power is fundamental for understanding how the Communist regime functioned, an excessive adherence to the institutionalized conception of power can easily ignore other possible historical narratives and explanations of life at the time.[5]

For example, as some previous studies indicated, queer people in Socialist Czechoslovakia had a powerful, even if rather invisible ally: Czechoslovak sexology and sexologists who played an important, and mainly positive, role in the process of decriminalizing homosexuality in the late 1950s and early 1960s.[6] While acknowledging this positive influence, most studies by historians examining Czechoslovak sexology have placed emphasis on the represive aspects of the sexological discourse, which through its authority defined homosexuality as a perversion and disease. Historian Josef Řídký and sociologist Kateřina Lišková both analyzed the process in which the heteronormative definition of the 'homosexual' subject was constructed, even though they examined different time periods and different source materials. Řídký focused on the popular sexological self-help literature during the interwar period, while Lišková studied broadly the entire discourse on sexuality and the "science of desire" during the period of state socialism. Performing deconstructive discursive analyses of sexological definitions and arguments — and taking the texts at face value — they both concluded that Czechoslovak sexology played a pivotal role in creating the category of a 'deviant' and 'perverted' homosexual, who was inhibited from forming a positive sexual identity and leading a satisfied and happy life.[7]

5   Vera Sokolova, *The cultural politics of ethnicity: discourses on Roma in Communist Czechoslovakia* (Stuttgart: *ibidem*-Verlag, 2008), 44–54.

6   Seidl 2012; Jiří Hromada, *Zakladatelé: Cesta za rovnoprávností českých gayů a lesbiček.* http://gay .iniciativa.cz/www/index.php?page=clanek&id=266 (2000); Ivo Procházka, "Czech and Slovak Republics." In *Sociolegal Control of Homosexuality: a multi-nation comparison*, edited by Donald James West and Richard Green (New York: Plenum Press, 1997), 243–254.

7   Kateřina Lišková, *Sexual Liberation, Socialist Style: Communist Czechoslovakia and the Science of Desire, 1945-1989* (Cambridge: Cambridge University Press, 2018). In the book, Lišková formulates this argument in a more complex way, which is a significant departure from her earlier

This book argues, to the contrary, that Czech and Slovak sexologists in their scholarship espoused complex and diplomatic attitudes towards homosexuality and non-heterosexual behavior, from which it often was not easy to discern whether they were a prolonged arm of the officially sanctioned heteronormative system, or its critics. Both the archival sources and the oral history narratives collected in this book suggest that the science of sexology and sexologists themselves played an influential role in gradually improving not only the state's treatment and attitudes towards homosexuality and 'homosexuals,' but, perhaps more importantly, also the self-perceptions and self-worth of gay men and lesbian women in Communist Czechoslovakia. With a bit of exaggeration, one can argue that since the late 1970s some sexological offices became the first gay clubs in Czechoslovakia. Medical doctors — as trusted expert-messengers of the official normative doctrines — contributed through their scientific writings to the creation of an unexpectedly open and complex framework for understanding and living out one's queer subjectivity. Indeed, this book goes beyond the existing research on the everyday lives of 'homosexual' people during the Communist period — research that focused primarily on the conditions and lifestyles of gay men.[8] Instead, the following chapters bring forth mainly the points of view of broadly defined queer women (lesbian, bisexual, transsexual, intersexual, and transgender). In its broader scope, the queer oral history project uncovers testimonies and experiences, which challenge the male-female and hetero-homo dualisms and provide evidence that even though such categories were not explicitly articulated during the Communist period, they existed and were lived.

Eastern Europe between 1945 and 1989 had in many ways more tolerant laws about homosexuality than the democratic West.[9] While some Socialist countries had strong anti-homosexual legislation (especially Romania, USSR,

---

articulations of this topic, as for example, in her article "Perverzní sex a normální gender. Normalizační sexuologie promlouvá o sexu a gender," *Gender, rovné příležitosti, výzkum* 13/2 (2012): 40–49; Josef Řídký, "'Neexistuje dobře přizpůsobený a šťastný homosexuál.' Pozice homosexuality v českých populárně sexuologických příručkách 30.–90. let 20. století." In *"Miluji tvory svého pohlaví': Homosexualita v dějinách a společnosti českých zemí*, edited by Pavel Himl, Jan Seidl, and Franz Schindler (Praha: Argo, 2013).

8   Jürgen Lemke, *Gay voices from East Germany* (Bloomington: Indiana University Press 1991); Fanel 2000; Radek Miřácký, *Proces coming-outu u homosexuálních mužů v Československu před rokem 1989*. Bakalářská práce. (Praha: Fakulta humanitních studií, 2009); Schindler 2013. A notable exception to this trend is the work of Francesca Stella on Soviet and Post-Soviet Russia (2015), discussed in the next chapter.

9   Margot Canaday, for example, in her pioneering study *The Straight State: Sexuality and Citizenship in Twentieth-Century America* reveals how systematically the United States penalized homosexuality and excluded many gays and lesbians (especially incoming immigrants) from full-fledged citizenship. Canaday argues that the opression of gays and lesbians in the United States in the 1950s was not a sudden abberation but rather the culmination of a long and persistent heteronormative state-building process.

and Cuba),[10] in most Socialist countries anti-homosexual laws became increasingly progressive over the decades.[11] In fact, the GDR, Czechoslovakia, Bulgaria, and Hungary gradually decriminalized consensual adult homosexuality in its entirety.[12] At the same time, the "absence of a commercial homosexual subculture" paralyzed any ability to create substantial alternative spaces that were common in the 'open' West.[13] In other words, for general ideological reasons, Socialist societies were unable to translate legislative advantages into the real-life advantages of more visibility or the development of subcultures and vibrant communal spaces for gays and lesbians. Gert Hekma, a Dutch historian and sociologist, provocatively argued that "Communist states were largely organized along homosocial lines, always an interesting playground for homosexual desires."[14] Along with other scholars, Hekma has pointed out that the specific patriarchal circumstances of Communist societies provided much larger spaces for subversion than is commonly believed. Slavoj Žižek similarly argues that, contrary to expectations, coercive socio-political contexts often offer more opportunities for transgressing normative borders than politically free environments because it is much harder for both the public and the state to "imagine beyond" such borders.[15] This thesis was applied and substantiated by historians studying queer lives in clearly defined and sexually restrictive historical contexts, as well as by the queer of color critique, which expands queer politics by situating transgressions within an intersectional framework.[16] Drawing on this literature and evidence from

---

10   Dan Healey, *Homosexual Desire in Revolutionary Russia: The Regulation of Sexual and Gender Dissent* (Chicago: University of Chicago Press, 2001); Laura Essig, *Queer in Russia* (Durham: Duke University Press, 1996); Marvin Leiner, *Sexual Politics in Cuba: Machismo, Homosexuality and AIDS* (Boulder: Westview Press, 1994); Lucian Turcescu and Lavinia Stan, "Religion, Sexuality and Politics in Romania," in *Europe-Asia Studies* 57:2 (3005): 291-310; Erin K. Biebuyck, "The Collectivisation of Pleasure: Normative Sexuality in Post-1966 Romania," *Aspasia* 4 (2010): 49-70; Luis Salas, *Social Control and Deviance in Cuba* (Westport, Praeger Publishers, 1979).

11   Richard Green and Donald James West, eds., *Sociolegal Control of Homosexuality: A Multi-nation Comparison* (New York: Plenum Press, 1997); Antonín Brzek and Slavomil Hubálek, "Homosexuals in Eastern Europe: mental health and psychotherapy issues." *Journal of Homosexuality* 15/1-2 (1988): 153-162.

12   Seidl 2012; Samirah Kenawi, *Frauengruppen in der DDR der 80er Jahre. Eine Dokumentation* (Berlin: GrauZone, 1995); Gudrun Hauer, Doris Hauberger, Helga Pankratz and Hans Vonk, *Rosa Liebe unterm roten Stern. Zur Lage der Lesben und Schwulen in Osteuropa* (Vienna: HOSI Wien and Christiane Gemballa Verlag, 1986); Monika Pisankaneva, "The Forbidden Fruit: Sexuality in Communist Bulgaria." *E-magazine LiterNet* 68/7 (2005): 1-10; Fanel 2000.

13   Frédéric Jörgens, "East" Berlin: Lesbian and Gay Narratives on Everyday Life, Social Acceptance, and Past and Present. *Beyond the Pink Curtain: Everyday Life of LGBT People in Eastern Europe*, edited by Roman Kuhar and Judit Takács (Ljubljana: Mirovni Inštitut, 2007), 119.

14   Gert Hekma, "Foreword. In *Beyond the Pink Curtain: Everyday Life of LGBT People in Eastern Europe*, edited by Roman Kuhar and Judit Takács (Ljubljana: Mirovni Inštitut, 2007), 9.

15   Slavoj Žižek, *The sublime object of ideology* (New York: Verso, 1989).

16   Charlene Carruthers, *Unapologetic: A Black, Queer, and Feminist Mandate for Radical Movements* (Boston: Beacon Press, 2018); Kimberle Crenshaw, "Mapping the Margins: Intersectionality,

the oral history research, this book argues that queer people in Communist Czechoslovakia also had particular opportunities for subversion and transgression, which allowed them to maintain a greater degree of personal agency and autonomy than one would expect in an authoritarian regime.

To be clear, queer encounters with Communist power and the Socialist state were not harmonious. Queer people living in Communist Czechoslovakia were not able to form a legal community,[17] did face many obstacles, were discriminated in many areas of their private and public lives, and at times were subjected to random acts of violence, surveillance, and political harassment.[18] However, the queer oral history project also revealed a large degree of autonomy and agency by individual queer people in the face of these hardships. People, who at the time had no means (either terminological or political) to officially identify themselves as gay, lesbian, bisexual, or transgender, nonetheless provided clear evidence of living such identities. This is a story of people who, despite various and often dire obstacles, lived their lives not only with fear and stress but also with invention, dignity, and passion. The book contributes to both the recent history of Czechoslovakia and the history of sexuality in several important ways. First, it fills the gap in oral history of our recent past by integrating queer people, whose voices have been so far largely silent and invisible. Second, it further complicates the picture of a singular, monolithic "Communist regime" by discussing the importance played by a variety of expert discourses in the functioning of the Socialist state. And third, the book contributes to the study of state socialism by utilizing the category of gender as its main analytical tool. Using this particular lens exposes not only the ways in which queer people formed their subjectivity or how they negotiated their identities *vis-à-vis* the heteronormative and ideological pressures of the state and society, it also reveals unexpected historical markers queer people considered important in their lives and thus offers an alternative periodization of the Socialist era.

Identity Politics, and Violence against Women of Color." *Stanford Law Review*, 43/6, 1991; Gloria Anzaldúa, *Borderlands: The New Mestiza: 25th anniversary* (San Francisco: Aunt Lute Books, 2012); Patricia Hill Collins, *Black Feminist Thought: Knowledge, Consciousness, and the Politics of Empowerment*. Revised tenth anniversary edition. (London: Routledge, 2000); Cherríe Moraga and Gloria Anzaldúa, *This Bridge Called My Back: Writings by Radical Women of Color*. Fourth edition. (Albany: SUNY Press, 2015); Pisankaneva 2005; Rupp 1999.

17   Kateřina Nedbálková, "The Changing Space of the Gay and Lesbian Community in the Czech Republic." In *Beyond the Pink Curtain: Everyday Life of LGBT People in Eastern Europe*, edited by Roman Kuhar and Judit Takács (Ljubljana: Mirovni Inštitut, 2007), 67–80.

18   Franz Schindler, "Život gayů za socialismu." In "'*Miluji tvory svého pohlaví': Homosexualita v dějinách a společnosti českých zemí*, edited by Pavel Himl, Jan Seidl, and Franz Schindler (Praha: Argo, 2013); Seidl 2012; Procházka, Ivo, David Janík and Jiří Hromada, *Společenská diskriminace lesbických žen, gay mužů a bisexuálů v ČR* (Praha: Gay iniciativa, 2003).

TERMINOLOGY

As can be discerned from the discussion so far, finding suitable terminology for this book was not an easy task. On a personal level, all the narrators had very different relationships to their own sexual and gender identities, to their biological bodies, as well as to questions of marriage, parenthood, and sexuality. At a more general level, they also had quite distinct relationships to Communist power and the membership in the Communist party, as well as questions of resistance or obedience and outward loyalty to the Communist political regime. When thinking about what characteristics and experiences define the narrators together, it was neither their 'homosexual,' 'lesbian' or 'gay' identity (because some of them do not identify with, or even hate, those terms) nor their 'same-sex' desires and sexual relations (because some of them did not see themselves as 'women sleeping with other women' or 'men sleeping with other men'). Some narrators complicated the temptation for a homogenizing terminology by questioning their biological body as 'female,' while others identified as 'transsexual,' with a note that this realization came much later in their lives, while growing up under socialism they had no idea that such an identity (by then well covered by sexological literature) even existed. The only thing that connected all of the narrators together was their rejection of heterosexual subjectivity, whether in terms of sexual orientation or gender identification. For that reason, in the earlier versions of this text I used the term "non-heterosexual" as the most fitting expression of the diversity of the narrators.

But defining queer people as 'non-heterosexual' is not satistying either. Such definition does address the nonconforming and subversive aspects of their identity and behavior through which they defied the heteronormative pressures and expectations projected at them by the Socialist state and society. The term does capture flexibility and the important dimension of transgressing the heterosexual norms in a variety of ways, but ultimately it does not solve the problem of naming. Defining queer people by a supposed standard, as the absence of the heterosexual norm, perpetuates their categorization as deficient or lacking. Lots of people, maybe most, would have non-binary gender identities and non-heterosexual affinities, if not for legal prohibitions and social pressures. Queer people worked their way out of being defined as deficient by appropriating that negative appraisal and owning it as an identity to embrace. Thus, when referring to non-heteronormative sexual identities and behavior, as well as when referring to the narrators and discussing their lives during the Socialist era, I use the term 'queer' which I believe best captures the complex and emancipatory nature of this proces.[19]

---

19   I would like to thank Kate Brown for inspirational discussions on this topic.

Most Czech scholars who recently wrote on the subject of queer identities and discourses from a variety of disciplinary perspectives most often opted for the term 'homosexual,' mainly because they analyzed written documents that explicitly operated with these terms: Seidl researched the topic of de-criminalization of homosexuality, Řídký studied the constructions of a "homosexual subject" in popular sexological handbooks and Lišková examined how homosexuality was linked with deviance in sexological discourse on perversion.[20] Jiří Fanel did not theorize or explain his terminological choices at all and simply used the term 'gay' for all same-sex desire and identities from the period of antiquity to the 1990s.[21] In a similar way, in order to capture a collective and transcendent essence of same-sex desire while simultaneously reflecting the historical consensus in writing about a recognizable identity, various anthologies examining homosexuality in the history of Czech culture and society also decided to use the term 'homosexual.'[22] Other colleagues, who conducted structured interviews or biographical narratives about the Socialist period used the category 'homosexual' as well, explaining that they did so because "it best captures who their respondents are," and "the narrators themselves identified that way."[23] Miřácký and Schindler went so far as to argue that they researched the life and topography of meeting places of a "homosexual community" during the Communist regime. Needless to say that all of these projects using 'homosexuality' as the umbrella term for same-sex desire and subjectivity were concerned with the study of male sexuality and men.

The mentioned studies are correct in that the sexological discourse of state Socialist period worked explicitly with the hetero-homo division and conceptualized men and women with same-sex desires as 'homosexual.' The same is true about other expert and popular discourses produced by the Socialist state and its institutions in Communist Czechoslovakia. When analyzing these discourses, I use the terms that appear in them. However, I purposefully do not use these terms for identifying personal subject positions of queer people living during the Communist period unless they explicitly attach such terms to themselves. I am equally reluctant to write about the lives of my narrators in a homogenous way because they were so vastly different. They did not form a community or collective body during the Communist period that would entitle me to treat them that way. The fact that after 1989 most of the narrators identified as gay or lesbian does not legitimize a retroactive

---

20   Seidl 2012; Řídký 2013; Lišková 2018.

21   Fanel 1999.

22   Martin Putna and Milena Bartlová, eds. *Homosexualita v dějinách české kultury* (Praha, Academia: 2011); Seidl 2012; Pavel Himl, Jan Seidl and Franz, Schindler, eds., *'Miluji tvory svého pohlaví': Homosexualita v dějinách a společnosti českých zemí* (Praha: Academia, 2013).

23   Miřácký 2009; Schindler 2013.

appropriation of such categories and subjectivities for past historical periods, especially since those terms did not readily exist in the discursive contexts of the Socialist state.[24]

Throughout the book I use several different terms relating to the topic of sexual identities and experiences during the Communist period, such as 'queer,' 'non-heterosexual,' 'homosexual,' 'lesbian,' 'gay,' and 'gay and lesbian.' When it comes to historical documents and archival sources, the terminology is used in strictly historically contextual ways. Medical discourse during the Communist period used only the term "homosexual," either by itself or in conjunction with the terms "inclinations" (*sklony*), "dispositions" (*dispozice*) or "origins" (*původ*). Also the Communist legal discourse worked only with the term homosexual or found ways to avoid this term altogether. The wordings of the 1950 and 1961 laws, the only two laws directly dealing with homosexuality during the Communist era, both referred to "sexual acts with a person of the same sex" (*pohlavní styk s osobou téhož pohlaví*) and nowhere used the term homosexuality or homosexual. In materials related to these laws, such as reports from committee meetings, correspondence and recommendations between ministries, Central Committee of the Communist Party and diverse state institutions, only the term homosexual appears. For this reason, when working with these documents or context, I also use only the term 'homosexual.'

The queer oral history project, which forms the most important research foundation of this book, was carried out mainly with older women (born between 1929–1952). Very few of them explicitly identified as being 'lesbian' and none referred to herself as being 'homosexual.' Occasionally, the narrators applied the term 'lesbian' to their identities retroactively, and when they did so, the citations used in this book kept their terminological choice. Most narrators resorted to a variety of alternative terms used in the Socialist past, such as "being into girls/boys" (*být na holky/na kluky*), "our kind" (*našinec, náš člověk*), or simply avoided any naming altogether. When discussing efforts to create queer communal spaces in the face of surveillance and censorship, narrators often used the term "*teplý*" or "*teplá komunita*," fittingly translated as "queer." The term 'homosexual,' in fact, rarely appeared in their recollections and when it did, it refered to 'other homosexuals' or to the perceptions of the narrators about how other people viewed homosexuality or homosexuals in the past. Some narrators, for example, mentioned that "homosexuality was a social taboo," "homosexuals had a difficult life" or that "homosexuality was never spoken about." The unwillingness to embrace the term 'homosexual' by the female narrators for their personal identity suggests there was a clear discursive abyss between the understanding of the Socialist medical science

---

24   Rupp 1999.

about who the homosexuals were and the self-perceptions of queer people themselves. The medicalization of their sexual identities in terms of sickness, disease, deviance, misfortune, and pity resulted in queer people's reluctance to associate with this term. Additionally, it also exposed the male-dominated and male-centered character of the state Socialist discourse on homosexuality in general.[25]

STRUCTURE

The book is organized into six main chapters. Following this introduction, chapter two elaborates on the relevance and importance of sexuality as, to paraphrase Joan W. Scott, a useful category of historical analysis.[26] Sexuality is situated into both historical and gender studies scholarship, suggesting what can be gained by inclusion of sexuality into contemporary Czechoslovak history of the Socialist period. In general, this chapter addresses conceptual questions and discusses the main methodological tools used in this project. Since the book is based on the combination of methods of discursive analysis of the sexological discourse of Socialist Czechoslovakia and oral history, the second part of the chapter explains the purpose of this methodological approaches and the productivity of the combination of analysis of medical documents with biographical narratives. The chapter is concluded by a discussion of power and agency in authoritarian societies.

Chapter three provides a detailed analysis of the Czechoslovak sexological discourse. Based on an original comprehensive research of more than 120 articles and books from the medical database of Czech National Medical Library from 1947 to 1989, this chapter offers an in-depth look into the attitudes and arguments of Czech and Slovak sexologists, and other medical professionals concerned with sexuality, towards the questions of homosexuality, intersexuality and transsexuality. Inevitably, the chapter dissects the

---

25 Male narrators were more willing to use the term "homosexual," both as a noun and adjective (in the Czech and Slovak languages, there is no customarily used female form of the noun "homosexual," most often it is used only as an adjective with the added designation "woman"). In this context, it is significant that some of the most visible male activists in the early 1990s refered to themselves as "homosexuals," for example Jiří Hromada, Šimon Formánek, and others, and that the very first civic organization after 1989, led and dominated by men, bore the name *The Movement for Equality of Homosexual Citizens* (HRHO — Hnutí za rovnoprávnost homosexuálních občanů) and later *Union of Organizations of Homosexual Citizens* (SOHO — Sdružení organizací homosexuálních občanů). While the LGBT movements and scholarship in the "West" thematized and articulated the problems with the term 'homosexual' since the 1970s, in the Czech context it was used until the late 1990s. Only since the turn of the millennium have civic activists used for their self-designation, activities and projects the terms "gay," "lesbian," or "queer."

26 Joan W. Scott, "Gender: A Useful Category of Historical Analysis, *The American Historical Review* 91/5 (1986): 1053–1075.

gendered nature of the Czechoslovak sexological discourse and examines what it tells us about the ability of Czechoslovak sexologistst to move beyond the hetero-homo dualities in their treatment of non-heteronormative sexuality. Significantly, the analysis of sexological writings in major medical journals, as well as in popular medical and cultural journals and books, from the early 1950s through the late 1980s' reveals a remarkable progress towards liberal and emancipatory understanding of human sexuality, which has not been yet adequately addressed by historical scholarship. This trend was reflected not only in the complicated arguments of Czechoslovak sexologists about the compatibility of homosexuality and marriage but also in the willlingness and ability of many doctors to turn their sexological practice into therapeutic coming-out sessions for homosexuals. Instead of being (only) the tool of heteronormative regulation and adversaries of queer people, many sexologists became their friends, advocates, and protectors. As a prominent sexologist of the Normalization era, Dagmar Bártová, put it, "we knew that we were basically substitutes for the non-existent gay clubs."[27]

The second half of the book delves into the everyday lives of queer people. Chapter four first leads us into the processes of the narrators' adolescence and their searching for queer points of reference. In this respect, the biographical interviews uncovered both quite predictable aspects of identity formation and gender socialization in the early childhood period of the narrators, as well as some extraordinary moments of queer growing up, which one would not expect in Socialist Eastern Europe. The narratives also made it clear that despite the informational vacuum about homosexuality, at least some young girls and boys in Czechoslovakia, who did not identify as heterosexual, found alternative reference points or succeeded in subverting the intended meanings of the heteronormative ones.

Chapter five examines in greater detail the subversive potential of queer lives, especially its gender dimensions. Since the majority of the narrators participating in this oral history project were women, their life experiences and memories provided so far unexamined aspects of homosexuality, transsexuality, and queerness during state socialism. Their recollections challenged some of the myths traditionally associated with femininity and female sexuality, such as passivity or longing for stable monogamous relationships. While proper gender performance often successfully functioned as a camouflage for 'improper' sexuality, this did not mean that under the performative cover of expected gender, queer women would necessarily behave in traditionally feminine ways. To the contrary, many of the biographical narratives revealed that traditional gender expectations were often used by

---

27 Luboš Koukal, "S negativními reakcemi jsem se nesetkala. Rozhovor s 'mámou homosexuálů' — MUDr. Dagmar Bártovou." *Lambda* 1/9 (1990): 3.

queer people, both women and men, in quite creative ways.[28] This creativity was, for example, responsible for a surprising ability of 'homosexual' women, looking for relationships with other women, to place same-sex ads in Socialist newspapers. This chapter also explores queer family constellations during state socialism, which were traditionally regarded as lonely or forcefully hypocritical. This section, building on the sexological discourse on homosexuality and marriage in chapter three, invites confrontation between the stereotypes of the family life of 'homosexuals' during socialism and the recollections of queer women, who lived in same-sex relationships, sometimes with children, as well as queer women, who entered into marriages with men. The last part of chapter five is devoted to solidarity between 'homosexual' women and men and discusses the existence of queer community and spaces in Socialist Czechoslovakia.

Chapter six explores queer encounters with institutionalized state power. One of the obvious concequences of the diversity of the narrators was their different positionality when it came to their relationships with the state and its institutions, the Communist Party and the privileges and (dis)advantages of the Socialist system. As already discussed, it has often been argued that 'homosexuals' were marginalized and repressed by the Communist 'regime' in Socialist Czechoslovakia. A corollary to this generalizing argument was an implicit assumption that, by the default of their minority sexual orientation, all 'homosexuals' stood on the opposing side of state power, Communist membership, and privileges enjoyed by loyal or passive citizens. Through three different individual encounters with the state in three different historical periods of Czechoslovak socialism from the early 1950s through the late 1980s and three different social contexts, the last chapter of this book scrutinizes this stereotype in order to discuss the relationship between (queer) sexuality and (Communist) power and to see what these discussions can tell us about the state attitudes towards homosexuality, as well as about the ordinary lives of queer people living in Czechoslovakia before 1989.

I conclude with a comprehensive summary of its main arguments, but only after unraveling the story of the last article about homosexuality published in the Socialist era, printed on September 9, 1989 in the main Communist daily *Rudé právo*, and discussing all 39 letters from the readers that arrived in the editorial office of *Rudé právo* after its publication: an archival gem which provides a fitting end to the book.

---

28   For an insightful theoretization and examples of creative notions of family forms and intimate relationships see, Jana Mikats, Susanne Kink-Hampersberger and Libora Oates-Indruchova, eds. *Creative Families: Gender and Technologies of Everyday Life* (London: Palgrave Macmillan, 2021).

CHAPTER 2
WHY SEXUALITY?

In 1999, Dáša Frančíková, then a student of mine at Charles University in Prague who went on to get a doctorate in gender history from the University of Michigan, was working on an article about the personal correspondence between the revered 19th century Czech writer, Božena Němcová, and her friend Sofie Podlipská. The letters that Frančíková found in regional archives and started to study contained remarkably similar sentiments and formulations as the intimate correspondence that American historian Carol Smith-Rosenberg analyzed in her iconic article about the world of love and ritual in 19th-century America.[29] Familiar with and inspired by Smith-Rosenberg, Frančíková explored in her article what the sentiments expressed by Němcová and Podlipská in their letters could mean, how we should work with them and interpret them at the end of the 20th century and, above all, what they can tell us not only about female friendships and gender relations, but also about the mainstream academic narratives of 19th-century Czech history.[30] While I felt it was a great research topic and thus far unstudied aspect of a major Czech historical and literary figure, I remember the horror of one of my colleagues when I told her about Frančíková's endeavor. "What?! Is she suggesting that Němcová was a lesbian? That's ridiculous! It's complete nonsense. We can't support such stupid questions!" Frančíková was not suggesting that Němcová was a "lesbian," she was studying female intimacy through the lens of the history of sexuality. But the simple suggestion that unspoken romantic relationships could contain a dimension of sexual intimacy terrified some Czech historians. They adhered to the well-established and safe ways of approaching Czech modern history, in which feminist investigations of sexuality (let alone a queer one) did not have a place.

Czech historiography has changed dramatically over the past twenty years, producing a wealth of insightful and inspirational work in the field of history of sexuality. The story, however, aptly illustrates why some historians are still afraid and doubtful of sexuality as a relevant and legitimate category

---

29 Carroll Smith-Rosenberg, "The Female World of Love and Ritual: Relations between Women in Nineteenth-Century America." *Signs* 1/1 (1975): 1–29.

30 Dáša Frančíková, "Female Friends in Nineteenth-Century Bohemia: Troubles with Affectionate Writing and "Patriotic Relationships." *Journal of Women's History* 12/3 (2000): 23–28.

of 'proper' historical scholarship, fearing it would devalue serious academic work by asking 'inappropriate' or 'ridiculous' questions. Such concerns seem exacerbated especially when the study of sexuality threatens to challenge established narratives of the national past, dominant interpretations of certain historical events, or uncontroversial understanding of major historical figures. The Czech historian Anna Hájková, for example, skillfully reveals these anxieties and tensions in her study of same-sex desire in prisoner societies of ghettos and Nazi concentration camps. She maps out queer biographies of Holocaust victims and explores how attention to gender and sexuality, and queer sexuality in particular, enriches and transforms the study of the Holocaust in general. In her pathbreaking work, Hájková convincingly complicates the current narratives of the Theresienstadt ghetto and unveils the importance of queer Holocaust history.[31] These, and similar, efforts reveal that placing (queer) sexuality into the center of historical inquiry provides us with a valuable opportunity to reexamine the dominant frameworks of understandings the past, especially in contexts that are generally understudied from this perspective, such as the Holocaust, as well as the period of state socialism in the postwar period.

SEXUALITY IN HISTORICAL SCHOLARSHIP

One of the important insights that the study of sexuality has brought over the past forty years to the discipline of history is the recognition that human sexuality is not a mere biological category that would be instinctual, innate, and immune to historical forces. Indeed, the challenge that Smith-Rosenberg confronted was to get historians to view same-sex relationships "within a cultural and social setting rather than from an exclusively individual psychosexual perspective."[32] Following inspiration in anthropology and sociology, scholars studying sexuality in vastly diverse historical periods and societies accumulated overwhelming evidence that people learn to behave and express themselves sexually and that knowledge depends on particular historical contexts.[33] As American historian John D'Emilio argued in his pathbreaking work,

---

31 Anna Hájková, "Sexual Barter in Times of Genocide: Negotiating the Sexual Economy of the Theresienstadt Ghetto," *Signs: Journal of Women in Culture and Society* 38/3 2013: 503–533; "Den Holocaust queer erzaehlen," *Humanities Commons* 2020 (PDF available from http://dx.doi .org/10.17613/4qtz-sy02); Anna Hájková, Elissa Mailaender, Doris Bergen, Patrick Farges and Atina Grossmann, "Holocaust and the History of Gender and Sexuality," *German History*, 36/1 2018: 78–100.

32 Smith-Rosenberg, 2.

33 Robert Padgug, "Sexual Matters: On Conceptualizing Sexuality in History," in *Radical History Review* 20:2/1979, 3–23; Estelle B. Freedman, "Sexuality in Nineteenth-Century America: Behavior, Ideology, and Politics, in *Review in American History* 10/4 (1982): 196–215; Jeffrey Weeks, *Coming*

while concrete sexual practices, "from heterosexual intercourse to mastur-bation and sodomy, have a universal existence," the ways how individual men and women interpret their sexual activities and desires, and the meanings that different societies and cultures assign to such behavior, are incredibly diverse both in geographical and historical senses, as well as individually.[34] Since sexuality, along with other intersectional categories, namely class, race and gender, is one of the fundamental ways to organize societies and enact power relations within them, it also forms a salient analytical category to examine any given society and particular historical contexts. The following sections will provide an overview of some of the main contributions the his-tory of (queer) sexuality has made over the past thirty years to the science of history in general, and to the study of states and societies during state socialism in Eastern Europe in particular.

The most significant development in the recent historiography of queer sexualities in Eastern Europe during the Communist period have been the fo-cused but diffused efforts, coming simultaneously from queer scholarship in all post-Socialist countries, to challenge the dominant understanding of both state approaches to homosexuality and the lives of queer people under com-munism as homogenized and uniform.[35] Scholars from different countries have adopted a variety of methods and conceptual frames to debunk the myth that all East European states approached homosexuality similarly and that queer people in Socialist countries experienced and lived the 'homosexual' label provided by the state in the same way. Moreover, as Robert Kulpa has ar-gued, the homogenization of East European Soviet satellites during the Cold War resulted in the conceptual framing of Central and Eastern Europe as the European (homophobic) Other in the current sexual nationalism debates.[36]

Out: Homosexual Politics in Britain from the Nineteenth Century to the Present (London: Quartet Books, 1977); Michel Foucault, *The History of Sexuality, vol. 1, An Introduction*; Lillian Faderman, *Surpassing the Love of Men: Romantic Friendship and Love Between Women from the Renaissance to the Present* (London: HarperCollins, 1998).

34 John D'Emilio, *Sexual Politics, Sexual Communities: The Making of a Homosexual Minority in the United States, 1940–1970* (Chicago and London: The University of Chicago Press, 1983), 3–4.

35 Lukasz Szulc, *Transnational Homosexuals in Communist Poland: Cross-Border Flows in Gay and Les-bian Magazines* (London: Palgrave Macmillan, 2018); Francesca Stella, *Lesbian Lives in Soviet and Post-Soviet Russia. Post/Socialism and Gendered Sexualities* (London: Palgrave MacMillan, 2015); Kateřina Lišková, *Sexual Liberation, Socialist Style: Communist Czechoslovakia and the Science of Desire, 1945–1989* (Cambridge: Cambridge University Press, 2018). Irina Costache, *Archiving De-sire: Materiality, Sexuality, and the Secret Police in Romanian State Socialism.* (Ph.D. Dissertation, CEU Budapest, 2014); Anna Borgos, "Homosexuality and Psychiatry in State-socialist Hungary: Representing Women's Same-sex Desire in the Psychomedical Literature." *American Psychologist*, 74(8), 2019: 925–939.

36 Robert Kulpa, "Western *Leveraged Pedagogy* of Central and Eastern Europe: Discourses of Ho-mophobia, Tolerance, and Nationhood," *Gender, Place & Culture A Journal of Feminist Geography*, 2014: 21/4, 431–448; Robert Kulpa and Joanna Mizielinska, eds. *De-centring Western Sexualities: Central and Eastern European Perspectives* (London: Routledge, 2016);

Lukasz Szulc broadened Kulpa's argument in his *Transnational Homosexuals in Communist Poland*, an inaugural volume of the new Palgrave Macmillan series on *Global Queer Politics*, by pointing out that the myth of homogeneity of Eastern Europe under socialism with respect to the LGBT issues has been accompanied by the persistent imagination of the West "as essentially progressive, that is post-racial, post-feminist and post-gay," while East Central Europe continues to be perceived as "essentially backward, that is racist, sexist and homophobic."[37] Both Kulpa and Szulc, among other scholars, thus call for the de-centering of Western sexualities by adopting pluralistic, intersectional and complex perspectives to the study of queer sexualities in Eastern Europe. Their call is doubly important for the context of state socialism.

More generally, the integration of the history of sexuality into mainstream historical narratives has led to a number of fundamental reassessments of historical periodization.[38] In her brilliant work on sexualities in twentieth-century Germany and Europe, German historian Dagmar Herzog convincingly showed how using sexuality as the main analytical category and focus of study can open new interpretations not only of German anti-Semitism but the entire 20th-century European history in general and redraw historical boundaries.[39] Focusing on changes in abortion law and women's freedoms during the re-unification of Germany in 1991, Eva Maleck-Lewy and Myra Marx Ferree revealed that the analysis of gender and sexuality can also bring into question what constitutes a turning point or a "new era."[40] Similarly, historians of the American South persuasively showed that the analysis of sexual relations between whites and blacks can challenge commonly accepted interpretations and periodizations of the Civil War, as well as bring completely new insights to slave studies.[41]

Historians of (homo)sexuality in Socialist Eastern Europe have emphasized the importance of medical discourses in shaping state policies and

---

37 Szulc, 2018, 5.

38 Michel Foucault, *History of Sexuality: An Introduction* (New York: Vintage, 1980); Thomas Lacqueur, *Making Sex: Body and Gender from the Greeks to Freud* (Cambridge: Harvard University Press 1990).

39 Dagmar Herzog, *Sexuality in Europe: A Twentieth-Century History* (New York: Cambridge University Press, 2011); Dagmar Herzog, *Sex after Fascism: Memory and Morality in Twentieth-Century Germany* (Princeton: Princeton University Press, 2005).

40 Ewa Maleck-Lewy and Myra Marx Ferree, "Talking about Women and Wombs: The Discourse of Abortion and Reproductive Rights in the G.D.R. during and after the *Wende*." In *Reproducing Gender: Politics, Publics, and Everyday Life after Socialism*, edited by Susan Gal and Gail Kligman (Princeton, N.J.: Princeton University Press, 2000).

41 Kathleen Brown, *Good Wives, Nasty Wenches & Anxious Patriarchs: Gender, Race, and Power in Colonial Virginia* (Chapel Hill: University of North Carolina Press, 1996); Drew Gilpin Faust, *Mothers of Invention: Women of the Slaveholding South in the American Civil War* (Chapel Hill: University of North Carolina Press, 1996); Suzanne Lebsock, *The Free Women of Petersburg: Status and Culture in a Southern Town 1784-1860* (Chapel Hill: University of North Carolina Press, 1984).

popular attitudes. In her study of homosexuality in Socialist Bulgaria, Monika Pisankaneva argued that Bulgarian psychiatrists and sexologists, while ardently claiming in the 1950s that homosexuality was a dangerous perversion, later played an important role in decriminalizing homosexuality in 1968.[42] Similarly, Samirah Kenawi pointed out that East German sexologists often played a positive role in the gradual emancipation of homosexuality in the GDR.[43] Most recently, Kateřina Lišková argued that the "science of desire" permeated all expert discourses in Communist Czechoslovakia, while Jan Seidl and Ivo Procházka described how sexology helped to facilitate the rise of gay and lesbian movements in Czechoslovakia after 1989.[44] Laurie Essig, on the other hand, insisted in *Queer in Russia* that Soviet sexologists and sex psychiatrists throughout the entire Communist period held a negative, gender-essentialist and dogmatically normative approach to sexuality. According to Essig, being an influential force they significantly contributed to making the Soviet Union's medical and legal treatment of sexuality the most repressive apparatus in the East European Bloc.[45]

Scholars of non-heterosexual sexualities in Communist countries also identified alternative histories, milestones and reference points for queer people. Samirah Kenawi and Dara Bryant, in their excellent analyses of gays and lesbians in the GDR, revealed one such historical narrative, which started in 1976 when the Protestant Church began to offer refuge and open dialogue to gay and lesbian groups. Kenawi and Bryant argue that unlike in other Socialist countries, in the GDR it was predominantly lesbian women, not gay men, who led the movement towards increasing the visibility of non-heterosexual identities. By gaining empowerment from the recognition of their double discrimination as women and as lesbians, women also organized the first large lesbian meeting in Dresden in 1982 and initiated the first discussions with the state. 1983 marked a crucial turning point in the LGBT movement in the GDR, when a group of lesbians from the Protestant Church visited the former women's concentration camp in Ravensbrück, identifying themselves as *Kirchliche Lesbengruppe* ("Lesbians in the Church") and laying a wreath with the words: "We honor the homosexual victims of fascism. – Lesbians in the Church, homosexual self-help working group." The group also signed the guest book of the memorial, again openly identifying themselves. Three days later, two of the lesbians discovered that the wreath and their entry in the guest book had disappeared. The women complained at the highest

42 Monika Pisankaneva, "The Forbidden Fruit: Sexuality in Communist Bulgaria." *E-magazine LiterNet* 68/7 (2005): 1–10.
43 Samirah Kenawi, *Frauengruppen in der DDR der 80er Jahre. Eine Dokumentation* (Berlin: GrauZone, 199.
44 Lišková 2018; Seidl 2012; Procházka 1997.
45 Essig 1999, 25–55.

level of the state; finally, as a result of their complaints, the Ministry of Interior replied that they would reconsider their approach to homosexuals.[46]
This story represents an alternative milestone for historical periodization,
identified by Judith Halberstam and other scholars as "queer temporality."[47]
In a similar though less dramatic fashion, my own queer oral history project
revealed that Martina Navrátilová's coming out as a lesbian in 1981 was one
of the most important formative moments in the lives of many queer people,
especially women, during the Communist regime.[48]

While the academic focus on the institutional dimensions of state approaches to homosexuality under communism is understandable, little attention has been paid so far to the individual experiences of queer people living
during state socialism in Eastern Europe. Moreover, the few available studies
that are concerned with queer memories during the Socialist period predom-
inately focus on the recollections and experiences of gay men. Shortly after
the fall of the Berlin Wall, Jürgen Lemke published his *Gay Voices from East
Germany*, a collection of essays based on interviews of fourteen East German
gay men in the mid-1980s, which revealed the diversity of gay experiences
behind the Iron Curtain.[49] At the same time, Lemke's work completely excluded lesbian women, an omission which Josh Armstrong aims to rectify
in his most recent study of homosexuality in the GDR.[50] Similarly, Franz
Schindler, Radek Miřácký, and Jiří Fanel provided much needed insights
into gay life in Socialist Czechoslovakia in their oral history research and
ethnographic work but they, too, presented a strictly male point of view.[51]

An extraordinary exception to this trend is the excellent work of Francesca Stella, who conducted an extensive ethnographic and oral history research
project of *Lesbian Lives in Soviet and Post-Soviet Russia*. Stella's work is remarkable not only because of her focus on lesbian women (broadly defined) but
also because she "aims to fracture essentialist notions of Russian sexualities
as the 'other'" by attending to both generational and regional differences.

46   Dara Bryant, "Queering the Antifascist State: Ravensbruck as a Site of Lesbian Resistance."
         In *Edinburgh German Yearbook, Volume 3: Contested Legacies: Constructions of Cultural Heritage in
         the GDR*, edited by Matthew Philpotts and Sabine Rolle (Rochester, NY: Camden House, 2009);
         Kenawi 1995.

47   Judith Halberstam, *In a Queer Time and Place* (New York: University Press, 2005). Halberstam's
         arguments are analyzed in a different place of the book.

48   Martina Navrátilová is a legendary Czech tennis player, who emigrated to the United States in
         1975 at the age of 18 after being warned by the Czechoslovak Sport's Federation that she was
         becoming "too Americanized" and should go back to school, making tennis only her secondary
         interest. ("Martina Defects for Love Set," *St. Petersburg Independent*, Sept. 8, 1975, p. 1–C).

49   Lemke 1991.

50   Josh Armstrong, "Homosexuality under Socialism in the German Democratic Republic," *Oxford
         Research Encyclopedia of Politics*. Published on 28 September 2020, available from https://doi
         .org/10.1093/acrefore/9780190228637.013.1264

51   Schindler 2013; Miřácký 2009; Fanel 2000.

During her fieldwork, Stella conducted 61 semi-structured interviews with Russian lesbian women aged 18–56, as well as 24 additional biographical narratives with older lesbian women born in the Soviet Union between 1946–1969 in several different areas of the Russian Federation. In its scope, as well as in the complexity of her approach and argumentation, Stella's book is highly inspirational and stands out in the current scholarship on queer sexualities in the Socialist period in East Central Europe.[52]

Besides the works mentioned above, the scholarship on non-heterosexuality and queer lives during the Communist era is quite limited. The paucity of academic work examining (not only non-heterosexual) sexuality in Eastern Europe during the period of state socialism is somewhat surprising when considering how many excellent and comprehensive monographs, anthologies, and journal articles across many academic disciplines have been devoted to sexuality in the region both before and after the Communist period. There have been a number of in-depth studies and specialized volumes devoted particularly to queer sexuality in both post-Communist period in Eastern Europe, as well as to East-West comparisons, including *De-centering Western Sexualities: Central and Eastern European Perspectives*; *Queer in Europe: Contemporary Case Studies*; *Beyond the Pink Curtain: Everyday Life of LGBT People in Eastern Europe*; *Sexuality and Gender in Post-Communist Eastern Europe and Russia* or *Queer Visibility in Post-Socialist Cultures*.[53]

The majority of historical scholarship of sexuality in the Czech lands and Czechoslovakia covers the pre-Socialist period, mainly the 19th century and first half of the 20th century. Czech historian Daniela Tinková, for example, focuses on the conceptual changes in the definitions and considerations of sin and mental disease and maps the historical changes in attitudes towards the body, sexuality, motherhood, and parenthood from the 16th to the 18th centuries.[54] In her emphasis on the intersections between the rise of the modern state and the creation of modern medical science, Tinková, albeit in different contexts, exposes the processes that formed modern deviant and marginalized subjects. She joins historians who argue (in different contexts) that 'the other,' is not a self-obvious and stable category of difference but a flexible

52 Stella, 2015.

53 Kulpa and Mizielinska, 2016; Lisa Downing and Robert Gillett, eds. *Queer in Europe: Contemporary Case Studies* (London: Routledge, 2011); Roman Kuhar and Judit Takács, eds. *Beyond the Pink Curtain: Everyday Life of LGBT People in Eastern Europe* (Ljubljana: Mirovni Inštitut, 2007); Aleksandar Stulhofer and Theo Sandfort, *Sexuality and Gender in PostCommunist Eastern Europe and Russia* (New York: Haworth Press, 2005); Nárcisz Fejes and Andrea P. Balogh, eds., *Queer Visibility in Post-socialist Cultures* (London: Intellect Books, 2013).

54 Daniela Tinková, *Hřích, zločin, šílenství v čase odkouzlování světa* (Praha: Argo, 2004); Daniela Tinková, *Tělo, věda, stát. Zrození porodnice v osvícenecké Evropě* (Praha: Argo, 2010).

social construct always depending on the historical context of its creation.[55] Also inspiratioonal is the work of Czech historian Pavel Himl. Himl's study of the creation of modern vagabonds, vagrants, and homeless in the Czech lands and institutional approaches to these marginalized groups convincingly documents the rise of the repressive-caring approach of the state to people perceived as 'problematic.'[56] In many ways, we can see aspects of this system in the state approach of many East European countries, especially the Soviet Union and Romania, to homosexuality and homosexuals after 1945. On the one hand, the state used a repressive apparatus to regulate and control homosexuals; on the other hand, it adopted a paternalistic and caring attitude towards their 'misfortune.' As a result, Dan Healey argues, through the definition of their identity and behavior as pathological yet understandable, such discourses created a framework which left no official space for crafting a positive queer subjectivity.[57]

The history of homosexuality in the Czech lands in the 19th century and the interwar period is competently covered by the broadly conceived and interdisciplinary three-volume project of independent publications (two anthologies and one monograph) on homosexuality in Czech culture from the 19th century to the present: *Homosexuality in the History of Czech Culture*; *From the Prison to the Altar: Emancipation of Homosexuality in the Czech Lands since 1867 to the Present* and *'I Love the Creatures of My Own Sex': Homosexuality in the History and Society of the Czech Lands*.[58] At the same time, an important lesson repeatedly demonstrated by historians of sexuality in a variety of geographical and historical contexts is the instability and complexity of the category of the 'homosexual.' They remind us that we should treat this category not as self-evident but as suspect, paying careful attention not only to its constructions but also to the varied manifestations and meanings of this category for individual people living different lives, in different circumstances. When it comes to post-WWII history, however, Czech historiography of sexuality has much less to offer and the study of queer sexuality during state socialism is close to non-existent.

---

55   See especially the work by Svatava Raková on the constructions of otherness in early American colonies, Svatava Raková, *Víra, rasa a etnicita v koloniální Americe* (Praha: Nakladatelství Lidové noviny, 2005); Karel Kubiš, ed. *Obrazy druhého v historické perspektivě: Identity a stereotypy při formování moderní společnosti* (Praha: Univerzita Karlova, 2003); or Jitka Malečková's work on representations of women and gender in nationalizing discourses, Jitka Malečková, *Úrodná půda: žena ve službách národa* (Praha: ISV nakladatelství, 2002).

56   Pavel Himl, *Zrození vagabunda: neusedlí lidé v Čechách 17. a 18. století* (Praha, Argo, 2007).

57   Healey 2001.

58   Putna and Bartlová 2011; Seidl 2012; Himl, Seidl, and Schindler, eds. 2013.

SEXUALITY IN THE STUDY OF WOMEN AND GENDER IN EASTERN EUROPE

Since the early 1990s, the position of women and gender relations during state socialism in Eastern Europe have been under increasing scrutiny by many feminist scholars, studying a variety of diverse topics across all satellite countries of the Eastern Bloc. Gradually, sexuality came to the forefront of research inquiry as a important analytical category to understand social dynamics and gendered relations of power in Socialist societies, as well as institutional ways of disciplining and controlling women's bodies, especially in the areas of population policy and reproductive healthcare. However, efforts to integrate the study of women, gender and sexuality together were undermined and discouraged by anti-feminist and homophobic sentiments, circulating in the public and media discourses of post-Socialist countries from the 1990s well into the first decade of the new millennium. As a result, academic investigations of heteronormativity, homophobia, and queer sexualities during state socialism have been appearing slowly.

The pioneering scholarship on women and gender culture in Eastern Europe during the Communist period strongly concentrated on women, both as subjects of research and as an analytical category.[59] One of the first accounts attempting to evaluate the advantages and shortcomings of state socialism for women, was Hilda Scott's 1974 study *Does Socialism Liberate Women?*[60] As the title suggests, the driving question of this work was whether state structures and the possibilities offered by state socialism provide (mostly economic) conditions for gender equality and women's emancipation; a question most recently revisited in a complex way by the provocative work of Kristen Ghodsee and Julia Mead.[61]A decade later, Alena Heitlinger provided the first comprehensive discussion of the Socialist welfare system, population policies and reproductive medicine in Eastern Europe from a gendered

59 See, for example, Sharon Wolchik and Alfred Meyer, eds., *Women, State and Party in Eastern Europe* (Durham: Duke University Press, 1985); Nannette Funk and Magda Mueller, eds., *Gender Politics and Post-communism: Reflections from Eastern Europe and the Former Soviet Union* (New York: Routledge, 1993); *Transitions*, 5:1 (January 1998): "Talking about Women and Men"; *Women's History Review*, 5:4 (1996): "Special Issue: Women in Central and Eastern Europe"; *Hypatia: A Journal of Feminist Philosophy*, 8:4 (Fall 1993): "Special Cluster on Eastern European Feminism"; *Czech Sociological Review*, 7:2 (Fall 1999): "Thematic Issue: The Position of Czech Women in the Society of the 1990s in the Spectrum of Research."; Oates-Indruchová 2012, 357–383; Dudová 2012; Denisa Nečasová, *Buduj vlast, posílíš mír: ženské hnutí v českých zemích, 1945–1955* (Brno: Matice Moravská, 2011).

60 Hilda Scott, *Does Socialism Liberate Women? Experiences from Eastern Europe* (Boston: Bacon Press, 1974).

61 Kristen Ghodsee, *Why Women Have Better Sex Under Socialism and Other Argument for Economic Independence* (New York: Nation Books, 2018); Kristen Ghodsee and Julia Mead, "What has Socialism Ever done for Women?," *Catalyst* 2018, Vol. 2/2: 101–133.

perspective, arguing that the rhetoric of gender equality under communism was largely a vacuous claim.[62]

Barbara Einhorn's work was the first effort to study women and gender under socialism from a comparative perspective.[63] Einhorn continued the focus on women's emancipation, exploring women's movements and Socialist women's ability to participate in "active citizenship." Einhorn analyzed the ways in which gender inequality was rendered invisible by state socialism — such as the double burden of conceiving of women as "workers" and "mothers" without also placing the same social responsibility on men to be both "workers" and "fathers" — and led to the creation of a gender-blind society.[64] Her book argued that East European women were relegated to 'second-class' citizenship — without, however, discussing how the same frameworks practiced by authoritarian regimes affected Socialist men and relations between women and men. While Einhorn carefully differentiated the varying situations in individual East European countries, she created an exclusionary division between 'women' and 'men,' assuming that all men and all women living under socialism shared in the same conditions and experiences. As a result, she treated men and women in East European countries in a homogenizing manner and contributed to the much criticized hierarchical duality of 'Eastern' and 'Western' women. Subsequent research demonstrated that these assumptions were unsubstantiated and rather obfuscated the efforts to understand the diverse social realities of women and gender relations during state socialism not only in the different East European countries, but also within them.[65]

---

62 Alena Heitlinger, *Reproduction, Medicine and the Socialist State* (London: MacMillan Press, 1987); *Women and State Socialism: Sex Inequality in the Soviet Union and Czechoslovakia* (Montreal: McGill-Queen's University Press, 1979); and "Passage to Motherhood: Personal and Social Management of Reproduction in Czechoslovakia in the 1980s," in *Women, State, and Party in Eastern Europe.*

63 Barbara Einhorn, *Cinderella Goes to Market: Citizenship, Gender and Women's Movements in East Central Europe* (London, New York: Verso, 1993).

64 Ibid., especially chapter 1, "The Woman Question." Einhorn's discussion of citizenship centers around ideas of famous Central European dissidents, Adam Michnik, Georgy Konrad and Václav Havel, who all proposed morally acceptable alternatives to Communist citizenship by arguing for politics from below, such as "active self-organization" (Michnik), "antipolitics" (Konrad) or "living in truth" (Havel). Based on these notions of active participation and subversion, Einhorn sees citizenship as "not simply formal voting rights... [but] rather it implies active agency and the assertion of full individual autonomy." 3. For further discussions of civil society and citizenship in East Central Europe see, especially, Václav Havel, et al., *The Power of the* Powerless; Adam Michnik, *Letters from Prison and Other Essays* (Palo Alto: University of California Press, 1986); Georgy Konrad, *Antipolitics: An Essay* (Longon: Quartet, 1984).

65 Hana Havelková and Libora Oates-Indruchová, eds. *The Politics of Gender Culture under State Socialism: An Expropriated Voice* (London and New York: Routledge, 2014; Susan Gal and Gail Kligman, *The Politics of Gender after Socialism* (Princeton: Princeton University Press, 2000) and by the same authors an edited volume *Reproducing Gender: Politics, Publics and Everyday Life After Socialism* (Princeton: Princeton University Press, 2000); Susan Bridger, ed., *Women and Political*

Feminist scholarship gradually shifted its attention from women's emancipation to examining the ways in which East European Communist regimes used institutional gendered practices to control their societies. Gail Kligman's study of the politics of reproduction in Ceaucescu's Romania, for example, demonstrated how policies and laws enacted in the name of national progress and growth were deeply gendered.[66] Kligman's pioneering work showed the brutal consequences of criminalizing abortion and contraception in order to promote national reproduction, exposed the institutional obstetric violence practiced by the Romanian Communist regime, and demonstrated how the politics of reproduction functioned as a mechanism of state control. Importantly, through combining research of institutional documents with a study of witness testimonies, Kligman located the locus of power to control women's reproduction and discipline their bodies not only in state policies, laws and court reports, but also in the agency of local doctors, nurses, and husbands, who often possessed the means to either significantly aggravate or alleviate the impact of the draconian laws.[67]

One of the striking features of feminist scholarship on East European socialism, especially in the first decade after 1989, has been its heteronormativity. This trend holds true in the Czechoslovak context as well. Most well-known works of Czech feminist and gender scholarship from the 1990s do not include a single study, essay, article, or chapter, which would utilize sexuality as an analytical category or thematize homosexuality, gays, and lesbians. The much cited special issue on gender and feminism of *The Philosophical Journal*

Change: Perpectives from Eastern and Central Europe (London: Macmillan, 1999); Sharon Wolchik and Jean Jaquette, eds., *Women and Democracy in Latin America and Central and Eastern Europe* (Baltimore: Johns Hopkins University Press, 1998); *Women 2000: An Investigation into the Status of Women's Rights in Central and South-Eastern Europe and the Newly Independent States.* (International Helsinki Federation for Human Rights, 2000); Insightful articles analyzing gender stratification in Czechoslovakia and the Czech Republic inlude: Hana Havelková, "Abstract Citizenship? Women and Power in the Czech Republic," *Social Politics: International Studies in Gender, State and Society*, 3:2–3 (Summer/Fall 1996): 243–260; by the same author, "Women in and after a 'classless' society," in *Women and Social Class — International Feminist Perspectives*, edited by Christine Zmroczek and Pat Mahony (London: Taylor and Francis Group, 1999), 69–84; Jiřina Šmejkalová, "Gender as an Analytical Category of Post-Communist Studies," in *Gender in Transition in Eastern and Central Europe Proceedings*, edited by Gabrielle Jahnert, Jean Gohrisch, Dana Hahn, Hannah Nickel, Iris Peinl and Karen Schafgen (Berlin: Trafo Verlag, 2001); and Angie Argent, "Post-communism and 'Women's Experience'?," in *Feminist Approaches to Social Movements, Communist and Power*, edited by Robin Teske and Mary Ann Tetreault (Columbus: University of South Carolina Press, 2000).

66 Gail Kligman, *The Politics of Duplicity: Controlling Reproduction in Ceausescu's Romania* (Berkeley: University of California Press, 1998).

67 For comparative studies on abortion politics and discourses in other socialist countries see, for example, Radka Dudová, *Interrupce v České republice: Zápas o ženská těla* (Praha: Sociologický ústav, 2012; Agáta Chelstowska, "Stigmatisation and commercialisation of abortion services in Poland: turning sin into gold," in *Reproductive Health Matters* 2011, Vol. 19/37: 98–106; Maleck-Lewy and Marx Ferree 2000.

in 1992; the *Czech Sociological Review* with the subtitle "Special Issue on the Position of Czech Women in the Society of the 1990s in the Spectrum of Research" (1999); a well-received and widely-read 30-essay book on *Feminism of the 90s through Czech Eyes* (1999); the first interdisciplinary collection of essays from gender studies, *Gender Aspects of Society of Women and Men* (1999); and a large research project entitled *Transformation of Contemporary Czech Family* (2000) — none of these feminist academic endeavors included a single essay or chapter devoted to non-heterosexual women.[68] On the other hand, in the first two decades of the post-Socialist era Czech scholarship on homosexuality and the gay and lesbian movement, for its part, was equally blind to gender as an analytical category and reluctant to associate with feminist argumentation and rhetoric.[69]

Unlike post-Socialist scholarship on gender and sexuality in Poland, the former East Germany, or Slovakia, for example, the discourses on gender and sexuality in the Czech Republic were until recently characterized by a significant gap between the discussions of 'women/gender' on the one hand, and 'homosexuality/homophobia' on the other hand. The separation between gender (read as relating to, mainly, women who were presumably all heterosexual) and sexuality (understood as dealing with 'pathological' sexualities, mainly homosexuality, gay men and lesbian women) went beyond terminology. These subjects or areas of study were understood and articulated by many scholars as two separate topics and thus were rarely integrated to expose how historical constructions and the functioning of patriarchy, heteronormativity, heterosexism and institutionalized homophobia work together and affect all people and identities alike. Applying a narrow understanding of identity politics into the study of both gender and sexuality, both discourses as a result lost half their argumentative and analytical potential for a productive critique of patriarchal and heteronormative institutional practices.

Czech feminist scholarship after 1989 gradually produced a wealth of excellent studies, which have successfully challenged the male-dominated mainstream narratives of history, society and culture in the Czech lands, but most of this scholarship did not utilize the category of sexuality. Sexuality remained conceptually locked in a heteronormative framework as applying only to the study of 'alternative' sexualities and hence not necessary for researching the history of women, gender relations, and power dynamics in the

---

68   *The Philosophical Journal* 5/1992; Marie Chřibková, Josef Chuchma and Eva Klimentová, eds. *Feminismus 90. let českýma očina* (Praha: One Woman Press, 1999); Eva Věšínová-Kalivodová, ed. *Společnost žen a mužů z aspektu gender* (Praha: Open Society Fund, 1999); Hana Maříková, ed. *Proměny současné české rodiny* (Praha: SLON, 2000).

69   For example Džamila Stehlíková, Ivo Procházka and Jiří Hromada, *AIDS, homosexualita a společnost* (Praha: Orbis, 1995); Pavlína Janošová, *Homosexualita v názorech současné společnosti* (Praha: Karolinum, 2000); Fanel, 2000; Procházka, Janík and Hromada 2003.

implicitly heteronormatively conceived state and society. Most of this scholarship used the category of gender to demonstrate the plurality of women's identities and voices as well as to analyze how gender, as a relational category, worked in diverse social and political processes from national revival, political culture, education, or sport to medical sciences and literature.[70] Without attention to the constructions of sexuality, however, women and men, as well as heterosexuality and homosexuality, remained oppositional and stable categories. As a result, such scholarship possessed a limited capacity to reveal how heteronormativity, crucial to the workings of the category of gender itself, functioned in particular historical or social contexts, and explore how differently various people might have understood and performed their gender and sexual identities. While most scholars writing on these topics were well-aware that gender and sexuality are interrelated categories, in their research projects they did not necessarily connect them conceptually and analytically together. The few notable exceptions only underscored the general sense of a gap in understanding, which characterized Czech feminist scholarship on women and gender in the early decades of the post-Socialist period.[71]

The reason for this separation can be found to a large degree in the way Czech media handled debates on homosexuality and feminism in the first decade after the collapse of communism. Both topics were exposed to virulent anti-feminism and homophobia in the early 1990s, especially in Czech tabloid media (bulvár), a journalistic trend that was only slowly replaced by more

---

70 Milena Lenderová, Božena Kopičková and Eduard Maur, *Žena v českých zemích od středověku do 20. století* (Praha: Nakladatelství Lidové noviny, 2009); Lenderová 1999; Jana Malínská, *Do politiky prý žena nesmí — proč? Vzdělávání a postavení žen v české společnosti v 19. a na počátku 20. Století* (Praha: SLON, 2005); Dana Musilová, *Z ženského pohledu. Poslankyně a senátorky Národního shromáždění Československé republiky* (Hradec Králové: Univerzita Hradec Králové, 2007); Marie Neudorflová, *České ženy v 19. století. Úsilí a sny, úspěchy i zklamání na cestě k emancipaci* (Praha: Janua, 1999); Denisa Nečasová, "Dějiny žen či gender history? Možnosti, limity, východiska." *Dějiny-teorie-kritika* 1 (2008): 81–102; Daniela Tinková, "Žena" — prázdná kategorie? Od (wo)men's history k gender history v západoevropské historiografii posledních desetiletí 20. století," In *Dějiny žen aneb Evropská žena od středověku do poloviny 20. století v zajetí historiografie*, edited by Kateřina Čadková, Milena Lenderová and Jana Stráníková (Pardubice: Univerzita Pardubice, 2006), 19–32; Jana Ratajová, "Dějiny ženy a koncept genderu v české historiografii," *Kuděj* 1/2 (2005): 159–174.

71 See mainly the brilliant essays from this period by Hana Havelková, most of which are collected in *The Courage to Disagree: Feminist Thought of Hana Havelková and its Reflections*, Věra Sokolová and Lubica Kobová, eds. (Prague, FHS UK: 2019); Libora Oates-Indruchová 2012 and *Discourses of Gender in Pre- and Post-1989 Czech Culture* (Pardubice: Univerzita Pardubice, 2002); Gerlinda Šmausová, mainly "Proti tvrdošíjné představě o ontické povaze gender a pohlaví." *Politika rodu a sexuální identity. Sociální studia* 7 (2000): 15–27; and "Normativní heterosexualita bez nátlaku k prokreaci?" *Gender, rovné příležitosti, výzkum* 2/3 (2004): 1–4; Kateřina Kolářová, "Já a moje Láska": Nad deníky Michaela Fielda Works and Days," in *Vztahy, jazyky, těla*, edited by Libuše Heczková (Praha: FHS, 2007), 405–424; and Kateřina Nedbálková, *Spoutaná Rozkoš: (re) produkce genderu a sexuality v ženské věznici. (Praha: SLON, 2006).*

serious and balanced discussions. The attacks on feminism and feminists in Czech media in the 1990s are legendary and covered in detail elsewhere.[72] As my interrelated parallel analysis of feminist and gay and lesbian discourses exposed, however, the hostile media coverage during this period of time, either skillfully or unwittingly, pitted feminists and gays and lesbians against each other. As the identities of 'feminists' and 'homosexuals' were singled-out and stigmatized separately in both media and public discourses in the 1990s, advocates of both groups had a tendency to articulate their legitimacy and claims for justice through the exclusion, ignorance, or silencing of the other.[73] In the first two post-Socialist decades, the discourse on gender and feminism in the Czech Republic was thus characterized by strong heterosexist undertones, and the discourse on homosexuality, on the other hand, had a distinct anti-feminist character. Both trends had a profound impact on Czech feminist and queer scholarship, influencing also the delayed scholarly attention to queer sexuality during the Socialist period.

THE QUEER ORAL HISTORY PROJECT

In the last two decades, oral history has become an influential and respected method for studying the recent past across the globe.[74] In Czechoslovakia, particularly through the pioneering work of Czech historian Miroslav Vaněk and his team, we learned about the unexpected dimensions and everyday details of the functioning of Communist power, differences in life experiences and attitudes towards the state and society among the workers and intelligentsia in the period of Normalization, or the motivations and visions

---

72   For example, Jitka Malečková, "Nation and Scholarship: Reflections on Gender/Women's Studies in the Czech Republic." In *New Frontiers in Women's Studies: Knowledge, Identity and Nationalism*, edited by Mary Maynard and June Purvis (London: Taylor and Francis, 1995); Jiřina Šmejkalová, "Strašidlo feminismu v českém ,porevolučním' tisku: úvaha, doufejme, historická." In *Žena a muž v médiích*, edited by Hana Havelková and Mirek Vodrážka (Praha: Gender Studies, 1998), 16–18; Libora Oates-Indruchová, "Gender v médiích: nástin sire problematiky," in *Společnost žen a mužů z aspektu gender*, edited by Eva Věšínová-Kalivodová (Praha: Open Society Fund, 1999), 131–152; Rebecca Nash, "Exhaustion from Explanation: Reading Czech Gender Studies in the 1990s," *The European Journal of Women's Studies* 9/3 (2002): 291–309.

73   Vera Sokolova, "Identity Politics and the (B)Orders of Heterosexism: Gays, Lesbians and Feminists in the Czech Media after 1989." In *Mediale Welten in Tschechien nach 1989: Genderprojektionen & Codes des Plebejismus*, edited by Jirina van Leeuwen-Turnovcová and Nicole Richter (München: Kubon und Sagner, 2006), 29–44.

74   Paul Thompson with Joanna Bornat, *The Voice of the Past: Oral History*, 4th edition. (Oxford: Oxford University Press, 2017); Prue Chamberlayne, Michael Rustin, and Tom Wengraf, eds., *Biography and social exclusion in Europe: Experience and life journeys* (Bristol: The Policy Press, 2002); Prue Chamberlayne, Joanna Bornat and Tom Wengraf, eds., *The Turn to Biographical Methods in Social Science: Comparative Issues and Examples* (New York and London: Routledge, 2000).

of the student leaders of the 1989 Velvet Revolution.[75] Oral history has become one of the major methodological tools in elucidating the process of democratization of the country after the collapse of communism and as such has been an invaluable tool facilitating the ongoing process of coming to terms with the Communist past. Oral history helped to open the sensitive and polarizing topic of the expulsion of ethnic Germans from Czechoslovakia in 1945 and 1946; made visible and vocal the victims of the Romani Holocaust (*Porajmos*); vocalized the life stories of the daughters of political prisoners; brought attention to the memories of people persecuted for their religious beliefs, political prisoners, soldiers serving in the black insignia (PTP) units. Oral history has been used to probe Normalization architecture as well as the rural communities of the Czech cultural underground during the 1970s and 1980s. Oral history constituted the main methodological lens in a unique student documentary project, *Children Document the Lives of Heroes (Děti točí hrdiny)*, in which elementary and high school students selected individuals whom they considered to be "heroes" during the Communist times and filmed biographical interviews with them.[76]

Yet these remarkable projects — even those exclusively or substantially focused on women — worked with the category of gender in marginal and rather descriptive ways, and ignored sexuality altogether. A much better job utilizing gender as an analytical category was implemented by feminist scholars, mainly from former Czechoslovakia and former Yugoslavia, in their extensive international project *The Memory of Women*, and its offshoot *The Memory of Roma Women*.[77] Even this project, however, while offering a complex comparative gender analysis from explicit (and diverse) feminist positions, is framed in an unspoken heteronormative way. While the question of

---

75 Miroslav Vaněk and Pavel Mücke, *Velvet Revolutions: An Oral History of Czech Society* (Oxford: Oxford University Press, 2016); *100 Student Revolutions* (Praha: ÚSD, 1999); Pavel Urbášek and Miroslav Vaněk, *Winners? Losers?: Political Elites and Dissent during the So-called Normalization (Biographical Interviews)* (Praha: Prostor, 2005; Vaněk, Miroslav, *Ordinary People...?! A Look into the Lives of the So-called Silent Majority: Biographical Narratives with the Members of Working Class and intelligentsia* (Praha: Academia, 2009); Miroslav Vaněk, Pavel Mücke and Hana Pelikánová, *Naslouchat hlasům paměti: Teoretické a praktické aspekty orální historie* (Praha: Ústav pro soudobé dějiny AV ČR, 2007); Miroslav Vaněk, *Orální historie ve výzkumu soudobých dějin* (Praha: Ústav pro soudobé dějiny AV ČR, 2004).

76 Zuzana Vittvarová, *Osudová kaňka: Příběhy dcer politických vězňů Československa* (Praha: Pavel Mervart, 2011); František Čuňás Stárek and Jiří Kostúr. *Baráky — souostroví svobody* (Praha: Pulchra, 2011); Monika Rychlíková, *... to jsou těžké vzpomínky (Holocaust Romů)*. DVD (Brno a Praha: Muzeum romské kultury a Asociace Film a sociologie, 2002); Jana Kramářová et al. *(Ne)bolí: Vzpomínky Romů na válku a život po válce* (Praha: Člověk v tísni, 2005); Barbora Klímová, *Replaced* (Kat.) (Brno: autorská edice, 2006).

77 Zuzana Kiczková et al., *Pamäť žien. O skúsenosti sebautvárania v biografických rozhovoroch* (Bratislava: Iris, 2006); Pavla Frýdlová, *Všechny naše včerejšky I. and II.: Paměť žen* (Praha: Gender Studies, 1998); Helena Danielová, Dana Zajoncová and Jana Haragaľová, eds. *Paměti romských žen: Kořeny I.* (Brno: Muzeum romské kultury, 2001).

sexual (self)identification of the narrators is not addressed by the authors of the project and the book presents them simply as 'women,' all interviewed women, more than one hundred of them, told their narratives from a heterosexual positionality. By not including sexuality as an analytical category in its theoretical-conceptual apparatus and by not analyzing it in the same way as other aspects of the women's identities, such as gender, ethnicity, social status, education, or age, for example, the project implicitly essentialized heterosexuality as an inherent aspect of the women's identities, not necessary to discuss.

The lack of scholarly interest in queer lives by oral historians of East European state socialism is stunning. In the past twenty years, there has been so much attention devoted by oral historians to a great variety of contexts, subjects and professional positionalities and personal identities under state socialism that the enduring ignorance of queer lives is staggering. In the mainstream and respected oral history narratives that have been gradually shaping the collective memory of socialism, influencing public discourses of the recent past and shaping educational approaches to the Communist era, queer people's voices and experiences have been invisible. It is as if queer people's voices were worthless for an 'appropriate' study of the Communist era and their memories were relevant only for a (narrowly defined) field of the history of sexuality, detached from the 'proper' historiography of socialism.

In 2015, in an effort to challenge this absence and denial, a group of Czech historians and activists formed the Society for Queer Memory (SfQM), inviting queer people to actively participate in shaping the collective memories and narratives of the recent Czechoslovak past.[78] Research for this book fits within the ongoing, broadly shaped queer oral history project promoted by the SfQM, which focuses on conducting and collecting biographical interviews with queer people, who spent most of their lives in Socialist Czechoslovakia before 1989. Creating a unique and valuable archival material, the stories and experiences continuously shared by queer narrators in this project remind us that the history of Socialist Czechoslovakia is far richer than is often discernible from its mainstream and most celebrated accounts. The story unfolded in the pages of this book is based on 54 narrative accounts of queer lives, covering the period from the late 1940s through 1989. Personally, I conducted sixteen oral history interviews with Czech queer seniors. The oral history subcollection of the SfQM archive contains additional 33 biographical interviews with LGBT seniors, conducted by different SfQM interviewers in

---

78   The Society for Queer Memory (SfQM) is a small, non-profit civic organization founded in 2015 by activists and scholars led by Czech historians Jan Seidl and Anna Hájková. SfQM is based in Prague and aims to collect historical artefacts and popularize the LGBT past. Among its many activities and projects, SfQM oversees an ongoing queer oral history project and supervises its archival collection.

the years 2009–2018. In addition to my own biographical narratives, in this book I also work with thirteen of the SfQM interviews accessible to scholars for research purposes (nineteen interviews remain inaccessible to the public for a variery of reasons; one was conducted with an American lesbian woman who started to live in Czechoslovakia only after 1989). Lastly, my research sources were enriched also by a collection of fifteen written transsexual autobiographical accounts from the Socialist era, which I was generously permitted to study in the private archive of Hana Fifková, a renowned Czech sexologist specializing in transsexuality. To protect the privacy of the narrators and in lieu with standard ethical practice, the real names of all 54 narrators, whose memories and experiences of their lives during Czechoslovak socialism I share and analyze in this book, remain confidential and they are identified only either by their initials or first names of their choice.[79]

Queer oral history is important not only for the empirical reason of filling in the blank spots of our recent past and for giving voices to continuously marginalized identities. It is crucial from a theoretical point of view as well. It provides evidence of the heterogeneity of queer identities and experiences during the period of state socialism and, equally importantly, also of the diversity and disunity of the apparatus of state power during the Communist regime. As already discussed, with a few notable and very recent exceptions,[80] the dominant accounts of queer experiences and lives in Eastern Europe during the Communist era painted quite a homogenizing picture of 'homosexual' or 'gay' past. The frequent homogenization and reduction of queer subjectivity and lived experiences into the unitary category of the 'homosexual' rests in taking at face value the pervasive medical discourse on non-normative sexuality, which centered on a dichotomous conception of sexuality and gave the impression that 'deviant' homosexuality was the only alternative to 'healthy' heterosexuality. Moreover, the homosexual/gay past has been overwhelmingly narrated and represented by male memories and voices.[81] Authors often explain and legitimate their focus on men's experiences by the alleged absence of women in public spaces, legitimized by shared myths about passivity and invisibility of female (homo)sexuality. Women's invisibility, interpreted as empirical absence, then analytically translates into a justified male-dominated picture of 'gay' past. Queer oral history breaks up these neat categories and connections and unearths much more flexible and complex pictures of queer sexualities lived by people in different countries of the Soviet Bloc.

---

79 Joan Sangster, "Telling Our Stories: Feminist Debates and the Use of Oral History," *Women's History Review* 3/1, 1994: 5–28.

80 Stella 2015; Szulc 2017; Armstrong 2020; Tomasz Basiuk and Jedrzej Burszta, *Queers in State Socialism: Cruising 1970s Poland* (London: Routledge, 2020).

81 Seidl 2012; Schindler 2013; Miřácký 2009; Fanel 2000; Lemke 1991.

Given the overwhelming attention paid by Czech historians of sexuality to the experiences of gay men,[82] my oral history research intentionally focused on female narrators (though men were not principally excluded). Eleven narrators were women, three were men, and two narrators identified privately as transsexual or transgender even though they never formally protested their officially assigned gender (which in both cases was female). The oldest narrator was born in 1929, the youngest in 1952. All thirty biographical narratives used in this book methodologically fulfill the classification of feminist oral history.[83] All narrators were interviewed at least twice in long biographical interviews lasting from one to (in a few exceptional cases) four hours. The narratives focused on the period before 1989 and were primarily grounded in free-flowing narratives along four main axes: 1) the formation and articulation of individual gender and sexual identity of the narrator; 2) the concrete sexual behavior, relationships, and experiences lived by the narrator during socialism; 3) relationship and power dynamics between the narrator and the 'state' and 'society'; and 4) resistance and/or conformity to the surrounding sex-gender system with special attention to specific strategies and tools for enacting personal agency and creating 'queer' spaces and solidarity. Choosing this interpretative grid for the analysis of the interviews enables teasing out commonalities as well as capturing unique individual differences among the narrators. Such an approach prevents generalizations and temptations to look for some all-fitting picture of 'homosexual lives during communism.' Instead, it exposes the diversity of queer identities and lives, and in doing so contributes to the study of East European communism by complicating the predominantly heteronormative historical narratives of Czechoslovak socialism produced so far.

The interviews reveal that, contrary to the belief that we somehow 'know' what it meant to be a 'lesbian' or 'gay' during the Communist period in Czechoslovakia, queer people lived varied lives and experienced socialism in many different and often quite contradictory ways. While there existed a unitary legal framework and structured patterns of discrimination, the oral history narratives help us remember that such systematic forms of control are experienced individually, making it impossible to place any generalization or theory on the nature of 'homosexuality' under communism. The stories independently demonstrated that in the absence of a common terminology, channels of communication and the ability to exchange information, people

---

82   As noted before, a noteworthy exception to the male-dominated trend in the Czech queer oral history is the work of Anna Hájková, who focuses primarily on the queer history of the Holocaust but also conducted oral history narratives with queer women about the socialist past.

83   Sherna Berger Gluck and Daphne Patai, eds. *Women's Voices: The Feminist Practice of Oral History* (New York and London: Routledge, 1991); Sangster 1994; Thompson and Bornat 2017; Kiczková 2006.

lived their lives and sexual and gender identities in a myriad of ways. Often, and perhaps surprisingly, it was not their 'homosexuality' that played the decisive role in their life opportunities and decisions.

Based on the complex web of memories shared in the queer oral history project, the book consciously works against simplistic and homogenizing assertions of early studies of gay and lesbian history in Czechoslovakia, which claimed that "during socialism gays were repressed into invisibility" or that "under communism homosexuals had to get married in order to hide their true sexual orientation."[84] In addition, I am cautious not to frame my narrators as either victims or heroes of their times. Instead, I search for concrete situations in their lives when they confronted institutionalized power or specific individuals in the positions of power and examine those encounters. At the same time, I explore moments, in which they exercised power and agency or transformed state control and scrutiny into their advantage.

The forty-five lives of queer seniors (in the time of the interviews in their sixties, seventies and eighties) who grew up and lived during Czechoslovak socialism, shared on the pages of this book are diverse and defy any simple divisions into binary or simple categories such as men and women, homosexuals and transsexuals. The narrators also differ very much in their complex social positions and attitudes towards the Socialist state, which cannot be easily understood by categorizing them as victims, dissidents, or supporters of the Communist regime. Sixteen narrators identified over the course of the interviews as 'homosexual,' 'gay' or 'lesbian' with varying degrees of acceptance or rejection of those terms. Fifteen considered themselves 'transsexual,' nine of which were FtM men and six MtF women, most of which professed their self-understanding as "heterosexual" women and men. Two narrators identified as both 'transsexual' and 'lesbian.' Only one narrator used the term transgender for their self-understanding, accompanied by a self-identified 'lesbian desire.' Ten narrators refused to attach to themselves any labels at all. Some narrators were members of the Communist Party of Czechoslovakia, and some moved within dissident circles. On occasions, they mingled together in the queer contexts of 'salons' or secret apartment parties, as well as in queer public spaces. Some narrators were deeply devout Christian 'gays' and 'lesbians'; others identified as atheist. Most female narrators lived in long-term monogamous relationships with another woman, sometimes along with their children, while some preferred anonymous sex with other women in public restrooms. There were women and men among the narrators who had no doubts about their homosexuality, as well as those who never questioned their homosexuality but until now they are not sure whether they are a man or a woman. There are those who consider the Communist period the "best

---

84 Fanel 1999; Janošová 2000.

times of their life" as well as those who are bitter about their lives during the Communist regime and feel their life was destroyed for political reasons. There are those, who were called 'faggots' since childhood and those who claim they were fully accepted by their peers. All of them were married (some to 'heterosexuals,' some to other 'homosexuals') or had at least one long-term relationship with another married man or a woman. Most biographical interviews were initiated by historians, who approached the narrators and asked them to share their life stories, but a few narrators came to the SfQM on their own and themselves offered to share their memories.[85]

The immense heterogeneity of identities and experiences, which is contained even in this small group of people who participated in the queer oral history project, exposes the myth and flaws of homogenous narratives of 'homosexual' or 'gay and lesbian' history during Czechoslovak socialism. The category of homosexuality is not complex enough to capture the nuanced dimensions of gender and sexual subjectivities, romantic sentiments, sexual desires and practices, as well as discrimination, fear and shame the narrators experienced in their lives. Due to the absence of public discussions of non-normative sexuality and the lack of naming, love and sexuality had no easy relation to sexual identity during the Communist regime in Czechoslovakia. At the same time, similar to the conservative and sexually repressive context of nineteenth-century America described by Smith-Rosenberg, Socialist Czechoslovakia created far more space for moving within and beyond the binary categories of homosexuality and heterosexuality than one might expect in an authoritarian regime of the Soviet Bloc.[86]

But despite this diversity, which prevents writing a history of homosexuals, gays or lesbians, there is obviously something that connects all the narrators together and forms a reason to bring their memories together on the pages of one book. The connection used in this book is a broad concept of queer subjectivity and desire that allows for diversity of identity feelings and experiences, while accounts for structural obstacles and limits posed by the binary understanding of gender and sexuality by the Czechoslovak Socialist state. Queer is not an easy choice either as it equally threatens to homogenize the narrators as 'other.'[87] The concept of 'non-heterosexuality,' which offers itself as a possible alternative, however, derives its name from the rejection of or definition against the heterosexual norm and thus perpetuates the negative grounding of non-heterosexual identities as not living up to the standard of the proper norm. The category of queer, while also a problematic and complicated one, at least contains a possibility for affirmative constructions

---

85 I would like to thank Jan Seidl from the SfQM for this insight.
86 Smith-Rosenberg 1975.
87 Stella 2015, 5.

of an identity that can stand on its own and is possible to embrace and perform in a myriad of authentic ways.[88]

Historically, heterosexuality has built an absolute conceptual dominance
through which it relegates all other kinds of sexual identities and practices
into marginalized or deviant positions. Homosexuality, according to Katz, is
just one of the marginalized sexualities, one that unlike queerness requires
stable and dichotomous historical subjects and explicit articulation.[89] The
concept of homosexuality argues for a specific sexual identity, which ultimately can be collectively shared and result in obtaining and advancing civil
rights. The concept of queer, on the other hand, emphasizes the awareness of
non-normative and marginalized identities, which are often hard to articulate
and unequivocally share with others. Lisa Duggan, to offer another strategy, suggested to get around these questions by using the model of religious
tolerance. She argued that instead of irritating the proponents of historical
essentialism by explanations of the socially constructed nature of gender and
sexuality, it might be worthwhile to point out that sexual desire, like religion, is not biological or fixed. At the same time, it is not frivolous or easily
changed. Sexual difference from the expected and heavily promoted heterosexual norm can be thus seen as a form of dissent.[90]

While working with the queer narratives from Socialist Czechoslovakia,
many of which exhibited an inability or reluctance towards naming, I was
continuously confronted by questions posed by the American historian Leila
Rupp. In her work, Rupp rejected the usage of the categories and terms 'lesbian,' 'gay' or even 'homosexual' in historical contexts, when we lack explicit
evidence not only that the terms existed and people actually used them but
also when we do not know what people meant by those terms. Rupp asks what
it actually means to say about someone that she was a lesbian or he was gay.
Considering this question in regards to her own aunt, who lived all her adult
life with another woman but never actually said aloud anything about her
sexuality, she wonders what she would answer: "That she identifies herself
that way? That she had sex with another woman? That she was in love with
another woman? That she saw herself in a conceptual category with other
women who loved women?" And what if I ask her, Rupp continues, and she
says no, I was not "one of those." Then what?[91]

These questions bring us back to the importance of oral history. Collecting the diverse voices and memories of queer people during state socialism

---

88 Butler 1990; J. Jack Halberstam, *Gaga Feminism: Sex, Gender and The End of Normal* (Boston: Beacon Press, 2012).
89 Katz 1990. Katz conceptualized this dominance as "erotic apartheid," 276.
90 Lisa Duggan, "Queering the State." *Social Text* 38/1994: 1–14.
91 Leila Rupp, *A Desired Past: A Short History of Same-Sex Sexuality in America* (Chicago: University of
Chicago Press, 1999), 5–10; "Thinking About "Lesbian History" *Feminist Studies* 39/2, 2013: 357–36.

is urgent for at least three reasons. First, given the lack of written first-hand accounts that could be used to document the lives and conditions of queer people under socialism, oral history accounts bring invaluable and irreplaceable individual narratives of those conditions that cannot be transmitted and told by anybody else. In most cases, queer identities were never explicitly articulated but what is important — they were experiences actually lived. These narratives bring an "authenticity of experience," as Joan W. Scott argued, which would otherwise stay hidden, forgotten and irretrievable. At the same time, the experiences themselves must be understood as objects of inquiry. It is important to analyze how such particular experiences were constructed and what they tell us about their historical and social contexts. The 'evidence of experience,' Scott urges, should be a part of the questioning and not a fact standing above analysis.[92]

Second, queer narratives can also serve as an apt example of a productive challenge to normative, static and antagonistic constructions of mainstream historical narratives.[93] As such, they can have an important impact on how we view both the collective and individual periodization of our lives. As Judith Halberstam argued:

> Queer subcultures produce alternative temporalities by allowing their participants to believe that their futures can be imagined according to logics that lie outside those paradigmatic markers of life experience — namely birth, marriage, reproduction and death.[94]

Halberstam's argument can be applied to oral history as well. She distinguishes between the concepts of 'queer' and 'family' time, arguing that "respectability and notions of the normal, on which it depends, may be upheld by middle-class logic of reproductive temporality." 'Family time,' 'time of reproduction' or 'generational time' are all synonyms used by Halberstam for normative practices, which are governed by the perceived biological clock for women, children's needs and the passing down of goods, morals, values and national past through "family ties from one generation to the next."[95]

92   Joan W. Scott, "The Evidence of Experience," *Critical Inquiry* 17/4 (1991): 773–797.
93   The following arguments, which I am revisiting here in the context of oral history have been developed together with Kateřina Kolářová in our common text "Gender and Generation in Mutual Perspective." In *Gender and Generation: Interdisciplinary Intersections and Approaches*, edited by Kateřina Kolářová and Věra Sokolová (Praha: Litteraria Pragensia, 2007), 1–20. See also, Joseph Allen Boone, Martin Dupuis, Martin Meeker, and Karin Quimby, eds. *Queer Frontiers: Millennial Geographies, Genders, and Generations* (Madison: University of Wisconsin Press, 2000); Corinne P. Hayden, "Gender, Genetics, and Generation: Reformulating Biology in Lesbian Kinship," *Cultural Anthropology* 10.1. (1995): 41–63.
94   Judith Halberstam, *In a Queer Time and Place* , (2005), 2.
95   Ibid., 3–4.

Her conception of 'queer time' then brings the potential of approaching oral history narratives shared by queer people in radically new (and gendered) ways. 'Queer time' refers to new understandings of history, community, sexual identity, embodiment, time and space, which are all based in highly subjective and non-normative experiences and behavior. Nonetheless, by challenging the oppressive weight of normative, homogenous constructions of biologized generational concepts and replacing them with a diffuse mode of temporality rooted in personal choice and self-understanding, 'queer time' can provide a new mode for the sharing of collective experiences and identities, and thus for creating new alternative bases for the (re)formulation of both gender and sexual experiences during state socialism.[96]

And third, queer oral history enables us to examine possibilities and ways of asserting individual subjectivities, which cannot be extracted from institutional documents. Enacted legislature or written definitions do not necessarily mean that they were applied in the same way as intended, and there are even larger discrepancies between laws and regulations and the actual ways in which people lived their lives. Biographical narratives are important for revealing social discrimination and homophobia during socialism on the one hand, as well as documenting transgressive and defiant behavior of queer people on the other hand, neither of which can be easily excavated from the written archival sources.[97]

In sum, rather than participate in the political-intellectual project of interpreting the identities of and differences between 'heterosexuals' and 'homosexuals' in Communist Czechoslovakia, I argue that a combination of queer oral history and analysis of the official discourses that were used to produce a particular understanding of queer people as deviant or deficient can more critically expose the pathways of marginalization as well as agency of queer people in the past. By focusing on biographical narratives and discourse as a site of political contestation and power, I reject theories of totalitarianism that locate Communist power more or less solely within the coercive political institutions of the party-state. Such theories not only problematically treat power as something 'above' society and alien to it, but also ignore the role of language in legitimating political practices and in producing truth claims about who the 'homosexuals' were and how they did or did not integrate within the larger Czechoslovak society.

---

96 Sokolová and Kolářová 2007.
97 Sokolova 2008.

POWER AND AGENCY IN AUTHORITARIAN SOCIETIES

In her reflections on the role of individual responsibility for sustaining Communist power, Hungarian philosopher Éva Ancsel pointed out that there is no such thing as collective guilt or collective responsibility. She argued that blaming the harmful effects of the previous regime "on the system" was a simple, but inadequate interpretation because "in reality everyone played their part in maintaining this system."[98] Her argument was a direct response to one of the most pervasive paradigms of historical writing on Eastern Europe during the Cold War: the idea that East European Communist regimes were monolithic leviathans controlling and ruling a mass of relatively passive people.[99] As Czech historian Karel Kaplan argued in 1987, the Communist regime in Czechoslovakia was Janus-faced: its "formal façade" of allegedly "democratic" party institutions covered up the "the real structure of the party... that results from its power mission, from its exercise of absolute control over society, from its efforts to resolve all social problems and direct every movement in society by means of its resolutions and instructions."[100]

Such conceptions of Communist regimes as having 'absolute control over society,' though largely discredited today, have still had a lasting and pervasive effect on how some historians of Eastern Europe conceive of 'power' under communism. The 'totalitarian thesis' of East European communism could be summarized in the following way:[101] With the Russian Revolution, Soviet history became determined by the totalitarian political dynamics of the Communist Party. Over time, party leaders solidified political power through centralized bureaucratic organization, police surveillance, ideological orthodoxy, disciplined leadership and party control over all social positions of prominence. Since the 1930s, Stalin perfected these mechanisms of power and asserted absolute control over society through mass terror, purges, the secret police and an evermore totalized party apparatus. According to the

---

98 Éva Ancsel, An interview with Barbara Einhorn, Budapest, May 26, 1990. Cited in Einhorn, 1993, 5. Václav Havel makes the same point in his "Power of the Powerless."

99 Richard Staar, *Communist Regimes in Eastern Europe* (Stanford: Stanford University Press, 1982).

100 Karel Kaplan, *The Communist Party in Power: A Profile of Party Politics in Czechoslovakia* (Boulder and London: Westview Press, 1987), xiii. By the "façade" Kaplan meant the structure of the party in a "system of tens," meaning that the ratio of party members to the total population is 1:10, a regional apparatchik oversees ten basic organizations, a region is made up of ten districts, the country is formed by ten regions, and so on, suggesting democratic rule, when in fact such a system is most suitable for effective control and surveillance. See also, Barbara Jancar, *Czechoslovakia and the Absolute Monopoly of Power: A Study of Political Power in a Communist System* (New York: Praeger Publishers, 1971).

101 No one particular author may accept all of this conception; it is simply meant as an illustration of a typical, "totalitarian" conception of communism's main aspects, which can be found in many different historical works. For a more sustained discussion of the thesis, see Stephen F. Cohen, *Rethinking the Soviet Experience* (Oxford: Oxford University Press, 1985).

totalitarian point of view, Stalin could be easily compared to Hitler, because they were both masters of using the state to terrorize their respective societies through total control of all the main aspects of life.[102] Stalinist zealotry subsided after his death in 1953, but the apparatus of the party-state remained more or less intact not only in the USSR but, to different degrees, in the countries of the Eastern Bloc as well. Up to 1989, the Czechoslovak party-state continued to exert total control of a passive, 'privatized' Czechoslovak society by punishing dissenters, pacifying people through consumer goods, deploying constant surveillance, preventing access to education for ideologically unfit subjects, and using party membership as an access to social mobility.

Today, the only research institution in the Czech Republic established by law (in 2007) to study authoritarianism in the 20th-century Czechoslovak history, bears the name The Institute for the Study of Totalitarian Regimes (*Ústav pro studium totalitních režimů*).[103] While the law defines the time of the Nazi control and occupation of Czechoslovakia, dating from the Munich Conference on September 30, 1938 and lasting until the end of WW II on May 4, 1945, as the "period of unfreedom" ("*doba nesvobody*"), it states explicitly that

The era of Communist totalitarian power (*období komunistické totalitní moci*) is understood as the period of Czechoslovak history from February 25, 1948, to December 29, 1989, and also the period directly preceeding this time period, in which events were under way preparing for the totalitarian takeover of power (*totalitní uchopení moci*) by the Communist Party of Czechoslovakia.[104]

The institute claims that it "studies and objectively evaluates the period of unfreedom and the period of Communist totalitarian power and the anti-democratic and criminal activities of state organs... criminal activities of

---

102 For a critical appraisal of this argument and relevant literature, see for example Ian Kershaw, "Totalitarianism Revisited: Nazism and Stalinism in Comparative Perspective," in *The Nazi Dictatorship: Problems and Perspectives of Interpretation*, edited by Ian Kershaw (London, Baltimore: Edward Arnold, 1985 and 2000).

103 The Czech Institute is the only one of similar institutions in all post-Communist countries in Eastern Europe that carries the term "totalitarian" in its title. In Romania, equivalent institution is called *The Institute for the Investigation of Communist Crimes and the Memory of the Romanian Exile*; in Bulgaria, *The Institute for Studies of the Recent Past*; in Poland, *The Institute of National Remembrance — Commission for the Prosecution of Crimes against the Polish Nation*; and in Slovakia the *Institute for National Memory* (*Ústav pamäti národa*). In Germany, there is *The Federal Commissioner for the Stasi Archives*. Hungarian *The House of Terror* in Budapest is exceptional in that, rather than being an academic research institution, it is a museum that emerged as a political project of Victor Orban's Fidesz party and covers Hungarian history only in the years of 1944–1956, from the Nazi takeover to the Hungarian Uprising, and interprets communism as an imported evil, thereby minimizing any complicity of the Hungarian state and society in both Nazi and Communist dictatorships.

104 Zákon č. 181/2007Sb, Ústavy ČR, *O ústavu pro studium totalitních režimů*, § 2. June 8, 2007.

the Communist Party of Czechoslovakia, as well as other organizations based on its ideology"; "analyzes causes and ways of the destruction of the democratic regime during the period of Communist totalitarian power"; "documents the participation of people in supporting the Communist regime and resisting it"; and "obtains and makes public documents revealing about the period of totalitarian Communist power"[105] — but by defining the Communist power, as well as the entire forty years of the duration of the Communist regime, as a period of Communist "totalitarian power," it inherently predetermines the nature of power (and thus the regime as such) it sets out to study and objectively analyze in the first place.

There is no need to rehearse all of the criticisms of the totalitarian conception of power here, but a few are noteworthy. First, the totalitarian consensus ignores forms of popular resistance that were quite common in many Communist societies, such as political subversion through folk and rock music, 'tramping,' literature and historical symbols, but also nudism and sports.[106] Second, the consensus conceives of the nomenklatura and other political actors as automatons of the party-state, not as agents with their own ideas, intentions, and sources of power. Third, East European history is conceived as primarily political, with cultural, social, religious and gender history allegedly determined 'from above' by the political dynamics. And fourth, the totalitarian thesis presupposes the normative claim that communism is inherently evil, coercive and violent.[107]

Even if many scholars do not accept the totalitarian thesis,[108] it has influenced how the workings of power during the Communist regime have been conceived — as intrinsically based in the political institutions of the

---

105 Ibid, § 4.

106 For example, see Josie McLellan, "State Socialist Bodies: East German Nudism from Ban to Boom," *The Journal of Modern History* 79/1 (2007): 48–79; Herzog 2011; Jan Kubik, *The Power of Symbols Against the Symbols of Power: The Rise of Solidarity and the Fall of State Socialism in Poland* (University Park: The Pennsylvania State University Press, 1994); Paulina Bren, "Weekend Getaways: The *Chata*, the *Tramp* and the Politics of Private Life in Post-1968 Czechoslovakia" in *Socialist Spaces: Sites of Everyday Life in the Eastern Bloc*, David Crowley and Susan E. Reid, eds., (Oxford and New York: Berg 2002); Petr Roubal, *Spartakiads: The Politics of Physical Culture in Communist Czechoslovakia* (Prague: Karolinum, 2019).

107 Stephen White, "Political Science as Ideology: The Study of Soviet Politics" in *Political Questions*, edited by B. Chapman and A. Potter (Manchester, 1975); Alexander Dallin, "Bias and Blunders in American Studies on the USSR," *Slavic Review* (September 1973). For other insightful critiques of the totalitarian thesis see, for example, Mary Fulbrook, *The Anatomy of a Dictatorship: Inside the GDR, 1949-1989* (New York: Oxford University Press, 1995); by the same author *Citizenship, Nationalism and Migration in Europe* (New York: Routledge, 1996); Svetlana Boym, *Common Places: Mythologies of Everyday Life In Russia* (Cambridge, MA: Harvard University Press, 1994); or Yuri Slezkine, "The USSR as a Communal Apartment, of How a Socialist State Promoted Ethnic Particularism," *Slavic Review*, 53:2 (Summer 1994): 414–52.

108 See, for example, Jacques Rupnik, *Dějiny komunistické strany Československa: od počátků do převzetí moci* (Prague: Academia, 2002).

party-state. Whether or not such power was totalized, some historians talk as if in Communist countries the only source of power with any impact was institutional. Yet an overly institutionalized conception of power can easily ignore other possible historical narratives and explanations of life during state socialism. The book challenges these assumptions in several ways. First, by looking at the discursive face of power rather than its overt, institutional form. Institutional conceptions of power, like the totalitarian thesis itself, ignore how laws, ideas and norms actually affect people in their everyday existence. They also ignore the role of "societal attitudes" and implicit biases in influencing how doctors, educators, editors, and other low-level state actors treated queer people in everyday contexts. A discursive conception of power, on the other hand, can bring the roles of societal attitudes, official rhetoric, cultural norms, and other factors to bear on the marginalization and acceptance of queer people in the country. As Foucault argued on numerous occasions, "power relations are rooted deep in the social nexus, not reconstituted 'above' society as a supplementary structure whose radical effacement one could perhaps dream of."[109]

Such an argument applies just as well to capitalist societies as Socialist ones: in each case, locating power involves looking at the concrete ways a group of people or individuals are objectified, defined and subordinated. Official laws may be one, but certainly not the only, site where such power was exercised. In fact, medical experts constituted a very important 'nexus' in Czechoslovakia because they were participants or purveyors of two different but interlinked discourses — popular discourses about 'non-heterosexuals' 'from below' and official discourses on 'homosexuality' 'from above' — and they thus had the potential of inflicting double harm on queer people by translating one discourse into the other. At the same time, they also had the power to alleviate the pressures and effectively obliterate the negative effects of one discourse through the other.

Second, policies written in the legal code of the regime are never immutable since they affect real people. This is because, even if local officials are ordered to follow directives from above, they still have the *discursive freedom* to interpret and apply laws according to the popular prejudices and stereotypes that inform their attitudes and behavior. This does not mean that low-level employees were free to do what they wanted or that they were not monitored by their superiors. Rather, it means that such officials, simply as interpretive beings, applied policies in ways that more directly related to popular consciousness and culture than according to the ideological straightjacket of the letter of the law. According to this view, local actors have

---

109 Michel Foucault, "The Subject and Power," cited in Hubert Dreyfus and Paul Rabinow, *Michel Foucault: Beyond Structuralism and Hermeneutics* (Chicago: University of Chicago Press, 1983): 222.

agency and are embedded in social and cultural networks that shape their behavior — precisely the types of 'state-society' relations that the totalitarian thesis rejects from the start.[110] Institutionalist conceptions of power create sharp conceptual divisions between state and society and have the potential to remove society from positions of responsibility for the harmful legacies of communism. On the other hand, theories of power rooted too much in social structures or overarching discourses lose sight of how people internalize ideas and exercise power in practice.[111]

Third, 'marginalization' by definition requires subjects to be marginalized. However, queer people in Socialist Czechoslovakia were not easily defined or visible 'subjects,' let alone a homogenous group. Unlike the Roma, for example, they were not characterized by any cultural characteristics, locality, social status or family background. As this book shows, individual queer people understood their sexuality in vastly different ways. As such, it was not possible for 'state power' to easily marginalize them or discriminate against them in the ways that available scholarship describes it. Some studies, discussed in the previous section, pointed out the necessity of 'homosexuals' to hide, their inability to meet and lead open sexual lives, impossibility to create a positive collective identity and subculture. While recognizing the state pressure on 'normality' and 'decency,' a more complex understanding of the relationship between queer people and the state and society is needed.

Lastly, one of the most important forms of power not grasped by institutionalist approaches to history has been the social regulation of normalcy. In Communist societies, in the supposed absence of socio-economic differences as signifiers of status, official discourse repressed class-based notions of difference, even though these societies had real class hierarchies of their own (such as between the nomenklatura and the majority population). Without these class signifiers, social differences between people were sometimes cast in terms of 'decency' or normality. To be 'decent' or normal was a key element of social citizenship. In order to be able to participate in the advantages offered by the Socialist citizenship, individuals and groups were expected to behave in 'normal' and 'proper' ways. The concept of 'decency' or normality

---

110 For an insightful discussion of discourse and agency in context, see also Pierre Bourdieu's concept of "habitus," in *Language & Symbolic Power* (Cambridge, MA: Harvard University Press, 1991).

111 Some interpreters believe that Foucault makes this mistake. According to Axel Honneth, for example, Foucault maintained a "systems-theoretic" position that all social interaction is essentially permeated by relations of subordination and domination. To the contrary, I think that Foucault never fully maintained a systems-theoretic conception of power. In the *History of Sexuality* and the essay "The Subject and Power," Foucault formulated a conception of subversive politics in which individuals interrupt "systems" of power while creating "new modes of subjectivities." For a critique of the systems-theoretic view, see Axel Honneth, *The Critique of Power* (Cambridge: MIT Press, 1991); chapters 5 and 6.

was regulated by both society and the state. On the one hand, it was one of the notions that kept the hegemony of the ruling class functioning; on the other hand, it was also an important way Czechoslovak heterosexual majority differentiated itself from the 'deviant,' yet largely invisible, 'homosexual' minority.[112]

Historically, a part of the Communist enterprise was purifying these differences, whether social, ethnic, or sexual.[113] In Czechoslovakia, these trends toward homogeneity were heightened by practices enacted even prior to the accession of the Communist party to power, such as the expulsion of ethnic Germans and Hungarians after WWII.[114] After the decriminalization of homosexuality in 1961, however, the Communist state did not attempt to enact any other punitive legislation against homosexuals. In fact, Czechoslovak Socialist legal discourse was rather lenient and progressive. Digressions from the prescribed social heteronormativity were regulated by the official sexological definitions of deficiency and deviance from the heterosexual norm. Next to biographical narratives, which can be revealing about how the marginalization of queer people happened from 'below' through prejudices and implicit biases outside of institutions, in Communist Czechoslovakia it is also important to study Socialist expert discourses, which exercised a high level of respect and authority, from both the general public and the leadership of the Communist party, and at the same time contained a large degree of autonomy and agency.[115] Rather than interpreting the identities and differences of 'heterosexuals,' 'homosexuals,' and 'transsexuals' in Communist Czechoslovakia, an analysis of the official discourses that were used to produce a particular understanding of homosexuals and transsexuals as deviant or deficient can more critically expose the pathways of marginalization of queer people in the past.

By focusing on discourse as a site of political contestation and power, I reject the concept of 'totalitarian Communist power,' which locates power more or less solely within the coercive political institutions of the party-state. Such a concept not only problematically treats power as something 'above' society

---

112 Průcha 2001.
113 See, for example, an excellent account by Kate Brown, *A Biography of No Place: From Ethnic Borderland to Soviet Heartland* (Cambridge, MA: Harvard University Press, 2005); Anastazia Karakasidou, *Fields of Wheat, Hills of Blood: Passages to Nationhood in Greek Macedonia, 1870–1990* (Chicago: University of Chicago Press, 1997); Yuri Slezkine, *Arctic Mirrors: Russia and the Small Peoples of the North* (Ithaca: Cornell University Pres, 1993); Roman Szporluk, *National Identity and Ethnicity in Russia and the New States of Eurasia* (Armonk: M.E. Sharpe Press, 1994); or extensive collection of essays *Cultures and Nations of Central East Europe: Essays in Honor of Roman Szporluk* (Cambridge, MA: Harvard University Press, 2000).
114 Eagle Glassheim, "Ethnic Cleansing, Communism, and Environmental Devastation in Czechoslovakia's Borderlands, 1945-1989." *The Journal of Modern History*, 78:1 (2006): 65–92.
115 Havelková and Oates, eds., 2014.

and alien to it, but also ignores the role of language in legitimating political practices and in producing truth claims about who the 'homosexuals' were and how they did or did not integrate within the larger Czechoslovak society. Next to oral history, which is my principal analytical tool to examine the experiences of queer people, this book is also based on discursive analysis of the medical discourse, which is by definition interpretive and qualitative, but it exposes important systems and mechanisms of marginalization and oppression enacted through language construction and usage.[116] Using the combination of oral history and discourse analysis of the medical discourse as my main interpretive lens of the history of Socialist Czechoslovakia serves two related purposes. First, in order to contextualize the limits and possibilities of living queer lives, for understanding how heteronormativity was achieved and perpetuated vis-a-vis the constructions of the individual and collective 'homosexual' and 'transsexual' subjects, and second, for understanding how queer people themselves interpreted these categories and negotitated their lives within them.

The book points to ideological associations and power dynamics of discourse, which are often oppressive and exclusionary, but tend to remain overlooked and under-analyzed. According to Václav Havel's famous analysis of power in "The Power of the Powerless," Communist societies are best understood as "post-totalitarian" states in which power is exercised not through coercive force, but through the diffusion of ideological discourse in society. Ideology, in Havel's view, links the political system to individuals by creating a linguistic arena where the political system self-referentially legitimates itself through the discourse of socialism. While the political system claims to be humanist, egalitarian and socially just, the "truth" of such a system is that it "serves people only to the extent necessary that people serve it."[117] Because ideology serves the interests of the state rather than being an interpretation of reality, ideology produces "a world of appearances, a mere ritual, a formalized language deprived of semantic content with reality and transformed into a system of ritual signs that replace reality with pseudo-reality."[118]

---

116 For discussions of discourse analysis, see especially, Norman Fairclough, "Critical Discourse Analysis as a Method in Social Scientific Research" (121-138); Siegfried Jäger, "Discourse and Knowledge: Theoretical and Methodological Aspects of a Critical Discourse and Dispositive Analysis" (31-62) and Teun A. van Dijk, "Multidisciplinary CDA: A Plea for Diversity" (95-120). All in *Methods of Critical Discourse Analysis*, Ruth Wodak and Michael Meyer, eds. (London: Sage Publications, 2001); See also, Norman Fairclough, *Analyzing Discourse: Textual Analysis for Social Research* (New York: Routledge, 2003); Nelson Phillips and Cynthia Hardy, *Discourse Analysis: Investigating Processes of Social Construction* (London: Sage Publications, 2002) or for a good application of the method, Roman Kuhar, *Media Representations of Homosexuality: An Analysis of the Print Media in Slovenia, 1970-2000* (Ljublana: Mirovni inštitut, 2003).

117 Václav Havel, "The Power of the Powerless," in *Open Letters* (London: Faber and Faber, 1991), 135.

118 Ibid., 138.

Without accepting Havel's assumption that we can know what is "real" and "true" outside of ideological frameworks, I appropriate his notion that ideology is not a set of ideas standing above society, but is a discursive field containing ideas that are internalized and projected by people in order for them to negotiate their lives in accordance with "official" norms.

If ideology is discursive and 'post-totalitarian' power is present when ideology is internalized, then the power to define *how* or *if* 'homosexuals' and 'transsexuals' fit or do not fit into Czechoslovak society should also be located in discourse. The different chapters of this book show this to be the case in two different ways. On the one hand, I argue that the medicalized and sexualized understanding of homosexuals and transsexuals as 'sick' or 'deficient' subjects have been a mainstay in Czechoslovak discourse on otherness. Talks about the "scientific" notions of sexual perverts have a long history dating back to the 18th century and therefore defy easy periodization.[119] On the other hand, under the conditions of state socialism, 'popular discourse' inevitably intersected with the 'official discourse' of the state and party organs. In official contexts, state actors and experts made ideologically correct but empirically vacuous claims about homosexuals and transsexuals as leading improper Socialist lives, as being sick, and so on. At the same, state actors and experts on occasions also lived and functioned as colleagues, friends, and relatives of people who considered themselves queer and, as we learn from the biographical narratives, approached and treated queer people in many different ways.

The marginalization of 'homosexuals' and 'transsexuals' in Communist Czechoslovakia took place largely within the space of language. This does not mean that real queer women and men did not experience discrimination or the world 'outside' discourse is somehow unreal or unimportant for history of sexuality, but rather that it is through discourse that the 'homosexuals' and 'transsexuals' have been defined, stigmatized, and forced to hide.[120] However, the millions of Czechs and Slovaks who were familiar with the popular and official conceptions of 'homosexuals' and 'transsexuals' would hardly have thought that such discourses could have been such a strong tool of marginalization. This is because these discourses were hegemonic: they had the power to establish the obvious or common sense understandings of 'homosexuals' and 'transsexuals' that are taken for granted as 'true' and which go without saying.[121] Unlike in democratic societies where marginalized groups can

---

119 Filip Herza, *Imaginations of "Otherness" and Freak Show Culture in the 19th and 20th century Prague* (Unpublished Ph.D. Dissertation, Charles University, 2018); Himl, Seidl and Schindler 2013.

120 In a different context, see also Joanna Richardson, *The Gypsy Debate: Can Discourse Control?* (Exeter and Charlottesville, VA: Imprint Press, 2006).

121 This conception of hegemony resembles that of Gramsci. Antonio Gramsci, *Selections from the Prison Notebooks of Antonio Gramsci* (New York: International Publishers, 1972).

appropriate language in order to contest the hegemonic power of popular be-liefs and official prescriptions, in Communist Czechoslovakia such a discur-sive arena was never officially sanctioned due to censorship, and queer peo-ple had few avenues of communication to 'talk back.' But, as this book shows, queer people and their supporters, often even while working in the official institutional structures, such as medical doctors or editors of state-censored media for example, found these avenues and used them in subversive ways.

Discourse was also the space where the identities of heterosexual and queer people were constructed and played out. As Joan W. Scott argued in a very different context, "identities and experiences are variable phenom-ena... discursively organized in particular contexts and configurations."[122] Who counted as a 'homosexual' in the eyes of the state and the public had often little to do with one's putatively 'real' sexuality. Rather, it was important how one was in their given context situated within the officially sanctioned categories of the healthy and sick, proper and improper, normal and deviant, loyal and disloyal. Such categories, moreover gendered, created an identity of the 'homosexual' regardless of how people may have felt themselves. But dis-course was not only a locus of power or a site of the production of identities, it was also the means for legitimating state policies that marginalized 'homo-sexuals,' as an umbrella term for diverse gender and sexual transgressions. As Foucault pointed out, Western discourse on sexual repression legitimized various institutions that mediated how people should interpret themselves;[123] in a similar vein, the discourse on sexual normalcy and deviance legitimated a wide range of institutional practices aimed at correcting such deviant be-havior, regardless of whether 'homosexuals' were enunciated as the official target of those practices.

In sum, I seek to sidestep the problems of narrating a 'history of homosex-uality' by instead positioning identity claims about homosexuals as themes within the discursive field of Communist power. Sexological discourse was the arena where ideologically correct conceptions of the 'homosexual' and 'transsexual' were defined, but also where institutionalized practices were enunciated and carried out. Popular discourse was the parallel arena where homophobicly charged notions of heterosexual/homosexual difference were circulated, but not repressed, because sexual categories were rarely dis-cussed in public spaces. This focus on discourse, however, does not mean that power was 'autonomous' or that agency does not matter. On the contrary, it

---

122 Joan W. Scott, *Gender and the Politics of History* (New York: Columbia U. Press, 1988), 5.
123 Michel Foucault, *The History of Sexuality: An Introduction* (New York: Vintage Books, 1985). Other works by Foucault that this book most significantly draws from include: *Discipline and Punish: The Birth of the Prison* (New York: Vintage, 1979); *The Order of Things: An Archeology of the Hu-man Sciences* (London: Tavistock, 1970); and *Birth of the Clinic: An Archeology of Medical Perception* (New York: Vintage, 1973).

was precisely low level-state employees, be they teachers, newspaper editors or police officers, who, by using their own authority to interpret the official medical discourse conceiving homosexuals as 'deviant' and 'deficient' had the power to translate these terms into officially sanctioned practices, or reject them to apply their own judgments of how 'homosexuals' should be treated. A detailed analysis of the Czechoslovak sexological discourse between 1947 and 1989, the subject of the next chapter, however, unveils that even the rigid and regulatory medical discourse was far from uniform, evolved over time, and contained internal contradictions and unexpected moments.

CHAPTER 3
INSTITUTIONAL APPROACHES
TO NON-HETEROSEXUALITY

The following chapter examines the legal and medical frameworks of state approaches to homosexuality and transsexuality in Communist Czechoslovakia in order to contextualize the conditions, in which queer people lived their lives during the decades of state socialism. After setting up the historical legal context, the chapter focuses in particular on the sexological discourse on homosexuality and transsexuality in Czechoslovakia from 1947 to 1989. It examines the development of its medical arguments, analyzes the transformation of curative practices and discusses the civic involvement of some medical doctors in the public sphere from the 1950s through the late 1980s.

LEGAL FRAMEWORK OF HOMOSEXUALITY

An outline of the legal development of the state approach to homosexuality in Communist Czechoslovakia in the late 1950s and early 1960s, culminating in the partial decriminalization of homosexuality in 1961, provides an important foundation for the subsequent discussion of the medical sexological discourse. It is also instructive for contextualizing both limits and opportunities that were available to queer people for building alternative, even if not outwardly articulated, sexual and gender identities during state socialism, and for exploring what impacts these measures had on their lives. Lastly, it contributes to a better understanding of the discourse on homosexuality in the official media in the 1970s and 1980s, including, for example, the possibility of placing same-sex personal ads in select papers, as well as the attitudes of the Socialist public towards queer people. It should be made clear at the onset of this discussion that while homosexuality and homosexual behavior was recognized and regulated by the legal provisions of the state, transsexuality and expressions of transsexual subjectivity were left squarely in the authority of the medical discourse. From a legal point of view, while homosexuals were approached as transgressive subjects whose sexuality it was necessary to control by a punitive institutional framework, transsexuals were completely ignored by the legal system. A non-binary understanding of gender was non-existent during state socialism and thus transsexual subjectivity was not recognized as an expression of transgender identity but merely as "defective syndrome" — a biological inversion curable by medical interventions.[124]

It is common knowledge that homosexuality was "decriminalized" in 1961 and Czechoslovakia became one of the first countries in the world with a relatively liberal state attitude towards homosexuality.[125] On the other hand, this decriminalization was only partial, giving state authorities the opportunity to interpret the law in flexible ways, enabling them to discipline and repress homosexuals, especially homosexual men, at they saw fit. Unraveling the process of decriminalizing of homosexuality exposes the pivotal role played by leading Czech sexologists, demonstrating how important expert discourse was in decisions at the highest levels of state power.[126] The legal framework of the criminalization of homosexuality since the middle of the 19th century and the decriminalization efforts in the Czech lands were competently described in detail by Czech historian Jan Seidl in his pioneering, comprehensive study *From the Prison to the Altar: The Emancipation of Homosexuality in Czech Lands since 1867 to the Present*.[127]

In his extensive work, Seidl focused primarily on legal efforts by both the 'homosexual community' itself and the diverse state and expert advocates of tolerance towards homosexuality. He documented in great detail the rise of the homosexual subculture in the interwar period of the First Czechoslovak Republic, as well as the establishment of the gay and lesbian community after the Velvet Revolution in 1989 and its fight for the legalization of same-sex unions (called "registered partnership" in the Czech context). However, only 50 pages of Seidl's lengthy 500-page book focus on the Communist era.[128] While Seidl closely maps the legal aspects of the decriminalization process, he has surprisingly little to say about how queer people actually lived during the Communist period. Moreover, his discussion of the "Communist regime" spans only the years from the liberation of the country by the Soviet Army in 1945 until the decriminalization of homosexuality in 1961. Leaving out almost thirty years of Czechoslovak history during state socialism, his otherwise

---

124 Hanka Fifková, Petr Weiss, Ivo Procházka, Peggy T. Cohen-Kettenis, Friedemann Pfäfflin, Ladislav Jarolín, Jiří Veselý, and Vladimír Weiss, *Transsexualita a jiné poruchy pohlavní identity* (Praha: Grada, 2008).

125 This information is mentioned in all available works dealing with sexuality in Eastern Europe and sexuality in Czechoslovakia in particular, always as a marker of liberal attitudes of Czechoslovak state and society towards homosexuality and also as an indicator of complicated nature of Czech Communist regime, which prevents its simplistic readings.

126 Havelková and Oates, eds., 2014.

127 Seidl 2012.

128 In a 500-page book, Seidl devoted about 100 pages to the Habsburg period (19–104), 150 pages to the interwar period (105–248) and almost 200 pages of his book to the post-Communist period (301–492). In contrast, the entire Communist era from 1945 to 1989 is covered only in the space of 50 pages (249–300).

impressively meticulous study then jumps directly into the late 1980s and the "emancipatory efforts of the homosexuals" just before the Velvet Revolution. This irregularity in his treatment of the Communist period is the result of Seidl's prime interest in the legal aspects of the state approach to homosexuality, as well as his dependence on Communist Party documents and other 'political' sources. Due to the detailed contributions by Seidl and other historians, the legal developments of the state approach to homosexuality are well documented, though we still know very little about how people actually moved within those frameworks, how they interpreted them, what choices they made and why, what experiences they had and how they translated them into their self-understanding.

Immediately after the end of WWII, 'homosexual' people in Czechoslovakia and their supporters had great hopes that homosexual behavior would soon be decriminalized. Even though in the USSR homosexuality was criminalized again (after a brief period of its legalization from 1922 to 1934),[129] in Czechoslovakia the situation was different. The Communist Party of Czechoslovakia, after it gained a monopoly on power in 1948, was quite tolerant and open towards the idea of decriminalizing homosexuality. During the interwar period, Communist representatives adopted the reform of the criminal law in relation to homosexuality as one of their election themes and the Communists occasionally even toyed with the idea of submitting the proposal for the decriminalization of homosexuality to the parliament.[130] Even though this never happened, proponents of decriminalization had good reason to believe that Communists would be still open to their cause, especially given the treatment of homosexuality by the Nazis and the Communist efforts to present the new Socialist direction as the very opposite of Nazi rule.[131]

Unfortunately, these hopes did not materialize as the new Criminal Law from July 12, 1950 stated in Paragraph 241 that:

1) A person, who has sexual relations with another person of the same sex, will be punished by up to one year of imprisonment.
2) A sentence of one to five years of imprisonment will be applied to an offender who commits an act mentioned in article 1) either
   a) with a person younger than 18 years old
   b) or in exchange for money

---

129 Healey 2001; Essig 1999.
130 A similar situation was in Germany, and consequently in the GDR, where it was also the Communist Party of Germany, which before WWII cooperated with Magnus Hirschfeld on his efforts to repeal the anti-homosexual Paragraph 175. Subsequently, the GDR was the only country of the Eastern Bloc in which some historians saw the "homosexual minority" as "coexisting" with the state under the auspices of the Communist regime. (Miller 2006, 215–230).
131 Seidl 2012; Fanel 2000.

3) A person who offers sexual services to a person of the same sex for money, will be sentenced to prison for six months to three years.[132]

In 1950, universal criminalization of homosexuality thus remained an integral part of the Czechoslovak legal system. As Seidl notes in his work, the current state of archival research and the lack of reliable sources do not allow one to ascertain the precise reasons why the Communists left the universal criminalization of homosexuality in effect. But he also cites Karel Malý, a professor of law at Charles University in Prague, who in a conference contribution about legal developments in Communist Czechoslovakia in 2004 warned against the danger that "behind the façade of the formal [Socialist] law one can easily miss the real life of the then-law, which was often in direct contradiction with the wording of the formal laws."[133] As the narratives from the queer oral history project make clear, queer people living their lives during State socialism indeed maneuvered quite skillfully around the limits of the criminal law formally prohibiting homosexual behavior.

The 1953 textbook *Criminal Law*, put together by scholars from the Law School of Charles University in Prague, argued that "Socialist criminal law protects the interests of the citizens of the Socialist state in all spheres of life, including sexual relations (*pohlavní vztahy*)." The homosexual offense fell under the general "criminal deeds against the dignity of man" and as such allegedly "grossly infringed on the Socialist morality." Such acts then were inevitably seen as "expressions of sexual perversion (*pohlavní zvrácenost*) of the offenders (*pachatelé*) and as deep and condemnable hangovers of the capitalist past."[134] The legal rhetoric in the textbook is quite revealing in terms of the state's ambition to regulate human sexuality through law. The explicitly stated protection of citizen's interests in the sphere of sexual relations through a codified criminalization of homosexuality is an apt example of the concept of "mandatory heterosexuality," as analyzed by Jonathan Katz.[135] Punitive practices are presented as protective ones in the name of the collective good, obfuscating the regulatory meaning and impact of the legal measure on the sphere of intimacy of all citizens. Normative gender and sexual behavior is regulated and sanctioned through singling out non-normative practices, which are presented as ideological leftovers from previous regimes. People, who profess such inclinations or engage in such behavior, are characterized

---

132 Zákon č. 86/1950 Sb., §241, July 12, 1950.
133 Karel Malý and Ladislav Soukup, eds. *Vývoj práva v Československu v letech 1945–1989* (Praha: Univerzita Karlova, 2004), 7. (Cited in Seidl 2012, 261).
134 Kolektiv autorů, *Trestní právo, část zvláštní* (Praha: Státní pedagogické nakladatelství, 1953), 379.
135 Jonathan Katz, "The Invention of Heterosexuality." *Socialist Review* 20: 6-301990. Katz later on extended his arguments in a book version of this article, Jonathan Katz, *The Invention of Heterosexuality* (New York: Dutton Books, 1995).

by the state discourse as "offenders," defining them as asocial, criminal and most importantly dangerous elements of society. Because such understanding of homosexuality 'from above' concurs with the implicit homophobic bias 'from below,' the chances for developing a positive individual identity (unlike, for example, the space for maintaining a religious identity within the confines of the family) is minimal.[136]

According to Seidl, the moral dictum of the 1950 criminal law represented the height of Stalinism in Czechoslovak criminal law and as such could not last long in its original wording.[137] After Stalin's death in 1953, social and political conditions started to rapidly change in all countries of the Eastern Bloc. Due to the heavy influence of the Soviet law on the Czechoslovak legal system, modifications of legal rhetoric and important passages in criminal and civil law came under scrutiny as well during the mid to late 1950s.[138] Developments emerging out of the specific East European macro-social and political circumstances during this time affected other gender-sensitive areas of civic law, such as, for example, the liberalization of abortion and divorce legislation in all countries of the Soviet Bloc.[139] However, the goal of the Socialist state was not necessarily to empower women (or men, for that matter) through these reforms.[140] Similarly, the principal objective of the changes in the law regulating sexuality was not necessarily to emancipate 'homosexuals.'

Important consequences of the changing political climate in the second half of the 1950s were the personal changes in the institutional structures of the state. In 1960, the newly appointed Czechoslovak minister of justice, Alois Neuman, began intensive work on the transformation of the rhetoric of the Czechoslovak criminal law to better reflect the liberalizing ambitions of the post-Stalinist era.[141] Within a year, the universal criminalization of same-sex sexual acts was replaced by a partial decriminalization of homosexuality, provided both persons involved in the act were older than 18 years of age, the

---

136 Ibid.; Rosalind Chou and Joe Feagin, *The Myth of the Model Minority*. 2nd edition. (Boulder, CO: Paradigm Publishers, 2015); Joe Feagin. *The White Racial Frame: Centuries of Racial Framing and Counter-Framing*. 2nd edition. (New York: Routledge, 2013); Sue Wing, *Microaggressions in Everyday Life: Race, Gender, and Sexual Orientation* (Hoboken, New Jersey: Wiley, 2010).

137 Seidl 2012, 264–265.

138 Michal Bobek, Pavel Molek and Vojtěch Šimíček, *Komunistické právo v Československu: kapitoly z dějin bezpráví* (Brno: Masarykova univerzita, 2009).

139 Radka Dudová, *Interrupce v České republice: zápas o ženská těla* (Praha: SoÚ, 2012). Dudová argues that instead of placing the decision to terminate unwanted pregnancy into the hands of women, this authority was vested in the hands of special official abortion committees, 170. See also Andrea Prajerová, *Za hranicemi: Analýza potratových diskurzů v (ne)demokratickém Československu*. M.A. Thesis. (Prague: FHS UK, 2012).

140 Kateřina Šimáčková, Barbora Havelková, Pavla Špondrová, eds., *Mužské právo: jsou právní pravidla neutrální?* (Prague: Wolters Cluwer, 2020).

141 Bobek, Molek, and Šimíček, 2009.

sexual intimacy between them was consensual and the sex did not involve financial payment. The law decriminalizing homosexuality under these circumstances was passed in 1961 and came into effect on January 1, 1962. The legal and political aspects of the process of decriminalization are covered in detail by Seidl, so there is no need to repeat them here. But it is worth looking closely at a few aspects of the proposal of this new law, which became known as the Neuman Report.[142]

The proposal of the new law was first articulated in a report, written by minister Neuman in February 14, 1961, and submitted to the Central Committee of the Communist Party on September 8, 1961. In this report, Neuman first openly admitted that "the existing criminal treatment in its universal scope leads to undesirable consequences, mental disorders, and sometimes even suicide" and pointed out that "people with homosexual tendencies are often used, abused, and blackmailed by various criminal elements." Second, he gave explicit credit for the idea of the moderation of the law to the sexological lobby, explaining that it was primarily the Psychiatric Association of J. E. Purkyně, which informed the Ministry of Justice about the alarming negative effects of the criminalization of homosexuality and recommended the legal change. Third, Neuman also utilized the then-new scientific findings in the understanding of homosexuality and used sexological evidence as his argumentative shield asserting that "according to the medical knowledge, the [homosexual] offenders (*pachatelé*) suffer from a sexual deviance that, within the current state of medical science, cannot be cured." And last, as his report outlined a new wording of the law, Neuman expressed the belief that "the proposed amendment will persecute only such cases of homosexual acts that are socially dangerous. In all other cases it will be up to the different organizations of the state to effectively enact the reformation of the offender (*náprava pachatele*)."[143]

The report is significant and remarkable in many respects. First, it exposes the influence of the experts, in this case medical/sexological discourses on the reasoning of the ruling political elite. Despite the centralized monopoly of the Communist Party on political power, authority was dispersed among many actors that influenced each other. Second, Neuman also admitted that for the Socialist state, which prided itself on its alleged humanity, it would be inhumane to punish people for a medical condition that they did not choose and cannot change. In doing so, he implicitly argued that the legal system and repressive forces should *not* interfere in the area of medical expertise.

---

142 Seidl 2012, 273–286.

143 Zpráva o splnění usnesení PB ÚV KSČ ze dne 14. února 1961. Národní archiv, Komunistická strana Československa — Branně-bezpečnostní oddělení, karton 155, složka MS-1-135. (Cited in Seidl 2012, 282–283).

Homosexuality was defined as an illness and as such should be addressed by medical professionals alone. In this way, the report further supported the division of authority over problematic areas among diverse institutional actors.

Viewing homosexuality as a stable (albeit still medical) condition was also a decisive departure from the Soviet understanding of homosexuality as a temporary (deviant) condition, which can be eradicated by properly chosen methods. According to historian Dan Healey, who analyzed official Soviet medical and legal writings on homosexuality in the 20th century, homosexuality in the Soviet Union was officially understood as a "transient identity." By the legal discourse it was viewed as a decadent hangover of the bourgeois past, while medical experts saw it as a problem of "improper alignment" of biological sex and gender identity, which could be cured by sex-change surgery. In both discourses, Healey argues, homosexuality was not viewed as a stable identity but rather as a "fleeting condition" at best.[144] While this view of homosexuality was influential in Bulgaria and Romania,[145] Czechoslovakia through Neuman's report and the partial decriminalization of homosexuality in 1961 set off on a completely different and much more emancipatory road for understanding human sexuality.

In a perhaps unintended way, Neuman also admitted the responsibility of the punitive legal framework for the mental problems and suicides of homosexuals. In other words, as one of the highest-placed Communist officials of the time, he openly stated that it was not homosexuality itself but rather its full criminalization that led to the tragic consequences in human lives. What is also quite remarkable in this particular report is its belief that Czechoslovak socialism was at such a high level of its development that it could proceed from the persecution of (the still believed) immorality of homosexuality to its prevention. In his report, Neuman drafted a rather Foucauldian concept of panoptical control and thus prevention of homosexuality in Czechoslovak society. In his view, the task of getting rid of homosexual behavior was supposed to be appropriated by the watchful eyes of social organizations, such as the Revolutionary Union Movement (*ROH*) or the so-called "comrade courts" (*soudružské soudy*), voluntary civic organizations involved in a number of less significant issues and disputes.[146] In other words, the Communist state (represented by the ministry of justice) did not necessarily change its view that homosexuality was perverse but promoted a conceptual change of the legal system, in which full authority over the definition and treatment of homosexuality was given to the medical discourse, and the regulation of

---

144 Healey, 2001.
145 Pisankaneva 2005; Turcescu and Stan 2005; Biebuyck 2010.
146 Bobek, Molek, and Šimíček 2009, 644–645.

homosexual behavior was transferred from the jurisdiction of the repressive apparatus of the state to the watchful heteronormative eye of the society in general.

Importantly, however, the new law also created a new category of offence, which was not necessary under the full criminalization of homosexuality and which in the end nullified much of the advance brought by the partial decriminalization. In the new paragraph §244, the law stated that "a person who creates public indignation (*veřejné pohoršení*) by engaging in a sexual act with a person of the same sex will be punished by one to five years of imprisonment."[147] Even though it appears to look harmless, this was a powerful weapon in the hands of both the state public police (VB — *veřejná bezpečnost*) as well as the state secret police (StB — *státní bezpečnost*), which could use it at will to harass selected individuals depending on how the police interpret the law in a given circumstance. Indeed, many narrators recalled in the biographical narratives that when queer people had problems with the police, most often the clause of "public indignation" was cited.

Even though it is clear that the political context of destalinization played an important role in the gradual reform of the legal code, the decriminalization of homosexuality exposed the strength and influence of the medical establishment on the articulation and regulation of gender and sexual norms under state socialism. As will become clear in the following pages, at least some sexologists were well-aware of this power and used it in rarely discussed ways to improve the ordinary lives of queer people. The respected and unquestioned authority of the medical expert voice also enabled some Czechoslovak sexologists to substitute the missing civil society in the 1970s and 1980s, by creating in their offices official meeting spaces for homosexuals and thus playing an important role in the rise of collective queer consciousness.

FROM CURE TO CARE: CZECHOSLOVAK SEXOLOGY IN ITS HISTORICAL CONTEXT

The academic treatment of Czechoslovak sexology in the 20th century contains three major scholarly contributions, which concentrated on two main aspects. First, as Seidl and his colleagues had done, historians looked into the contributions of Czech sexology in the process of decriminalization of homosexuality, both in the interwar period and after WWII.[148] And second, as historian Josef Řídký and sociologist Katerina Lišková did, scholars

---

147 Trestní zákon č. 140/1961 Sb., §244.
148 Seidl 2012.

looked into very specific contexts, in which Czech sexologists articulated and defined their visions of 'perversion' and 'deviance.' Based on the detailed study of legal documents and the archival sources of the Communist Party of Czechoslovakia, Seidl concluded that Czechoslovak sexology played quite an active and positive role in the process of decriminalization of homosexuality in 1961. Řídký and Lišková, who in their individual works concentrated on the definitions of the "homosexual subject" (Řídký) and on the construction of "sexual deviance and normality" (Lišková), argued that Czechoslovak sexology was full of theoretical and conceptual contradictions in its attempt to produce definite and stable truths about normative and healthy sexuality.[149] While both Řídký and Lišková assert that arguments of sexologists during the Socialist regime were ambivalent and internally divided, the overall picture of Czechoslovak sexology during those times painted in their works is rather negative, with an emphasis on the disciplinatory role of sexological authority.

The reason for the discrepancy between the conclusions of Seidl on the one hand, and Řídký and Lišková on the other hand, seems to rest in the fact that Seidl looked only at the arguments and activities of Czechoslovak sexologists connected to the issue of homosexuality as a legal category, while Řídký and Lišková both studied more complex discourses on the construction of sexual subjectivity and desire. Řídký studied quite a narrow body of popular sexological booklets published between 1930 and 1992, published in large representative volumes and designated for the broader public. Lišková, on the other hand, was concerned with the state approach to sexuality during the Socialist era in general and the sexological treatment of homosexuality constituted only a part of her focus. Her book comprehensively covers diverse dimensions of sexology as the "science of desire" and analyses its impact on the articulation and regulation of sexual and gender norms in different areas of Czechoslovak state socialism. The diversity of Řídký's and Lišková's sources, as well as their different (albeit overlapping) historical context covered, is useful in revealing how sexological knowledge and attitudes were produced and disseminated in different and specific contexts. Both scholars also concentrated on textual analysis of their sources. On the other hand, while they both investigated the broader picture of sexology and sexologists as a part of the state institutional authority over questions of sexuality, exploring what opportunities and limits the existence of such a particular sexological framework had for queer people themselves was not a part of their endeavor.[150]

Importantly, activities and writings of medical doctors demonstrate that there was no such thing as one official 'Communist' interpretation of

---

149 Řídký 2013; Lišková 2018.
150 Ibid.

homosexuality. In the field of sexuality, the 'regime' was represented by a rather diverse set of actors, who espoused different views on the topic and published numerous mutual polemics as a part of their research outcomes. The sexological evaluations and reports published during the Communist times serve as evidence that there was no unitary 'official' opinion or central directive from above on how to treat (homo)sexuality.

My own study of the sexological discourse during the Communist period began with similar questions to those Lišková and Řídký asked: How did Czechoslovak sexology construct sexual and gender deviance? How did it approach non-normative sexuality in its texts? My interest, however, went beyond the homo-hetero duality. The prevailing binary sexological construction of homo and hetero sexuality was without a doubt a dominant and authoritative notion of sexual difference that privileged homosexuality over all other non-heterosexual sexualities and forced all people, regardless of their sexual desire or gender identity, to fit in these dual categories. At the same time, official sexological writings also contain unexpected arguments, which show that not all Czechoslovak sexologists shared the binary and biologically determined notions of gender and sexuality. For example, in 1976 sexologists Eva Brauerová, Viera Satková, and Antonín Topiař argued that the "relative insignificance of the biological differences between the sexes mean[s] that the 'male' and 'female' are in the end nothing more than erotically conditioned ideals, which are subordinated to historical and individual changes."[151] Their social constructivist argument, formulated in the depth of the Normalization era, demonstrates that official Czechoslovak sexological discourse during the Socialist period was not uniform. It was also more liberal than is often presented. This diversity inevitably permeated into the way individual sexologists viewed their professional field, saw the role of medicine and the state in intimate sexual matters, interacted with their patients, cooperated with other state institutions and supported or rejected repressive elements of the state.

In the course of the research, I examined the comprehensive body of sexological literature that spans the entire Socialist period, as recorded in the database *Bibliographia medica Čechoslovaca* (BMČ) at the National Medical Library in Prague.[152] I located over 120 articles and books, which related to

---

151 Eva Brauerová, Viera Satková and Antonín Topiař. "K otázce transvestitických projevů v dětském věku," *Československá pediatrie* 31:1 (1976): 20–21.

152 *Bibliographia medica Čechoslovaca* (BMČ) is a national medical database of the National Medical Library in Prague. It was founded in 1947 and ever since it comprehensively records all medical scholarship published in the Czech Republic, including all publications of Czech authors published abroad. Until 1996 BMČ contains also all medical scholarship published in Slovakia and the production of Slovak authors abroad. Since 1996, BMČ continues uninterrupted only in the Czech Republic.

the medical constructions of homosexuality, transsexuality, bisexuality and intersexuality during this period. The sources retrieved from the database, founded in 1947 and functioning without interruption until the present, reveal that Czechoslovak sexologists were not only purveyors of a heteronormative disciplinatory discourse, but that they themselves also actively worked to complicate or even challenge the picture of the homosexual subject as (only) deviant and sick. However, they did so in subtle and diplomatic ways that were not immediately obvious. Moreover, since the late 1960s, sexology was also explicitly concerned with the issue of transsexuality and intersexuality, which the individual doctors tackled in sometimes unexpected ways. Finally, when considering not only their writings, but also the activities and behavior of some sexologists, as recollected by the narrators in the biographical interviews, the impact of the sexological discourse on queer lives broadens. When all pieced together, this chapter shows that, contrary to the generally negative mainstream assessment, Czechoslovak sexology played a complicated, and sometimes unexpectedly positive, role in attempting to create a conceptual (and physical) space for queer people to live their lives during Czechoslovak socialism with as much freedom and dignity as possible.

When it comes to the state attention to sexuality, Czechoslovakia has always played a unique and leading role. In many ways, Czechoslovakia was, along with countries like Germany and the United States, at the vanguard of changes in the field of sexuality. Already in May 1921, by the presidential decree of T.G. Masaryk, a Sexological Institute was established as a part of the Medical School of Charles University in Prague, becoming the first institute of its kind in the world. In 1934, the founder of Czech sexology, Prof. Josef Hynie became the first tenured medical doctor (*docent*) of sexology in the country and was named the director of the institute, having established the first sexological outpatient clinic (*ambulance*) already in 1929. One of the reasons behind Hynie's indisputable reputation was his studies at the prestigious Hirschfeld Institute in Berlin and other sexological institutions in Vienna in the late 1920s and early 1930s. Hynie was lucky to complete his studies and move back to Prague before the Nazis came to power, abolished all those institutions, and mercilessly persecuted their employees. After WWII, Hynie became heralded as a scientist who saved Central European sexological knowledge, traditions, and experiences and was able to transfer them to postwar Czechoslovakia.[153]

---

153 Jaroslav Zvěřina, "Historie sexuologie." In *Sexuologie*, edited by Petr Weiss et al. (Praha: Grada, 2010), 1–10; Josef Charvát, "Josef Hynie, zakladatel československé sexuologie." *Časopis lékařů českých* 109 (1970): 631; Jan Raboch, "K sedmdesátinám prof. MUDr. Josefa Hynieho, DrSc." *Časopis lékařů českých* 109 (1970): 632.

In 1946, Hynie became the first full professor of sexology in the country and gradually set the Sexological Institute (then called the Institute for Sexual Pathology), and Czechoslovak sexology as a whole, on an extraordinary path towards a progressive (for its times) approach to diverse sexualities. This road has been complex and often contradictory but viewed with the hindsight of a century, it is possible to see a surprisingly perspicuous and steady development, which continued without interruption even through the dramatic changes of fundamentally different political and social epochs of the interwar democracy, the Nazi occupation, the Communist one-party rule and the post-Socialist democratic transformation. Czech sexology benefited from its long historical tradition, and its leading international reputation in the field enabled Prague's Sexological Institute to retain its strong position throughout the entire Communist period.[154]

In the late 1940s, the BMČ database does not register any sexological articles related to non-heterosexuality. The last sexological text dates to 1940, when Prague publishing house of Josef Svoboda published Hynie's *Introduction to Medical Sexology*. The only sexological publishing activity in the 1940s was the repeated edition of Hynie's 1937 popular booklet for the wider public called *Sexual Life and its Deficiencies*, which was published seven times between 1937 and 1948.[155] The publishing absence during this period is logical because the existence of Prague's Sexological Institute was interrupted during WWII and its reestablishment after the war dates only to the accession of the Communist regime to power in 1948.[156] Even though the postwar institute rebuilt its vision, structure, and professional activities directly on the prewar legacy, plus it was continuously led by professor Hynie, in the 1970s its existence was heralded as "the evidence of the progressive nature of our Socialist society."[157] Communist official writings on the Socialist medical establishment tried to disconnect the postwar Sexological Institute from its prewar roots in order to ideologically and historically distance Czechoslovak Socialist sexology from the German influence, which was formative and obvious.[158]

The first postwar sexological research publications, which focused on non-heterosexual sexuality date to 1950, when professor Hynie and sexologist Karel Nedoma presented papers on the nature and treatment of homosexuality in one of the regular monthly meetings of the Purkyně Psychiatric

---

154 Lišková argued that the reason why the Sexological Institute was allowed to function in relative peace during the Communist regime, when the Communist Party strived to limit and regulate all potential independence of state institutions, was that it viewed sexology as a part of the "hard science" of medicine, which investigates and objectively presents "facts of life and nature." Lišková 2012, 40.

155 Josef Hynie, *Sexuální život a jeho nedostatky*, Praha (1937, 1939, 1941, 1942, 1946, 1948).

156 Zvěřina 2010, 3.

157 Jan Raboch, *Očima sexuologa* (Praha, Avicenum, 1977), 227.

158 Zvěřina, 2010.

Society.[159] In their contributions, they both argued that contemporary sexology knows only very little about homosexuality, especially when it comes to its origins. But they shared that the sexologist Kurt Freund from the Psychiatric Clinic of Charles University was currently working on a large study of male homosexuality. The first findings from this extensive project were published by Freund and Jan Srnec in *The Medical Journal* (*Sborník lékařský*) in 1953. Their 60-page article was also the first version of the most well-known book on homosexuality during the Socialist period, *Homosexuality in Men*, published by Freund in 1962. Freund's research, which involved 222 homosexual men, studied the results and influence of then-practiced methods of aversion therapy, electric shock therapy, inhaling CO_2, application of Metrazol, and other procedures developed by the team to cure homosexuality. In the 1953 study, Freund and Srnec described in detail those inhumane methods and the reactions of their patients to those procedures. For a better illustration of the brutality of these methods, it is worth citing the published description of the so-called aversion therapy in full:

The procedure has two phases: In the first phase, the patient drinks coffee or tea with emetin and in 10 minutes receives an injection of a mixture of emetin, apomorphin, pilokarpin, and ephedrine. Then he watches films and slides with men, first dressed, then athletes in bathing suits, and then naked men. As a result of the given pharmaceuticals, approximately after 5–10 minutes from the beginning of the session the patient will start to get sick and will begin to vomit. The procedure lasts about half an hour to 45 minutes. The patient is instructed ahead of the procedure to picture the men in the slides as partners of homosexual intercourse.

The second phase of the therapeutic procedure consists of projecting films showing women in situations, which in normal men arouse sexual appetite. These films are shown in the evening before going to bed, after the patient had received in the morning an injection of 10mg of Agovirin. This procedure is repeated 5 to 10 times, either daily or in longer intervals, depending on the patient's condition… Currently, the experimental procedure is repeated every day besides Sunday for four weeks. To provoke nausea and vomiting, we now use emetin only occasionally, maximum six times in one course of the treatment. Most often we work with the mixture of apomorphine and caffeine… At the beginning, we treated the patients individually, now we submit the whole group of patients to the treatment together.[160]

159 Josef Hynie, "Několik poznámek k podstatě a therapii homosexuality," *Neurologie a psychiatrie československá* 13 (1950): 327; Josef Hynie and Karel Nedoma, "Homosexualita v sexuologické praxi," *Neurologie a psychiatrie československá* 13 (1950): 328.

160 Kurt Freund and Jan Srnec, "K otázce mužské homosexuality: Analýza změn sexuální appetence během pokusné léčby podmiňováním." *Sborník lékařský* 55 (1953): 125–164, 129–130.

In the article, Freund and Srnec expressed optimism about the effectiveness of the aversion method. They argued that "it is very probable that the approach, which we chose, has therapeutic effects and in some cases of this deviance provides a tool for its adaptation."[161] Freund also noted that in the study,

> most patients were recommended by Prof. Hynie. Only a very small number of the [recommended] patients were women. None of those women expressed unhappiness with their deviance, only male patients thus underwent the procedure.[162]

It is remarkable that the deciding factor of which patients to include or exclude from the curing procedure of aversion therapy were the patients' own feelings of personal satisfaction with their 'deviant' identity. It is perhaps even more striking that the 'satisfactory' feelings with one's 'deviance' were held by all the women, who came to the facility. Later on, Freund elaborated on this aspect by writing that "none of the patients, who came, were rejected. However, [the research procedure] was carried out only on male patients because none of the homosexual women, who came, desired to change her [sexual] disposition (*žádná netoužila po změně svého zaměření*)."[163] In other words, no one was *rejected* from the study, but women, who expressed satisfaction with their homosexual orientation, were *excluded* from the study. Does that mean then that all the men, who took part in the study, came with the desire to change their homosexual orientation? If so, it begs the question, why did the women come there in the first place? And what does "women's satisfaction with their deviance" say about the nature and social dimension of homosexuality? Why, in the Stalinist Czechoslovakia of the early 1950s, were women allegedly satisfied with their homosexuality, while men desired to change it? Neither the article, nor the book answers these questions. One can only speculate that for men, homosexuality, which was then still fully criminalized, presented greater social obstacles and political risks than for women. At the same time, one of the women narrators in the queer oral history project shared that already in the 1950s people at her work knew about her sexual orientation and "no one cared" (Heda). Also, the biographical narratives here, as well as in the interviews that Schindler carried out, revealed that some men used the sexological research facility as a meeting point to meet other homosexual men.[164]

---

161 Ibid., 147.
162 Ibid., 131.
163 Kurt Freund, *Homosexualita u muže* (Praha: Avicenum, 1962), 231.
164 Schindler 2013.

But clearly, the whole aversive therapy procedure, based on a "routine anti-alcoholic treatment," seemed to be designed for and directed towards only men. There is no discussion anywhere in Freund's work on the significance of this fact or of potential modifications of the procedure for female patients such as, for example, changing the objects of erotic arousal or a different mixture of pharmaceuticals more adequate for female organism. Freund does not go any further in explaining this phenomenon nor does he elaborate further on the absence of women from all his studies and writings. But the fact that he simply notes such an obvious dimension of his experiments but does not feel compelled to seek an explanation for it testifies to a gender blindness, common in the medical science of the times, and suggests that Freund did not consider female (homo)sexuality as equally relevant (or interesting) as the male one.

Aside from allegedly personal reasons,[165] Freund's lack of interest in studying female homosexuality likely stemmed from the generally dismissive attitudes toward female sexuality in the immediate postwar period, which presented a continual trend from previous decades. As the bibliography lists of their publications reveal, the entire Czech sexological school was well-read in foreign, mainly Western literature from Richard von Krafft-Ebing, Havelock Ellis, Magnus Hirschfeld, and Sigmund Freud to John Money, and others, who all espoused in their works the view that female sexuality, as a derivate of male sexuality, does not have the same potential to advance scientific knowledge.[166] In other words, Freund was neither the first nor last sexologist, who expressed minimal interest in female sexuality whether it be 'healthy' or 'deviant.' At the same time, Freund's book includes references to the studies of Alfred Kinsey, who published his famous *Sexual Behavior in the Human Male* in 1948, followed only five years later, in 1953, by *Sexual Behavior in the Human Female*.[167] Moreover, unlike in Western sexology, in East European sexology, including sexology in Socialist Czechoslovakia, women doctors were integral parts of the medical teams and institutions.[168]

---

165 Some colleagues and patients of Freund informally claimed that Freund personally was much more interested in men than women but this rumor is impossible to verify (Cited in Seidl 2012, 294).

166 Richard von Krafft-Ebing, *Psychopatia Sexualis* (Stutgart: F. Enke, 1886); Havelock Ellis, *Sexual Inversion* (London: F.A. Davis, 1901); Magnus Hirschfeld, *Homosexuality of Men and Women as Biological Phenomenon* (1914 in German, Prometheus Books, 1922 in English.); Sigmund Freud, *Three Essays on the Theory of Sexuality* (London: Imago Publishing, 1949, first published 1905); John Money, *The Psychological Study of Man* (Chicago: Thomas, 1957).

167 Alfred Kinsey, *The Sexual Behavior in the Human Male* (Philadelphia: W.B. Saunders Company, 1948) and *The Sexual Behavior in the Human Female* (Philadelphia: W.B. Saunders Company, 1953).

168 On the other hand, this trend should be attributed rather to the equal access to university education for women in the countries of the Soviet Bloc and their greater success in achieving medical degrees in comparison with women from Western democratic countries than to any increasing gender awareness in the field itself. Freund himself worked until his emigration to

In 1957, however, Freund admitted that the results of the aversive therapy treatment were "less than satisfactory."[169] Moreover, Seidl in his book points out the memories of Ota Tasinato, one of the 222 homosexual men, who participated in Freund's study. Tasinato claimed in 1994, that in the clinic "there was a room with four beds [where the patients-subjects stayed during the study] but our spies immediately saw through it and turned it into a meeting point."[170] Tasinato's testimony, which Seidl does not interpret any further, is remarkable because it suggests that at least some men could have participated in Freund's study not in order to 'cure' or 'change' their homosexuality but to the contrary, to meet other homosexual men. It presents an extraordinary reversal of meaning and a moment of subversion of state authority, when the expert endeavor itself, examining presumably ignorant and passive subjects, is used by the 'objects' of the study to their own means. It also shows that official documents from the Communist period, for example this particular sexological study, should not be taken at face value and points to the importance of oral history and the history of everyday lives to uncover multiple meanings, subversive uses, and new interpretations of texts and events. Several major studies that Freund and his team conducted during the 1950s exposed for them quite clearly that it is impossible to cure homosexuality. Based on this knowledge, Freund along with several of his colleagues subsequently embarked on a systematic effort to decriminalize homosexuality in Czechoslovakia. Quite a few sexological articles from the late 1950s thus represent an interesting hybrid of medical and social argumentation, in which sexologists promoted and argued for the decriminalization of homosexuality.[171]

By late 1950s, sexology established itself worldwide as a legitimate medical science. By this time, Prof. Hynie himself was an internationally respected expert, who built around him a team of inspired and promising young

Canada in 1968 with sexologist Vlasta Březinová, who later became well-known for research on withdrawal and effects of caffeine. Czech sexology had also many other leading female figures, which are going to be mentioned later in the chapter, such as Dagmar Bártová, Iva Šípová, Jaroslava Pondělíčková-Mašlová, and others.

169 Kurt Freund, "Otázka pohlavní úchylnosti z hlediska sociálního," Problémy psychiatrie v praxi a ve výzkumu (Praha: Státní zdravotnické nakladatelství, 1957), 50.

170 Seidl 2012, 290.

171 Karel Nedoma, "Nový trestní zákon a trestné činy lidí s odchylnými sexuálními tendencemi," Praktický lékař 33 (1953): 316–318; Kurt Freund, "Diagnostika homosexuality u mužů," Československá psychiatrie 53 (1957): 382–394; Kurt Freund and Václav Pinkava, "K otázce věkové preference u homosexuálních mužů," Československá psychiatrie 55 (1959): 362–367; Karel Nedoma and Kurt Freund, "Otázka příčetnosti a nápravných opatření u sexuálních delikventů," Československá psychiatrie 55 (1959): 264–269; Kurt Freund, "Tři úvahy o práci psychopatologa," Československá psychiatrie 54 (1958): 177–183; Jiří Roubíček, "Ze života Čs. psychiatrické společnosti. Zpráva o odborné činnosti, sjezdech a pracovních schůzích v roce 1960," Československá psychiatrie 57 (1961): 133–139; Kurt Freund and Václav Pinkava, "K otázce souvislosti mezi homosexualitou a nepřítomností rodičů," Československá psychiatrie 55 (1959): 334–336.

sexologists. Hynie was a life-long supporter of a medical rather than criminal approach to sexual deviance. He always promoted accessible sexual education, argued for open and truthful information about human sexuality and urged for responsible sexual and marital relationships.[172] As can be inferred from the writings of a whole subsequent generation of Czechoslovak sexologists from the 1950s through the 1980s, under his leadership these values became shared and promoted by Czechoslovak sexology in general. This context also largely explains why Czechoslovak sexology played such a complex role in promoting heteronormativity and the traditional family on the one hand, while also supporting the emancipation of homosexuality and attending to questions of transsexuality and intersexuality on the other hand.

The Sexological Institute in Prague became an inspiration for a number of new departments and centers of sexology in hospitals, clinics, and medical schools springing up throughout the whole of Socialist Czechoslovakia from the early 1960s. One of the important tasks of such departments and centers was to promote healthy sexuality and treat its problematic and deviant aspects. But a detailed look into the activities and publications of Czechoslovak sexologists throughout the Communist period from the early 1950s to the late 1980s indicates that Czech and Slovak sexologists actually paved the way not only for the decriminalization of homosexuality in 1961, but also for the gradual emancipation of homosexual subjectivity as well. In the late 1950s, these doctors were the motor behind the process of decriminalization of homosexuality. Thirty years later, during the 1980s, they were the leading personalities organizing psychotherapeutic and social groups for homosexuals, which effectively functioned as meeting points and clubs for all interested queer people in Prague and Brno.[173] The Sexological Institute in Prague was unique in other respects as well. It was conducting not only medical and clinical research, it was also focusing on psychosocial therapy and social work with its patients. Such a broad and complex array of services enabled the Institute to be at the forefront of world sexology, which in turn allowed its members, even in the era of deep Normalization, to participate in international medical and academic forums, read and actively work with Western (mainly Anglophone and German) research studies, and publish in Western academic journals. Over the years, experts from the Sexological Institute developed prestige, which translated into legislative power and institutional trust.

---

172 Josef Hynie, *Sexuológia pre každého* (Bratislava: Osveta, 1970); *Základy sexuologie* (Praha: Universita Karlova, 1974); *Dospíváte v muže* (Praha: Avicenum, 1976); "Několik poznámek k podstatě a therapii homosexuality." *Neurologie a psychiatrie československá* 13 (1950): 327; "Principy sexuálního chování a sexuální morálky." *Časopis lékařů českých* 108/19 (1969): 553–556; Hynie and Nedoma 1950.

173 Seidl 2012; Procházka 1997; Bártová 1979.

The most important argument resulting from his clinical research, which distinguished Freund's work and consequently Czechoslovak sexology and Socialist Czechoslovakia in general, was the belief that it is not possible to cure homosexuals from their "disease" and thus it would be wrong to criminalize them for their disposition. This effort peaked in May of 1960 at the legal-psychiatric seminar in Hradec Králové. A team of sexologists, lawyers and members of the police engaged in a round-table discussion about the potential novelization of the criminal code of Socialist Czechoslovakia. Freund made it very clear in his book that it was the sexologists, who initiated the whole meeting: "On behalf of the Psychiatric Clinic of Charles University in Prague, together with Dr. Nedoma from the Sexological Institute, *we* invited representatives of other psychiatric clinics from Prague, Plzeň, Hradec Králové, Brno, Olomouc, and Košice, and relevant public institutions, as well as lawyers and representatives of the State Public Police (VB)."[174] The debate resulted in a proposal to abolish criminal code §241/1 criminalizing homosexual encounters between consenting adults. The criminal law was changed in 1961 and Communist Czechoslovakia became one of the first countries in the world to decriminalize homosexuality.[175]

Another extraordinary aspect of Freund's work, published in 1962, complementing his belief that homosexuality was incurable, was also his conclusion that, in fact, there is one form of "help" that homosexuals need and the society can provide:

There is one thing, with which we can help them… and that is that we could relinquish them from all forms of persecution and pressure. This could perhaps help them develop erotic relations better compatible with the surrounding society than when the hostile attitude of heterosexual people and criminal sanctions force them into the same position as chronic criminal asocial psychopaths.

There is, however, one thing that society has the right to ask [of homosexuals] much more than from heterosexuals: discretion in sexual matters. [Homosexuals] exude scandal with their sexual behavior much easier than heterosexuals and thus they have to conform to it. This is valid *mutandis mutatis* for any minority different in any way [from majority], when it is so small.[176]

---

174 Freund 1962, 248. (Italics mine).
175 Hromada 2000; Procházka 1997. It is important to note here that the effort of sexologists went against the dominant view of the Ministry of Interior. The work of Czech historian Jan Seidl shows that the Minister of Interior himself was against the decriminalization and attempted to create a version of civil courts that could still prosecute homosexual behavior regardless of the change of the law. The fact that such courts were never created and the legal decriminalization successfully passed shows not only the strong position of sexologists in the machinery of power but also the fragmented ambitions and efforts of the leading members of the Communist Party themselves.
176 Freund 1962, 247.

Freund's notion presents a complex argument blending together an articulation of the existence of latent homophobia in Socialist Czechoslovakia and its dangers with the need for social respect and acceptance of homosexuality as the only ways leading to improvement of the social situation of homosexuals. Freund stated very clearly that the main problem was the social attitudes of heterosexuals towards homosexuals and not homosexuality itself. He also quite openly distanced himself from associating homosexuality with asocial elements, a trend, which unfortunately continued in other medical research (mainly venereology, epidemiology, psychiatry) through the Socialist period. Most remarkable is Freund's recognition and open articulation that as members of a societal minority, homosexual people should be held to a higher moral standard than heterosexuals. In other words, Freund implicitly recognized a stigma that according to him homosexuality carries and stated bluntly that it is not the homosexual behavior itself, which is problematic but rather the fact that homosexuals form a minority of "others." At the same time, he reinforced the view that simply because of its size, the minority must conform to the rules and norms of the majority.[177]

As already mentioned, in 1961 homosexuality in Czechoslovakia went through a successful legislative milestone with its partial decriminalization and, interestingly, for almost a decade appeared less frequently in the pages of sexological writings. In 1964, Brno sexologists Milan Bouchal and Dagmar Bártová published a short article in the English-language journal *Activitas nervosa superior*, in which they presented their findings from a small survey of ten homosexual men and their "attitudes after the change in the Criminal Code."[178] Bouchal and Bártová concluded in their study that the decriminalization of the law had pretty much no effect on their respondents, at least not an effect that they could articulate. Bouchal and Bártová took the opportunity, however, to argue in this article that it was not surprising that the respondents did not feel any, presumably positive, changes in their lives given the "hostile moral attitudes [of society], which have not changed with the amendment of the law." They continued with a remarkable statement that there were still "homosexuals," who, despite the new law, come for

health and especially psychiatric care. If our therapeutic possibilities to do away with the deviation will not be effective, *we will consider psychotherapy aimed at strengthening*

---

177 To what extent this view was influenced by Freund's own experience as a Jew, living during the Nazi occupation, is not clear. Because of his Jewish origin, Freund had to divorce his wife in 1943 in order to protect her and their newborn daughter. After the war, he remarried his ex-wife again. Freund's articulation of stigma is very similar to Erwin Goffman's work on stigma. (Goffman 1963).

178 Milan Bouchal and Dagmar Bártová, "The attitude of homosexuals after the change in the Criminal Code." *Activitas nervosa superior* 6/1 (1964): 100–101.

the homosexual consciousness, the removal of the feelings of exclusion, guilt, and inferiority.
The amendment of the law itself may be of help in this psychotherapy.[179]

By this time, it was public knowledge in Czechoslovak sexological discourse for almost a decade that homosexuality cannot be "cured" or "done away with" by any means. Bouchal's and Bártová's argument can be thus interpreted as one of the first explicit expressions of commitment and support of Czech and Slovak sexologists to homosexual people, telling them that if they come to sexological clinics, they will find 'care' there instead of a 'cure.' It was an explicit statement that homosexuals, who come to sexological offices will not be subjected to humiliating curative procedures but rather find understanding and real therapeutic help aimed at the social aspects of their feelings of exclusion, guilt and inferiority. The declaration to help the incomers "strengthen their homosexual consciousness" in order to overcome their internalized homophobia is an extraordinary and unexpected statement from the ink of leading sexologists in a Communist country in 1964. It demonstrates, I argue, the increasingly complex role Socialist sexology came to play for queer people in the 1960s and 1970s. Knowing this context and this particular article, it is not surprising then that it was Dagmar Bártová herself, who started the first socio-therapeutic group for homosexuals in Brno in 1976.[180]

While Seidl locates the origins of these activities only to the second half of the 1970s and early 1980s, and moreover has a tendency to see the positive role of sexologists as a form of some default because "homosexuality somehow 'naturally' fell under the authority of sexology that was authorized by the state to alleviate suffering,"[181] my analysis of the long-term development of the sexological discourse during the Socialist era indicates that it was not coincidence but rather a bold and conscious step forward. In this way, many sexologists actively took authority into their hands and as a part of the official expert discourse applied their power in ways that they considered true and fit. However, it would be erroneous to perceive their arguments and actions as going *against* "the state" or "regime," because the sexologists were *a part of* both "the state" and "the regime." Rather, this agency provides evidence of the plurality of agents and of the dispersed nature of "the state." Instead of one central 'regime' authority on the question of homosexuality and other queer sexualities, evidently there were sexologists with differing

---

179 Ibid, 100. (Italics mine).
180 Dagmar Bártová, "Skupinová psychoterapie pacientů s poruchami psychosexuální identifikace," *Moravskoslezský Referátový Sborník* 11 (1979): 92–94; Dagmar Bártová and Vlastimil Škoda, "Příspěvek k psychiatrickým aspektům homosexuality," *Časopis lékařů českých* 116/33 (1977): 1029–1030.
181 Seidl 2012, 306.

and autonomous views. And many of them held liberal and lenient attitudes towards non-normative sexuality. Their voices thus challenge the myth of Czechoslovak sexology as a mainly disciplinary and regulatory tool and prolonged arm of the heteronormative ideology of the Socialist state. They also provide us with a glimpse of the complex 'official' frameworks, which were far from clear, and within which queer people lived their everyday lives.

The 1960s also brought the first boom of 'popular' sexological literature directed at the general public. While in the 1940s and 1950s only Hynie's work on sexuality and sexual behavior was available, the 1960s saw a radical increase in popular literature about sexuality, marriage and family, which continued into the 1970s and 1980s. Clearly, the Communist Party considered all of these areas important to its efforts to "build socialism" and at the same time hoped to utilize them to retain its monopoly on power. Heterosexual marriage, a dominant institution of the proper gender order, regulating relationships between men and women, represented the pivotal building stone of Communist ideology. Marriage was considered by all sexological texts as an automatic institution, a necessary presumption for a healthy sexual relationship between man and woman. But as sociologist Dana Hamplová argues, the ideological attitude of the Communist regime towards the institution of family was always ambivalent. Immediately after the accession to power in 1948, the regime was hostile towards the traditional family and was trying to belittle and weaken its power because it considered a strong nuclear family its competition, both in terms of loyalty (which should be directed toward the social collectivity and not wasted within family) and in terms of traditions and values, which could be transmitted within the family outside of state supervision.[182] Milan Kučera supports this view and argues that, for example, the liberalization of divorce legislature in the 1950s can be seen as a concrete step of the state attempt to destabilize the institution of marriage through an argument that "marriage without love is not in the interest of the Socialist society."[183]

According to sociologists Ivan Vodochodský and Petra Klvačová, who studied the image of marriage in Socialist popular literature, the 1960s saw a reversal of this trend, partly as a result of psychological research on children's deprivation and partly out of fears about decreasing fertility. Vodochodský and Klvačová documented the dramatic rise of popular marital handbooks since the 1960s, which shows that while only three guides were

182 Dana Hamplová, "Stručné poznámky o ideových přístupech k rodině v období socialismu," in *Cahiers du CeFReS No 22, Česko-francouzský dialog o dějinách evropské rodiny*, edited by Antoine Mares and Pavla Horská (Praha: CeFReS, 2010).

183 Milan Kučera, "Rodinná politika a její demografické důsledky v socialistickém Československu," in *Cahiers du CeFReS No 22, Česko-francouzský dialog o dějinách evropské rodiny*, edited by Antoine Mares and Pavla Horská (Praha: CeFReS, 2010).

published in the 1940s and seven in the 1950s, 24 books were published in the 1960s. During the 1970s, the production of popular books about sexuality, marriage, and family almost doubled to 45, followed by 42 new titles in the 1980s. Altogether, the Czechoslovak state published 121 popular books on these interlinked topics during the Socialist period, 104 of which were published between 1965 and 1989.[184]

Such intense attention to questions of interpersonal relations, sexual intimacy and parenting of course went hand in hand with sexological studies of sexuality and informed inquiries into non-heterosexual sexuality. In 1964, based on his novel idea of a confidential crisis hotline called *Linka důvěry* (*Trust Line*), psychiatrist Miroslav Plzák officially started a new field of "matrimoniology," as a separate interdisciplinary discipline focused on heterosexual partner and marital relationships interlinking sexology, psychology and psychiatry.[185] This opened a completely new and highly influential channel for the dissemination of essentialized heteronormative views of complementary (and thus oppositional) masculinity and femininity within "healthy" and "natural" interpersonal and marital relationships. But it also brought a new angle to grasp and approach queer sexuality. Already in 1962, Freund argued in his book on male homosexuality that "in exceptional cases, marriage can be recommended as an auxiliary tool in adaptive psychotherapy."[186] Based on his research into the marriage of homosexual men in his project, he found that 62 out of the 222 patients were currently, or in the past, married. From additional interviews and observations, into which he also invited the wives of the homosexual men, he concluded that "not all marriages of homosexual [men] have to be unsuccessful." To the contrary, his findings seemed to indicate to him that

there is most likely close causality between marriage and the heterosexual adaptation of homosexual men. No unmarried patient was able to sustain the heterosexual adaptation for longer than a few months. What we don't know, however, is what the nature of this causality is. It is, for example, possible that only [homosexual] men that have the energy to get married also have the energy to endure long-term heterosexual adaptation. On the other hand, it is also possible that marriage is important for the longer-lasting adaptation of a homosexual man as a form of therapeutic intensifier (*adjuvans*).[187]

---

184 Ivan Vodochodský and Petra Klvačová, "Obraz manželství v předlistopadové populárně naučné literatuře," In *Proměny genderové kultury v české společnosti, 1948–1989*, edited by Hana Havelková and Libora Oates-Indruchová (Praha: SLON, 2013).

185 Miroslav Plzák, *Manželské judo* (Praha: Avicenum, 1970) and *Taktika a strategie v lásce* (Praha: Mladá fronta, 1970).

186 Freund 1962, 246.

187 Ibid.

As we will see later in this chapter, homosexuality and marriage were very compatible categories for Czechoslovak sexologists during the Socialist regime, but the period of its main intensity and significance was to come only in the late 1970s and the early 1980s.

BEYOND THE HETERO-HOMO DUALITY: SEXOLOGICAL ATTENTION TO TRANSSEXUALITY

Besides the emerging changes in family and population policies, and significant liberalization of divorce and abortion legislation, mentioned earlier, the 1960s also witnessed an intensified interest and shift of attention into other forms of queer identity, especially intersexuality and transsexuality.[188] This testifies to the unique dimension of Czechoslovak sexology, which, unlike its counterparts in other East European countries, followed international trends, was familiar with cutting edge research, and discussed developments in the field in Western countries. Lists of references and bibliographies in Czechoslovak sexological publications from the Socialist era, both scholarly articles and popular books, are also remarkable. From the first report by Freund and Srnec in 1953 to the last 'Socialist' book on homosexuality called *The Third Sex?* by Jaroslava Pondelíčková-Mašlová and Antonín Brzek, published in 1992, every sexological publication I opened was contextualized primarily in Anglo-Saxon and German sexological scholarship, rather than Soviet. Clearly, the inspiration and knowledge in the field of sexology came from the Western side of the Iron Curtain and this leaning was accepted by the higher authorities in the Ministry of Health and the relevant publishing houses, such as Avicenum or Státní zdravotnické nakladatelství, responsible for the ideological censorship of transmitted knowledge and information in the country.

Most historians argue, based on diverse approaches to the study of the subject, that it was not possible to find any publicly available and open information about homosexuality because the topic was 'taboo' during the Communist period.[189] Sexological discourse on homosexuality and transsexuality during the Communist period, however, was quite prolific and sexologists openly referenced the research and theoretical and conceptual approaches of their Western colleagues. Consequently, and contrary to prevailing interpretations of Czechoslovak sexology during socialism, Czechoslovak sexologists

---

188 Between 1966 and 1989 there were more than twenty articles published by Czech sexologists, which devoted their attention exclusively to the topic of transsexuality. To this should be added additional twenty articles that mentioned transsexuality in relation to other issues, as well as articles focusing on intersexuality and bisexuality.

189 Seidl 2012; Fanel 2000; Schindler 2013.

also shared surprisingly complex understandings of human sexuality. Their texts also suggest that even though they believed in their own authority and the superiority of medical knowledge over "experience," they were able to shift their views based on new research and the responses of their patients. The main imperative has always remained 'to help' but the forms of that help kept changing. Increasingly, the well-being of the non-heterosexual subjects was being placed at the center of the sexological attention. In other words, while Socialist sexological discourse always paid a lip service to the "interests of Socialist society" and the "protection of the heterosexual majority," between the lines the main message and priority was quite often the emotional prosperity and emancipation of the queer individual. It does not mean, of course, that the result met the goals but it does reveal that the main aim of Czechoslovak Socialist sexology was to help and not to repress. The sexological treatment of transsexuality since the mid-1960s is revealing about both the positive intentions of sexologists 'to help' and the limits of such approach.

The first mentions of transsexuality in Czechoslovak sexological discourse dates to 1966, when Karel Nedoma and Jiří Mellan published an article called "Syndrom transsexualismu" (*The Transsexuality Syndrome*).[190] In the text, they summarized the latest (Western) research on the topic, and pointed out that the newest developments indicated that there must be a distinction made between transvestitism, as a desire to cross-dress, and transsexuality, as an expression of an "opposite" gender identity, when "people consider themselves to be members of the opposite sex than how their genitals developed." Already in 1966, Nedoma with Mellan urged that it is important to understand the "complexity of the problem."[191] In 1969, Prof. Hynie followed with an article, in which he already outlined the main medical and legal steps in the process of transformative sex-change therapy and surgery. Hynie argued that

> the [transsexual] disorder does not start and end with sexual orientation and activity but rests in transformed personality, which is the reason why I would not call it a deviation and perversity, as for example Imielinski does.[192]

Hynie defended transsexuals as "unfortunate" but "otherwise worthy (*hodnotní*) people" and argued against the then-current Polish and Soviet conceptions of transsexuality as a perversion in need of eradication or criminalization. To the contrary, Hynie listed most up-do-date Swedish, American

---

190 Karel Nedoma and Jiří Mellan, "Syndrom transsexualismu," *Československá psychiatrie* 62:1 (1966): 42–47.

191 Ibid.

192 Josef Hynie, "Lékařská opatření při transsexualismu." *Československá psychiatrie* 65/5 (1969): 295–299, 295.

and German sexological scholarship in order to dispel views of the Polish and Soviet sort, which he openly called "inappropriate."[193] Remarkably, having established in the beginning of the article that because of the "inborn and unchangeable" sex inversion, we should consider the gender identification, as well as sexual desires, of transsexual people as "natural"; Hynie spent the rest of the article listing out recommendations on how to make the lives of transsexual people easier and more comfortable. He pointed out that the "lack of social understanding causes for [such people] difficult conflict situations," which can lead to "heavy depressions and suicidal tendencies in almost half of them." With reference to Hirschfeld he stressed that it is "the duty of the medical profession to help [these people] lead a socially bearable life." Hynie's list of proposals included not only surgical and hormonal medical suggestions, but mainly recommendations of a social and institutional nature:

> What can we do for such people?... Most of all, we are trying to accommodate these people... It is not enough to walk around in clothing of the opposite sex. R.Z. looks so masculine in women's clothing that she was directly stopped by security organs (*bezpečnostními orgány*) and accused of being a man in women's dress. She was also prevented [it is not clear by whom] from entering a women's bathroom with the argument that she is not a woman. We recommended to the organs of ONV and VB [the local municipal office and the police] to enact a name change and issue such a person a new ID card. If the picture in the ID card shows a male-looking person, no one even thinks about it and addresses such person as a man [and hence presumably she can also easily live like a man, entering, for example, a male restroom]. In other administrative documents you can then find all the appropriate information about the fact that the biological sex of this person is female so that the organs of public power will not be disappointed... I would recommend that the name is changed into a neutral one and the picture ID is replaced so that there is not such an ostentatious discrepancy between the person's looks and his or her name.[194]

Hynie's examples from his practice (he worked "with about 30 persons, mostly women, quite masculine, who demand to be changed into a man") indicate that regular police officers in the streets or state officials in public institutions did not understand or empathize with transsexuals and either harassed them or at least made their lives very difficult. However, Hynie did not share such a dismissive attitude and argued against it by explicitly distancing himself from other "organs of public power." This little detail shows again that there was not one "official state discourse" on transsexuality

---

193 Ibid, 296–297.
194 Ibid, 297. Hynie repeats similar arguments in his subsequent article with Iva Šípová, "Transsexuálky," *Československá psychiatrie* 71:1 (1975): 48–52.

during socialism that could be easily grasped and simply narrated. Hynie's article (as well as other examples in the oral history recollections later on) unravel intersections of several different "state approaches," that were all a part of the 'regime' or "state authority" during the Communist period.

Hynie's approach to transsexuality is not an arrogant expression of superiority of sexological knowledge and assertion of medical authority as a voice of the state but rather an attempt to make sexology a vanguard and responsible agent for advocating for social change, which supported the inclusion and accommodation of queer people within mainstream society. Hynie appealed to state institutions to enact these changes at the administrative level, shielding the recommendations, including the defense of sexual diversity as an integral part of Socialist society, with his professional authority.[195] Hynie did not argue, as many sexologists in other Socialist countries did, that transsexuality (or homosexuality) was a perverse hangover from the bourgeois past or of decadent capitalism. Nor did he argue that sexual diversity did not have a place in "advanced Socialist society" or that it was incompatible with Communist ideology or Socialist morality.[196] To the contrary, along with other Czechoslovak sexologists, Hynie was one of the leading personalities, which made Czechoslovakia one of the first countries to perform regular and fully subsidized sex-reassignment surgeries.[197] Similarly, in 1980 sexologists Antonín Brzek and Petr Krekule published an article, in which they asserted that transsexual people, both men and women, should not be subjected to the (often-despised) mandatory military service. While their argumentation was problematic in its essentialist outlook, in times of mandatory military service during state socialism their expertise provided the basis for a so-called "blue book," a much-desired medical document exempting young men, in this case transsexuals, from the hated mandatory military service.[198]

To be clear, the Czechoslovak sexological discourse during the Socialist era *was* heteronormative, gender-blind, and worked with essentializing

---

195 The fact that Hynie was successful in this process is evidenced by the fact that all the administrative changes he suggested in 1969 were gradually implemented into the legislative framework of transsexuality in 1970 and 1977. It must be also mentioned, however, that one of the most restrictive and discriminatory aspects, mandatory castration (povinné „znemožnění reprodukční funkce"), also argued for by the sexologists, remains a part of the legislature on transsexuality up to this day, being heavily and repeatedly criticized by transsexual and queer civic activists. „Změna jména, příjmení a zápisu pohlaví u transsexuálních osob," *Věstník ministerstva zdravotnictví* 28:1–2, 1980, 3.

196 Pisankaneva 2005; Essig 1999.

197 Fifková, et al. 2008; Hana Fifková, Petr Weiss, Ivo Procházka, Ladislav Jarolím, Jiří Veselý, and Vladimír Weiss, *Transsexualita: diagnostika a léčba* (Praha: Grada, 2002); Antonín Brzek and Iva Šípová, "Dnešní možnost změny pohlaví u transsexualismu," *Praktický lékař* 59:19/20 (1979): 752–756.

198 Antonín Brzek and Petr Krekule, "Posuzování shcopnosti k vojenské službě u transsexuálů po změně pohlaví," *Vojenské zdravotnické listy* 49:3 (1980): 114–116.

gender and sexual stereotypes. The extensive research and analysis of the sexological discourse indicates, however, that it was *also* liberal and emancipatory in many ways. While the Czechoslovak Socialist sexological discourse was undeniably complex, its ambiguously positive character often gets lost in the prevailing accounts of its disciplinary and regulatory roles, routinely focused on its rigidity and imprisonment in authoritarian ideology.[199] It is thus important to tease out and highlight also the positive dimensions, in which the Czechoslovak sexological discourse contributed to the emancipation and empowerment of queer people during state socialism. It represents a crucial even if much less-known historical narrative, but more importantly, queer people themselves in their biographical narratives often recalled how important sexologists were for them and what positive roles they played in their lives during state socialism.

In 1968, Richard Kluzák, a sexologist in a clinic in the small Moravian town of Třinec, published a case-study article about one of his patients, a transsexual woman, who in 1963, at the age of 25, decided to undergo sex-reassingment surgery.[200] Even though Nedoma's article from 1966 was the first published piece, the sexological treatment of transsexuals in Czechoslovakia obviously had already started several years before that. Kluzák described at length the case and the individual phases of the sex-change process. The article is characterized by respectful understanding and commitment to help the patient enact the desired change, which was successfully and "to great happiness [of the patient] completed in 1966." Kluzák ended his article by stating that

> It is logical that the patient was strongly instructed that he is required to truthfully inform every woman, with whom we would like to enter into an intimate or even long-term relationship, about his physical state . Already before the end of the [sex-change] process, he introduced to me his fiancé, a young girl, who was completely normal psychosexually. She was informed in detail by the patient about everything. My own information, given to the girl, was completely redundant, and my attempt to talk them out of the marriage was futile. In the time of the publication of this article, their marriage is going on two years and it's completely harmonious. The last picture [a photo of a smiling "heterosexual" couple in wedding dress, getting married, attached to the article] thus illustrates the end point of the surgery excursion into the so-far not-studied-enough realm of psychosexual relationships.[201]

---

199 Lišková 2018 and 2012; Řídký 2013.

200 Richard Kluzák, "Chirurgická transformace pohlaví u ženského transsexualismu," *Rozhledy v chirurgii* 47:4 (1968): 253–261.

201 Ibid., 257.

Along with Hynie's approach to transsexuality, Kluzák's article is an example of the unexpected nature of Czechoslovak sexology during the Socialist times. First, Kluzák's article demonstrates that the attitudes and arguments held by Hynie and doctors around him were not espoused only by "informed" and centrally located sexologists in Prague or Brno but were also shared by their colleagues in smaller cities and towns around Czechoslovakia, such as Třinec, Olomouc, Ostrava, Košice, and Opava. Moreover, Kluzák matter-of-factly documents that transsexuality was not only an integral part of sexual diversity in the time of Communist Czechoslovakia but also that under the façade of the officially sanctioned picture of unitary normative identity of a "Socialist person," such allegedly "normal" people sometimes lived overt 'heterosexual' lives with covert complex sexual and gender identities. The oral histories of queer people, which invite complex readings of the allegedly stiff and uniform authoritarian regime, are sometimes dismissed as being too random or too individualistic. Kluzák's article provides a window into such lives from the other side and challenges the monotonous picture of hetero-homo and male-female duality presented so often in the histories of recent Czechoslovakia as well.

Other sexologists from different hospitals around the country shared similar case studies, reporting on the social adaptability and everyday lives of transsexual patients in Socialist Czechoslovakia. Similar to Kluzák, in 1980 sexologists Jana Myšková and Martin Mocek from the Ostrava psychiatric clinic described stories of well-adjusted transsexual women, who underwent sex-change surgeries and now "live in very satisfying relationships."[202] Myšková and Mocek provided the readers with more insight into the everyday lives and strategies of these transsexuals and their partners.

The most interesting are three couples... who met already before the end of the therapy. None of the partners of the transsexuals exhibit any mental insufficiencies... The transsexual women in these partnerships take on male roles and live in the apartments of their partners. All three partners have children from their previous marriages (two of them have two children, one has one child, the youngest child is three-years-old, the oldest child is eight-years-old). The transsexual women assumed the role of the father and are also addressed as such by the children... The partners negatively evaluate the personalities of their ex-husbands and describe them as irresponsible asocials (asociálové), while they very positively value their current transsexual partners, especially in their relationship to the family. They [the partners] emphasize their attention to a harmonious family life, that they pay attention to the children, and value the home and the woman... In their neighborhoods, all three couples formed a "defensive

---

202 Jana Myšková and Martin Mocek, "K osobnostem partnerů transsexuálů." *Praktický lékař* 60:15/16 (1980): 548–550.

mechanism" — any potential remarks by their neighbors they [both people in the cou-ple] mercilessly liquidate (*nekompromisně likvidují*) and they prefer the feelings of their own satisfaction over the reactions of those around. None of them consider moving away [because of the neighbors].[203]

Like the marriage of the couple in Kluzák's article, the lives of the three couples in Myšková's and Mocek's study also challenged the view of simple heteronormativity. On the one hand, it is obvious that Myšková and Mocek tried hard to fit the discussed transsexual lives and their family patterns into a binary and complementary understanding of heterosexual gender and sexuality. At the same time, they also matter-of-factly presented such family constellations as compatible with Socialist ideology and morality and openly approved the fact that transsexuals in Socialist Czechoslovakia raised chil-dren in "harmonious family" settings. They also implicitly suggested that if there was any problem in the described situations, it was the homophobia of the neighbors or potentially at school or work, not the transsexuality itself, and seemed to agree that "preferring the feelings of one's own satisfaction" was the best defensive strategy. In other words, the sexologists were not sug-gesting or recommending that the transsexuals and their partners should hide. To the contrary, they indicated that they should live their lives as they saw fit. Last, but certainly not least, it was not insignificant that many of the homosexual and transsexual lives discussed as case studies in sexological literature came from small cities and villages in Czechoslovakia. This aspect shows that at least for some queer people, it was possible to live queer lives outside of the largest cities, such as Prague and Brno with a degree of open-ness and dignity.

The sexological discourse on transsexuality during Socialist Czechoslova-kia was arguably more complex than the discourse on homosexuality, grap-pling with internal inconsistencies and theoretical contradictions, as well as possessing a veto power that could destroy people's lives. For example, in the same article in which Myšková and Mocek discussed with approval the non-normative lives of more than ten transsexual people, they also stated that "we are refusing to start treatment of one young female transsexual, who displays psychopathic personality structures and a tendency towards al-cohol-abuse."[204] Sadly, the "tendency towards alcohol-abuse" was authorita-tively dismissed by the authors as a symptom of mental instability, ultimately prohibiting the young queer person from receiving the desired treatment, without a hint of a discussion that rather than a symptom the "psychopathic"

---

203 Ibid., 549.
204 Ibid, 548.

personality could have been a consequence of transphobia, rejection and despair.[205]

The Socialist sexological treatments of transsexuality also contained some hard-to-believe approaches. Since 1966, for example, sexologist Iva Šípová tried to use toxic LSD therapy in order to treat male and female transsexual patients and help them "find harmony" in their lives. The therapeutic use of LSD in the sexological treatment of transsexuality, officially sactioned by the state, exposes once again just how much authority and power medical doctors had during state socialism and how trusted their "expert voices" were.[206] Šípová accepted into her study "only those homosexual men and transsexual women, who indicated their spontaneous interest in this method and absolutely refused to live in a homosexual way (*a za žádnou cenu nechtěli žít homosexuálně*)."[207] She did not discuss anywhere in her article how or where she found her subjects, nor did she explain the choice of including in her study homosexual men and transsexual women. Why them? Was there some medical or theoretical reason for this? Or were they simply available? The composition of her group suggests the already presented view expressed by many sexologists that homosexual men attended sexological offices in much greater numbers than homosexual women ever did. It would help explain why Šípová used only men as her "homosexual group." Similarly, Hynie already voiced his surprise that in Czechoslovakia "I did not encounter too many transsexual men, as the scholarship has it. For example, Walinder [states] that there are distinctly more of them [than transsexual women]."[208]

A partial explanation of this trend was proposed by the authors of the first ever popular book devoted solely to the questions of transsexuality published in the Czech Republic in 2002, who argued that in the countries of the former Socialist Bloc, FtM (Female-to-Male) transsexuals outnumbered their MtF (Male-to-Female) counterparts 5:1, which was dramatically different from the "Western world," where the MtF transsexual prevailed 3:1.[209] The authors suggested that one of the reasons for this discrepancy was the "influence of different social factors, which made it more difficult for the MtF transsexuals to successfully assert themselves in the conditions of the Socialist states."[210] Such an interpretation would be supported by the fact that since 1989, the number of MtF transsexuals in post-Communist Eastern Europe has

---

205 Warner, 1999.

206 Havelková, 2015.

207 Iva Šípová, "Terapie LSD u homosexuálů a transsexuálek." *Časopis lékařů českých* 113:48 (1974): 1491–1493.

208 Hynie 1969, 297; Myšková and Mocek reported the same ratio as Hynie in 1980 when they stated that their own clinic "registers distinct outnumbering of [transsexual] men by women — there are seven women to one man" (548).

209 Fifková et al. 2002.

210 Ibid. 17.

steadily grown and currently, like in the other democratic countries, MtFs already outnumber FtMs. The authors also suggested, however, that another reason might be "differences in diagnostic criteria" now and then.[211] While the authors see these two reasons as separate, from a gendered perspective it is likely that they are very much interconnected.

The great majority of sexological writings on transsexuality published during the Socialist period posited a fundamental belief in innate and oppositional gender differences between men and women, which could be observed, described and studied as stable and indisputable "facts." Based on these arguments, the Czech sexological school asserted that it is paramount to make sure that a potential sex-change surgery results in a "good looking woman who can pass as such."[212] The 1980 Decree on the "Change of name, surname, and sex registration of transsexual people" issued by the Ministry of Health of Czechoslovakia even officially demanded that transsexual people, who could be subsequently permitted by a special expert committee to undergo the sex-change surgery must first demonstrate that they "have achieved an adequately satisfactory appearance of the opposite sex."[213] Since the requirements for male "beauty" were not as demanding as they were in the case of women, this officially stated attitude also likely translated into more difficult conditions for MtF transsexuals to convince the sexologists that they would pass the aesthetic test.[214]

In 1974, however, Šípová concluded that "despite their [the transsexual women's] excellent cooperation during the therapy, the absolute hopelessness (*naprostá beznadějnost*) of attempts to alter their socio-sexual disposition was obvious." Interestingly, while Šípová praised the transsexual women in the study for their cooperation, she complained that the homosexual men "do not cooperate... they either express aversion towards the drug or they refuse to share their experiences." To her own surprise, however, despite their antagonistic attitudes towards the study, in the end the homosexual men, unlike the "hopeless" transsexual women, "reached the best results."[215] Based on these findings, Šípová gradually stopped with LSD therapy and turned instead into the research of social influences on transsexual people during their early childhood. Here, her findings represented a battery of gender stereotypes, which she presented as obvious truths. In her articles on this topic, she did

211 Ibid., 18.

212 Fifková et al. 2008; Fifková et al. 2002.

213 "Změna jména, příjmení a zápisu pohlaví u transsexuálních osob," *Věstník ministerstva zdravotnictví* 28:1–2 (1980): 3.

214 Jozef Medvecký, "Prípad transsexualizmu," *Československá psychiatrie* 69:4 (1973): 236–240; Lubomír Neoral, "K soudní lékařské problematice kastrace při transsexualismu," *Soudní lékařství* 14:3 (1969): 33–36.

215 Šípová 1974.

not question her fundamental premises and points of departure, such as whether there is such a thing as a "toy of one's own sex" or "colors belonging to the other sex."[216] She also supported the view that "family environment and proper gender role models were crucial for normal healthy development." At the same time, in her own research she herself often provided challenges to her own gender stereotypes. For example, in the 1980 summary of her longitudinal study of 100 transsexual women and 27 of their sexual partners, she stated that her incoming hypothesis was that

> the dominance of transsexual women will manifest itself in their behavior towards their sexual partners. We expected that the transsexual will identify with the male role [in the relationship]. The image of the male role she could have derived from her father, as is common for boys. However, this expectation was not fulfilled. And not even the transsexual women themselves expressed expectations that their partners would consider them based on the reference images of their fathers: as dominant authorities. In consensus with their expectations, their partners judged them as competent, strong and responsible, but at the same time as kind, tolerant and affectionate: that is, similar to their mothers.[217]

Šípová's own research demonstrated the falsity of gender-stereotypical expectations. What is commendable on her article is that she does not try to hide or manipulate her findings but openly admits the failure of her hypothesis. But she never seems to ask what such a conclusion means for her own theorizing about gender and sexuality, as well as for other sexological research. Examination of the sexological production on transsexuality during the Socialist era shows both the contradictions and the positive aspects of Czechoslovak sexological discourse during state socialism. The point of discussing the Socialist sexological discourse is to reveal the institutional and value frameworks of state attitudes towards non-normative sexuality, which created conditions for the everyday lives of queer people. In the process, the sexological writings provided an opportunity to get a glimpse of these lives. If *these* lives, recorded and presented by the sexologists themselves, did not conform to and support gender and sexual stereotypes, with which the sexologist set to study them, the question is how other queer people, who did not even express any need to cross paths with Czechoslovak sexology, actually

---

216 Iva Šípová, "Dětství intersexuálních osob, *Československá pediatrie* 31:8 (1976): 450–453; Iva Šípová, "Rodinné prostředí u intersexuálních lidí," *Československá pediatrie* 31:11, 1976, 629–63; Even though Šípová titled her articles Childhood of Intersexual People and Family Enviroment of Intersexual People, in both texts themselves she uses the term transsexual, Iva Šípová, "Intelektová úroveň u transsexuálů," *Československá psychiatrie* 71: 2–3 (1975): 131–136.

217 Iva Šípová, "Interpersonální vztahy transsexuálních žen," *Časopis lékařů českých* 119:17/18 (1980): 509–511, 511.

lived their lives. As the following chapters will unfold, even though many queer narrators shared the gender stereotypes of Czechoslovak sexology in theory, in practice they often lived their lives in ways which transgressed such stereotypes and made them irrelevant.

GENDER STEREOTYPES IN CZECHOSLOVAK SEXOLOGY

In 1976, a team of sexologists from the small north-Moravian town of Opava argued surprisingly that

> biological differences between the sexes are relatively insignificant and are rather a stimulus than a cause for the different formation of the female and male role, which is, in the end, fixed only socially. Each culture standardizes and institutionalizes the female and male roles in a certain way. It can be concluded from that that the "male" and "female" are in the end only erotically conditioned ideals, which are subordinated to historical and individual changes... Transsexuality [is] a feeling of harmony. [218]

It is the most explicit articulation of social constructivism in Socialist sexology found in the entire period studied. While Czechoslovak sexological discourse produced during state socialism was not completely unitary and predictable, the critical and open tone of this article is exceptional. Most Czechoslovak sexological texts, however emancipatory and liberal, built their study of human sexuality on the presupposition of stable and oppositional male and female bodies, and a corresponding binary gender. As Řídký demonstrated in his analysis of the popular and widely disseminated literature on homosexuality, this was also the view officially promoted by Czechoslovak sexology towards the public. Symptomatically, among the popular handbooks on homosexuality published between 1930–1992 that Řídký studied, there was not a single publication that would consider or be concerned with female homosexuality. Řídký thus argued that what Czechoslovak sexology produced was a definition and a picture of a "male" homosexual and "male" homosexuality, with the female one defined as an unspoken opposition. A homosexual male was deviant and inadequate precisely because he was "unmanly" and effeminate through his association with the female body and psyche. A homosexual female, Řídký asserted, was deviant simply by her biological opposition to the male norm.[219]

---

218 Brauerová, Satková and Topiař, 1976, 20–21.
219 Řídký 2013.

However, it would be incorrect to conclude from this that female sexuality was not discussed in Czechoslovak sexology at all. First, female transsexuality was at the forefront of sexological attention and during state socialism transsexual women had much easier access to sex-reassingment surgery than transsexual men did. And second, sexuality as such was an important component of ideological attempts of the Communist Party to remain in power by collectivizing private and intimate matters.[220] Claiming that sexuality was a public, collective point of interest, and the concern of the entire Socialist society dates to the late 1960s and early 1970s. Open discussions about sexuality were not seen as incompatible with Socialist morality. To the contrary, sexuality was one of the important tools to strengthen Socialist morality and to create an obedient and complacent public, which was loyal but apolitical. It makes a lot of sense from a historical point of view that the enormous rise, both in terms of number of publications and number of copy counts, of literature about sexuality, intimacy and interpersonal relations dates to the beginning of Normalization. Interestingly, among these publications were not only original works of Czechoslovak sexologists, heavily referenced by "Western" scholarship, but also direct translations of American, British, Canadian and French authors.[221] The aura of liberal and open sexuality discussed in a "communal way" on the pages of popular books and on radio waves worked to support the illusion of personal freedom, openness and control over one's private affairs and helped to build a "collective amnesia" about 1968.[222] The arguments, disseminated and "supervised from above" by renowned sexologists, presented a complex mixture of sexual freedom, personal power, collective responsibility and adherence to gender stereotypes, which together helped to maintain both heternormative social order and political stability all the way to the late 1980s.

Whether talking about heterosexuality or homosexuality, gender stereotypes informed most of the sexological writings. In 1979, Antonín Brzek published (in one of the most widely-read popular medical journals *Zdraví*), an

---

220 Havelková and Oates-Indruchová, eds., 2014.

221 William Masters and Virginia Johnson, *Lidská sexuální aktivita* (*Human Sexual Response*) (Praha, nakladatelství Horizont, 1970) — 25,000 copies; Oswalt Kole, *Kouzlo lásky* (Praha, Avicenum, 1970) — 100,000 copies;, Theodor Hendrik Van de Velde *Dokonalé manželství: Studies o jeho fyziologii a technice* (Praha, Avicenum 1968 a 1972) — 55,000 copies; Ivo Pondělíček and Jaroslava Pondělíčková-Mašlová, *Lidská sexualita jako projev přirozenosti a kultury* (Praha: Avicenum, 1971) — 70,000 copies, reprint in 1974 — 50,000 copies; Josef Hynie, *Dospíváte v muže*, (Praha, Státní zdravotnické nakladatelství, 1976) — 60,000 copies; Ivo Pondělíček and Jaroslava Pondělíčková-Mašlová, *Sexuální zrání mladého muže* (Praha: Avicenum, 1977) — 50,000 copies; Miroslav Plzák, *Manželské judo* (Praha: Avicenum, 1970) — 100,000 copies; Miroslav Plzák, *Taktika a strategie v lásce* (Praha: Mladá fronta, 1970) — 100,000 copies; *Důvěrné hovory: rozhlasové besedy o problémech sexuálního života* (Praha, Státní zdravotnické nakladatelství, 1968) — 60,000 copies.

222 Paulina Bren, *The Greengrocer and His TV: The Culture of Consumerism after the 1968 Prague Spring* (Ithaca: Cornell University Press, 2010).

article called "Man or a Woman?" (*Muž nebo Žena?*), in which he explained homosexuality to (presumably) the general public from a medical point of view. He pointed out that "such a defect is undoubtedly inborn" and that "indisputable are also psychological factors in the period of early childhood, which lead to manifestation of inborn dispositions. Today's knowledge proves that there are some deficiencies in the social environment of the child, such as the absence of correct parental male and female examples, excessive harshness or pampering, unclear visions of parents into what life role (in terms of gender role [*pohlavní role*]) they actually want to raise their child."[223]

Brzek shared a whole battery of gender stereotypes, which allegedly indicated a homosexual predisposition. He argued that "very often [homosexual] boys play with dolls, enjoy domestic housework, like dressing in their mother's or sister's dresses, and dislike aggressive sports. [Homosexual] girls, on the other hand, enjoy aggressive sports, crafts, and rogue behavior. Contrary to a transsexual, however, such a child never dreams of becoming a person of the opposite sex with all that it involves."[224] The list of gender biases espoused in 1979 is not surprising and discloses the depth of gender stereotyping, which informed sexological attitudes during the Socialist era. Even though Czech sexologists often complained that "not enough has been researched about female homosexuality" and that there is "a lack of knowledge about homosexuality in women," they themselves significantly contributed to the trend of a problematically gendered approach and attitude to human sexuality and all its variations.

Sexological articles, however, often were not just simple exercises in gender essentialism but contained elusive points. Without touching at all on female homosexuality, Czech sexologists distinguished between "virile" or "masculine" and "feminine" homosexualities. A "virile" or "masculine" homosexual was such a man who "feels like a man but towards other men projects the same feelings as normal men to women." "Feminine" homosexuality, on the other hand, was manifested by "deviation in other spheres" than purely sexual attraction. Such homosexuals, according to Brzek, for example, "behave and dress in effeminate ways, and for some a full female role would be appropriate. It seems that there is a number of fluid, gradual passing stages between homosexuality and transsexuality."[225] While Brzek informed the public about a flexible spectrum of sexuality between homosexuality and transsexuality, he did not extend this argument to fluid passing between heterosexuality and homosexuality as well. But if the readers were to apply just a little bit of logic, they could come to that conclusion anyway.

---

223 Antonín Brzek, "Muž nebo žena?" *Zdraví* 27/2 (1979): 18.
224 Ibid.
225 Brzek 1979, 18.

As elsewhere, gender-biased views of sexuality had complex consequences and not always were they only negative for queer people. For women, who preferred same-sex relationships, for example, it meant more freedom to live out their sexuality without the scrutinized attention of both medical professionals and the police. Moreover, it was not just the attention of the "state organs" but parental interests as well. In a complicated two-way street, society at large was adopting expert views of sexuality as scientific truth and in turn sexologists were influenced by the attitudes of their patients, in this case parents, who displayed a great gender bias as well. The detailed case studies contained in the articles of sexologists show that it was mostly parents themselves who brought young boys to sexological offices, either for diagnosis or directly for cure.[226] Interestingly, the 70 examined case-study articles from the Socialist era do not contain a single case about any girl who would be brought in by her parents for an alleged homosexual tendency. When it came to parental fears of transsexuality, however, parents were much more willing to bring their daughters in for an expert examination because they "behaved like a boy." In other words, parents seemed to be more concerned with their daughters crossing the expected boundaries of female behavior and correct performance of female gender roles than they were with the objects of their sexual desires. For boys, on the other hand, it was the other way around. The boys could behave in feminine ways as long as they exhibited sexual interest in the opposite sex, which was taken as an adequate proof of their proper masculinity.[227]

The writings of Czechoslovak sexologists from 1947 to 1989 disclose that throughout the Socialist era, Czech and Slovak sexologists were struggling between their efforts towards an emancipation of non-heterosexual sexuality in Socialist Czechoslovakia, presented primarily by their tireless efforts to argue for the "value" and "worth" of homosexual or transsexual individuals and their right for "respectable lives," and at the same time their inability to step outside their own prejudices and beliefs in the "normality" of heterosexuality and strong essentialist interpretations of gender subjectivities and relations. Consequently, the sexological writings were locked in conceptual imperialism, an uncritical acceptance of cultural categories without the ability to reflect on their instability and dependence on contextualization. Since the point of departure of all officially sanctioned medical writings on sexuality

---

226 See, for example Freund and Srnec1953; Freund 1962; Bártová, 1979; Antonín Topiař, M. Vilč and E. Gladr, "Homosexuální agresivní počínání v alkoholovém opojení," *Protialkoholický obzor* 21/2 (1986): 73–75.

227 As the following chapters will disclose, some of the women narrators shared similar experiences from the waiting rooms of sexological offices. While they went there as young adults and of their own will "to learn something new," they recalled "waiting rooms full of anxious mothers with their terrified young sons."

during the Communist period was the intertwined belief in the normality of heterosexuality and the defaulting abnormality of homosexuality, even the most ambitious pieces could not have moved beyond the constraining framework of heteronormativity. The Czechoslovak sexological writings from this era are thus full or contradictions and paradoxes, exposing the complex nature of Czechoslovak sexology and its constitutive impact on medical and social perceptions of both gender and sexuality in Socialist Czechoslovakia.

In one of her articles, Lišková argues that even though in general sexuality was approached in very essentialized ways, at the same time sexologists viewed sexuality, especially in its "non-normal/deviant forms" as unstable, originating in the social locus of family and thus malleable through variety of treatments. According to her, because the family was seen as the "origin of deviance" it was then also perceived as the most logical site of redress for the (homo)sexual deviance.[228] In addition, Lišková asserted that "some sexologists found it important to return to sexological terminology 'guilt' and together with it the need to punish."[229] Such an argument is surprising and contradicts the published sexological sources. The comprehensive study of the written sexological discourse on non-heterosexuality during state socialism in Czechoslovakia did not reveal any texts that would support such a reading. Perhaps, it is because, as Lišková herself states, she concentrated "particularly on texts focused on perversity" in order to analyze what they tell us about the construction of gender and (homo)sexuality under Normalization.[230] In other words, Lišková's choice of sources, focused on a series of sexological roundtables during one year and then stretched to characterize the entire Normalization period, predetermined her findings. In 1978, when her particular study took place, homosexuality was charged with "perversity" only in connection with generally criminalized pathologies, such as pedophilia or sexual aggression. By 1978, I did not come across any sexological texts that would define homosexuality (or transsexuality) *itself* as "perversion." Nor have I found any sexologists, who would want to reintroduce "guilt and punishment" for homosexual or transsexual identities and behavior alone. To the contrary, Brzek argued in 1979, that "parents cannot and should not be blamed for the homosexuality of their children."[231] As we will see later, it was, in fact, sexologists themselves, who argued that it was excessive to include specific mentions of homosexual orientation in the criminal code. They actively fought for further and full decriminalization of homosexuality based on their argument that homosexuality is dangerous *only* when

---

228 Lišková 2012, 40–41.
229 Ibid, 42.
230 Ibid.
231 Brzek 1979, 18.

connected with other criminal behavior (such as sexual violence, pedophilia, prostitution or blackmail), and that such behavior is already addressed by the general criminal code anyway.

MARITAL ADAPTATION THERAPY: HOMOSEXUALITY AND MARRIAGE

It is not news that many 'gays' and 'lesbians' living in different countries of the Soviet Bloc during the Socialist period were often married. It is much less known, however, that sexologists, at least in Socialist Czechoslovakia, were actively urging them to do so. Freund suggested already in 1962 that homosexuality and marriage were, according to him, quite compatible. One of the most important therapeutic methods for dealing with homosexuality from a sexological point of view, which by the late 1950s replaced the grossly unsuccessful method of behavioral aversion therapy, was so-called "marital adaptation."[232] This procedure consisted of a controlled and professionally coached marriage by a team of sexologists and matrinoiologists, who from the outside monitored the marriage of a "homosexual" patient, who expressed the desire to cure his "homosexual appetite by a heterosexual adaptation process."[233]

Strikingly, the approach was not only sanctioned by Czech and Slovak sexologists, but was even recommended and promoted as the best therapeutic strategy for the "successful socialization" of homosexuals from the late 1950s to the late 1980s.[234] While in the 1960s and 1970s the marital adaptation method was discussed only in specialized medical journals, in 1981 Brzek described this method at length for the wider public in the popular medical journal *Zdraví*, in an article aptly entitled "Marriage and Homosexuality."[235] In his text, Brzek, by then one of the most renowned and respected Czech sexologists, argued that it made a perfect sense that homosexuals enter heterosexual marriages and explained four major rules that should be observed for the "successful [heterosexual] marriage of homosexual persons."[236]

To begin with, Brzek pointed out that homosexuality is incurable and thus "it is not possible to raise any objections to the program of many homosexuals

---

232 Freund and Srnec 1953; Freund 1962.

233 Brzek 1979, 18.

234 Kurt Freund and Václav Pinkava, "Homosexuality in Man and its Association with Parental Relationships," *Review of Czechoslovak medicine* 7/1 (1961): 32–40; Bouchal and Bártová 1964; Brzek 1979, 1981 and 1986; Procházka 1987; Antonín Brzek and Slavomil Hubálek, "Homosexuals in Eastern Europe: Mental Health and Psychotherapy Issues." *Journal of Homosexuality* 15/1–2 (1988): 153–162.

235 Antonín Brzek, "Manželství a homosexualita." *Zdraví* 29/7 (1981): 18.

236 Ibid.

to not marry but live in a steady partnership with a partner of the same sex." Despite that, he pragmatically stated, "for rational reasons, many indisputably homosexual people (*nezpochybnitelní homosexuálové*) aspire for marriage, i.e. a legal union with a person of the opposite sex." Brzek went on to list several reasons why, in his opinion, this was the case:

> First, the society of the 'normal' people (*společnost 'normálních'*) makes the life of homosexuals difficult and often even unbearable. More sensitive individuals are not able to tolerate such discrimination and hope that entering marriages will mask their true orientation. The second reason tends to be the fear of loneliness in old age... Last, but not least, is the desire for one's own progeny (*potomstvo*). Especially homosexual men, probably because of the presence of some female characteristics in their personalities, often have a stronger need to take care of their own children than heterosexual, 'normal' men.[237]

Even without using the term 'homophobia,' Brzek recognized and openly blamed the majority society for being responsible for the behavior and atmosphere which made the lives of homosexual men and women difficult. Remarkable was also his overt usage of the term "discrimination," which was not common in Socialist texts during Normalization, as well as his open support for same-sex partnerships. Both of these points meant walking a fine line in 1981, as medical and social experts were expected to function as the messengers of correct social behavior for the masses.[238] What is fascinating, especially in the context of the current frenzied debates about the potential legal right of gays and lesbians to adopt children, is Brzek's explicit recognition of the desire and right of homosexual people to raise children and his pragmatic presentation of a traditional family as a practical trick to do so. His officially published argumentation demonstrates the remarkable openness of Czechoslovak Socialist sexology and points to the discursive freedom of sexologists to advocate for complex social constructions and false façades.

However, Brzek also exposed that his medical expertise, and thus his analytical potential when dealing with sexuality and sexual orientation, rested on deeply ingrained gender stereotypes — in this case one that automatically connects women with care and naturalizes the connection between women and children. At the same time, Brzek's use of this particular gender stereotype was complicated by an interesting twist, in which he claimed that homosexual men actually had stronger desires to have their own children than heterosexual men did — because of their (feminine) ability to take care of them. The important difference in Brzek's argument was the implicit meaning of

---

237 Brzek 1981, 18.
238 Havelková and Oates-Indruchová, eds., 2014.

having children. While heterosexual men might want to have their own children because of their biological predisposition to procreate, homosexual men do not desire children simply because they want to *have* them. Presumably, homosexuality erases such a simple, virile masculine desire, but instead replaces it with a feminine, innately possessed ability to *care*.[239]

Brzek's subsequent explanation of the precondictions and rules for a successful marriage between homosexuals and heterosexuals is even more striking. First, according to Brzek, the homosexual person "must realize that even in marriage his or her homosexual orientation will persist."[240] When a homosexual person makes the decision to get married, he or she "should definitively end all existing homosexual contacts, including only friendly ones. It is even advisable to leave the environment, where a person can easily get seduced, such as bigger towns."[241] Second, he or she must find such a person of the opposing sex, who will be "at least pleasant as a human (*lidsky příjemná*) to be around and with whom personal contact is not completely abhorrent." Third, Brzek advised that it was important to first make sure that both potential partners had the ability to enact mutual sexual intercourse. Brzek argued that

> certainly for a homosexual woman this is technically easier but even she can gradually become disgusted by having sex with a man. Of course, a more appropriate husband for a homosexual woman is a man with a low need of sexual intercourse... It is, however, surprising, how often homosexual men have no problems having sex with women, which is true even for very effeminate men.[242]

And fourth, Brzek recommended that because such marriages were not free of risks, "the other person should be informed about this situation [the partner's homosexuality] before the marriage... However, if the fact of homosexuality was not communicated early enough before the marriage, then *during the marriage the homosexual person must never admit it*. Such information could not only destroy the marriage, it could also be abused by the other party."[243] Brzek additionally warned that whatever the individual marital situation of any given homosexual person was, "nothing should be

---

239 A reverse analysis of how such an argument would work in the case of homosexual women, who were routinely read by Czechoslovak sexologists through the prism of aggressivity and masculinity, is missing from Brzek's article.

240 Ibid.

241 Other medical literature from the era speaks as well of this therapeutic trend of recommending to homosexuals moving away from towns to villages and small, isolated places (for example Karel Nedoma, "Homosexuální prostituce u mladistvých," *Československý psychiatr* 58/5 (1962): 312–314).

242 Brzek 1981.

243 Brzek 1981. (Emphasis mine).

undertaken without continual and systematic consultations with a specialist, a sexologist, with whom it is advisable to stay in regular touch even in the course of a successfully functioning marriage." Brzek ended the article by stating that "all this, which was said here, of course does not apply to purely formal marriages, in which both partners know about each other's [homosexuality] and eroticism plays no role, as it is for example in marriages of homosexual men with homosexual women. The point of those unions is, of course, totally different... but that is no longer the territory of a sexologist."[244]

All gender stereotyping about "technically easier" sex for homosexual women aside, the most fascinating, and important detail for the Socialist context, is the openness and matter-of-factness with which a medical expert promotes double lives — for both men and women — on the pages of an officially sanctioned and state-controlled popular journal. It is amazing that on the one hand, homosexuality was officially defined as an illness and a medical diagnosis, and on the other hand, sexologists, as the expert agents of the Socialist state, were recommending and professionally couching arranged marriages between 'homosexuals' and 'heterosexuals.' In the absence of legislature, which would enable queer people to live in legally recognized same-sex partnerships, marital adaptation therapy through arranged marriages presented for sexologists the only avenue to officially (even if awkwardly) help queer people enter long-term, legal partnerships that would enable them to raise children and have security in old age. The price for such security, however, was high. While homosexual people were no longer subjected to medical attempts to *change* their sexual identity through biological interventions to *be* heterosexuals, they were still "socially motivated" to *suppress* their identity and sexual behavior through marriages to *pretend and perform* heterosexuality. Moreover, the conducting and functioning of marriages described by Brzek required participating and fully-aware heterosexuals. Their motivations for engaging in such marriages are not mentioned at all in the article. Brzek's article also made it clear that sexologists were well aware that rather than entering arranged marriages with heterosexuals, some queer people simply married each other to reach the social advantages and security mentioned by Brzek.

Similar to Brzek's article five years earlier, in 1986 and 1987 the popular weekly *Zdraví* published yet another extraordinary series of four articles by several authors on the topic of "contemporary homosexuality."[245] To an uninformed reader, it was simply an exchange of three experts, who argued

---

244 Brzek 1981, 18.

245 Each issue of the journal had different sections for diverse medical fields. All of the mentioned articles were published on pages 18 and 19 reserved for "Sexology." From the late 1970s, *Zdraví* regularly published academic articles about homosexuality.

the pros and cons of the current criminalization of homosexual acts under certain conditions and the position of homosexuality (and homosexuals) in a Socialist society. But the interconnection and sequence of the texts was designed in advance and purposeful.[246] In the first article, Brzek explained the currently accepted definition of homosexuality as "harmless deviance" and argued that homosexuality was a permanent (albeit diversely deep) state of mind and sexual disposition not caused by the carrier. He also discussed the current trends in sexological therapeutic treatment known as "marital adaptation," which should help "exceptionally motivated individuals" suppress their "natural desire" within a functioning marriage. Brzek noted that "there are always some homosexually orientated people, who are not capable of any successful marital adaptation." He ended his article by a strong plea for the social and legal acceptance of homosexuality. Brzek argued that "the only sensible and appropriate solution to the problem of homosexuality, which would be worthy of a humane and developed society, is the acceptance of such individuals as fellow citizens, fully valued and equal." He believed that "only with full acceptance of homosexual orientation is it possible to raise members of the homosexual subculture to the dignified practices of sexual life... in permanent partnership. Such partnerships [would] also provide them with all positive aspects a partnership [offers] in non-sexual matters."[247]

Brzek's first article also presented noteworthy arguments about allegedly gendered foundations of homosexuality. According to him, "homosexuality happens to both men and women, but manifests itself differently in each gender." Brzek noted that "a sexologist sees [homosexual] women infrequently" because homosexual women "seek his help only very rarely." He reasoned that

one of the reasons is perhaps the passivity of the female sexual role, which makes it much easier to mask female homosexuality by marriage... There are probably also other factors, which lead homosexual women to seldomly seek help. [Those factors] are related to the personality structure of such women and have not yet been researched in detail... To the contrary, homosexual men seek out professional help much more often... Unlike women, homosexual men also have a greater ability to create a subculture, to join together, and they tend to be more promiscuous."[248]

On the one hand, Brzek admitted that "female homosexuality" was not researched enough, on the other hand ventured out to offer and support with the weight of his authority biased arguments about homosexual women and

---

246 Interview with Ivo Procházka, 12.3. 2011.
247 Antonín Brzek, "Láska k témuž pohlaví." *Zdraví* 34/5 (1986): 19.
248 Brzek 1986, 18.

their sexuality, that lacked any evidence and simply corresponded to common gender stereotypes about "passive" and prudish female sexuality, which allegedly results in less promiscuity and women's inability to create a functional subculture.

The second article in this exchange was written by East German sexologist Prof. Erwin Günther, the director of a sexological clinic in Berlin. Günther went much further than Brzek and openly argued that "homosexuality is a natural variation in a very broad spectrum of sexual experience and behavior. Homosexuals have the same rights. They are entitled the same sexual harmony, love and respect... They have no reason to seek out a medical cure because they are not ill."[249] Günther posited that "if a homosexual [person] suffers from any disorder or a problem, those are most commonly related to conflicts with the heterosexual majority, especially with those intolerant citizens who want to push their style of thinking on others." According to him, the most important task for "a Socialist society is to secure equality for the homosexual minority." Günther also pleaded for sexual education, openness in marital advice, and, importantly, the empathetic upbringing of teenage homosexuals by parents.[250]

The third article was a critical response to Brzek's first article by Radomil Resch, J.D., one of the divisional directors of the General Prosecutor's Office of the Czech Republic, who argued that the current criminal law is sufficient and justified, especially in the sense that "some homosexual acts... are socially unbearable... and can cause public indignation or endanger the proper development of youth." Resch asserted that the point of the Socialist legal system was to "support and protect undisturbed mental development of youth, which is the condition for forming Socialist relations among people, including healthy sexual relations."[251]

The key to understanding the strategy of Czech and Slovak sexologists in disseminating progressive knowledge about homosexuality among the general public in the context of ever-present censorship is the fourth article, Brzek's response to Resch. In his response, Brzek partially conceded to Resch's critique and stressed that the "Czechoslovak sexological school has always understood and understands homosexuality as a sexual deviance — that is a defect of medical substance, not caused by the bearer."[252] He argued that the role of Czechoslovak sexology was to "minimize the unfavorable manifestations [of homosexuality]," which was the same procedure as with "all other medical defects, which we cannot cure or remove." He also explicitly

---

249 Erwin Günther, "Homosexualita a společnost." *Zdraví* 34/12 (1986): 19.
250 Ibid.
251 Radomil Resch, "Jde jen o lásku k témuž pohlaví?" *Zdraví* 35/4 (1987): 19.
252 Antonín Brzek, "Ještě o homosexualitě." *Zdraví* 35/8 (1987): 19.

distanced himself and the whole of Czechoslovak sexology from Dr. Günther's interpretation of homosexuality. "Contrary to some of our colleagues abroad, Czechoslovak sexologists do not consider homosexuality a fully normal and equal variety of human sexual behavior. Such an extreme view, officially held by experts in the GDR, was explained in the December issue [of *Zdraví*] by Dr. Günther. This view is also included in the last statistical classification of the USA (DSM III), which completely removed homosexuality from the list of medical diseases and defects."[253]

This exchange is noteworthy in several respects. First, it discloses subversive practices of going around censorship. According to sexologist Ivo Procházka, a close colleague of doctor Brzek from the Sexological Institute, the whole series of these four articles in the magazine was actually published *in order* to get Günther's article and arguments in the journal.[254] Brzek got permission from the editor-in-chief to publish Günther's article provided he write a critical commentary to Günther's "extreme view," which would not have a chance to appear in a popular medical journal on its own. On the one hand, Brzek thus distanced himself from Günther but on the other hand repeated again his exact arguments, additionally pointing out where to find its original version and adding on top another source of a supporting argument from an American classification of illnesses. In the end, the series of texts, presented as a series from the beginning, had no problem finding its place on the pages of the popular and widely read journal. Equally importantly, this episode showed that editors of journals during the 1980s not only had a relatively free hand in choosing articles and accepting potential risks upon their own shoulders, but also that they sometimes actively did so.

These writings also contained a less obvious subversive dimension. On the one hand, the publications of Czech and Slovak sexologists formally affirmed the primacy of heterosexuality. On the other hand, the motivations of Czechoslovak sexologists in writing about marriage was often a carefully thought-out strategy to make the topic of homosexuality more visible. Situating homosexuality *within* the framework of heterosexual marriage protected information about diverse sexual desires and behavior from censorship and improved the chances of such texts appearing in popular media, such as the weekly *Mladý svět* or the daily *Svobodné slovo*. Sexologist Ivo Procházka pointed out this conscious strategy in an interview, reminiscing about a series of articles he himself wrote for *Svobodné slovo*.

I was asked to write something about homosexuality but it was clear that it coud not stand on its own. So we [together with the editor-in-chief] prepared a series of ten

253 Ibid.
254 Interview with Ivo Procházka, 12.3. 2011.

texts on contemporary issues in sexuality, one of which was also the topic of homosexuality… I didn't want to call it just "homosexuality" and after a brief thought I decided to use the title of Zemek's iconic article from 1973 "They Live among Us."[255]

Intentionally, the whole series of the ten articles published during the 'cucumber season' in July-September 1987 was called "Questions of a Healthy Marriage."[256] In his text, Procházka, like Brzek, situated the question of homosexuality within heterosexual marriage, arguing that heterosexual marriage might be a logical and practical option for many homosexuals. Like Brzek, he also pointed out that homosexuality is an existing variety of human sexual behavior. Most importantly, he himself saw as the main contribution of his article the fact that "again we could make something public and get information about the reality of homosexuality out among people."[257]

As Brzek remarked in his text on heterosexual marriage and homosexuality, there were quite a few queer people who got married only as camouflage. While there are no statistics on such marriages, such unions were mentioned not only in the official sexological discourse, but also routinely during the biographical interviews. More than half of the participants in the queer oral history project were married during the pre-1989 period and almost all of them were personally engaged in sexual relationships with other queer married people. Scholarship often depicts 'gays' and lesbians married during the Communist period as passive victims of an oppressive regime, which gave them no choice and forced them to get married and suppress their identities.[258] As the following chapters will reveal, many queer people who got married during state socialism, whether it was in the 1950s or the 1980s, did so with the full knowledge of their queer identity and with a clear, subversive motive and strategy.

Sexological writings from the Socialist era provide an important context of state approaches to non-heterosexual sexualities, both in terms of content and argumentative strategies. Equally important, often more so from the point of view of queer people themselves, were the personal relationships among individual medical doctors and their 'homosexual' patients, who were regularly coming to the sexological offices, officially for therapy. It is this unique relationship between 'doctors and patients,' that illuminates the powerful and emancipatory dimension of sexology in Socialist Czechoslovakia perhaps the most. As already mentioned, the first such group was

255 Interview with Ivo Procházka, 12.3. 2011. (The detailed context of Zemek's iconic article is discussed in the following chapter).

256 Ivo Procházka, "Hovoříme o zdravém manželství. Part VIII: Žijí mezi námi." *Svobodné slovo*, August 9 (1987): 4.

257 Interview with Ivo Procházka, 12.3. 2011.

258 Janošová 2000; Hromada 2000; Fanel 2000.

started already in 1976, by sexologist Dagmar Bártová in Brno. Bártová, who was heralded by the post-1989 gay and lesbian community as the "mom of homosexuals" said herself in a 1990 interview that already in the mid 1970s she and her colleagues "realized that [they] were basically substitutes for the non-existent gay clubs... which was something they [the homosexual people] knew only from literature or hearsay."[259] In 1983, a similar "psychotherapeutic group for homosexual patients" was organized also in the Sexological Institute in Prague. Psychologist Slavomil Hubálek, one of the leading doctors in these groups, noted quite openly in a 1988 article that among mostly therapeutic reasons for seeking professional sexological help, homosexual men also came to the Institute with a hope that "we will help [them] in finding a partner." Hubálek noted in his article, written still during the Communist regime, that among homosexual men, the sexological clinics were seen as "safe places to meet and discuss their identity."[260]

An emphasis should be placed here on Hubálek's phrase "meet and discuss identity." Clearly, both sides understood the sexological therapy as a positive process of coming to terms with one's sexual identity and coming out in healthy ways. It is also obvious that "healthy identity" in this case meant *non-heterosexual*. The sexological writings also indicated that the rumors about "gay clubs," operating at the sexological clinics, were getting out among queer men by the men themselves. Citing Bártová's own article from 1977, Hubálek noted that "among 76 homosexual men who sought out sexological help in Brno between 1964–1973, almost half (47.4 %) asked for therapeutic help with heterosexual adaptation. However, among 70 men, who visited Prague Sexological Institute between 1983–1985, only seven men (10%) asked for adaptation therapy."[261] In other words, fewer and fewer men were coming to sexological offices with an expressed desire to help to change their sexual orientation. Likely, they were not coming with this desire there earlier either but at least they felt compelled to articulate their reason for coming in those terms. By the mid-1980s, ninety percent of homosexual men voluntarily coming to the Sexological Institute in Prague openly stated that they came there to discuss their identity, coming out and perhaps also meet a new partner.

Moreover, queer men and women who participated in the therapeutic groups for many years gradually transformed from patients into partners, even in the eyes of the doctors themselves. As Ivo Procházka shared in the interview:

---

259 Koukal 190, 3.
260 Slavomil Hubálek, "Skupinová psychoterapie homosexuálních pacientů," *Praktický lékař* 68/5 (1988): 187–188, 187.
261 Ibid, 188.

Tonda [Brzek] never told any of them to stop coming. I think that it was pleasant for his ego that they kept coming. It was a somewhat narcissistic matter. They [the patients] went there for example for ten years and they were still 'working out their coming out.' [laugh] Well, it's clear that they moved far beyond that. Some of them actually became co-therapists and Tonda really relied on their opinions and experiences. In group therapy, it's extremely useful when someone has the distance and experience that he or she can share with the others. It's very helpful for the doctor.[262]

Clearly, it was not a simple one-way street between the power of the medical experts and their helpless, passive patients but rather quite a complex and mutually beneficial relationship.

The doctors at the Sexological Institute in Prague also actively protected the personal and sensitive data of their patients, showing again how problematic it would be to characterize sexological discourse as a loyal agent of the state or simply a mindless disciplinary arm of Communist power and heteronormative order. Procházka recalled an incident from 1987, when the main director of the hospital came at night to the Sexological Institute with several Secret Police (StB) agents, who were searching for compromising data on the homosexual patients. The StB agents could not get into the Institute because the key to the main door was missing. Because the police did want to use force and cause a commotion, they left. "The next day," Procházka continued

Raboch [the director of the Institute at the time] made a huge fake scene, yelling at all of us for not leaving the key from the main entrance door at the reception desk. We all left keys from our individual offices there, it was standard practice. The main key was supposed to be there as well but it was a mutually known secret that Raboch kept it so that no one could get inside [without his knowledge]. I don't know if the StB wanted to look in the file registry or search our personal desks but certainly they were after some information about the patients. For example, we all knew that Tonda Brzek had a lot of information of religious substance and other independent information from his patients. But the reality is that they [the StB agents] didn't get in [the Institute]. Raboch of course knew why they didn't get in, because he had the key in his own pocket, but in front of the director of the hospital he screamed at all of us: 'Where is the key?!? Who has the key?!?' [laughing][263]

This story once again demonstrates that there was no simple dividing line between 'regime' and "people" during socialism and that even individuals in trusted positions of power and state authority exercised agency and autonomy to make free decisions. Like other expert institutions, the Sexological

---

262 Interview with Ivo Procházka, 12.3. 2011.
263 Ibid.

Institute was one component in the centralized mechanism of power, which together created the normative framework for regulation of ideologically acceptable notions of sexuality. Since 1980, an increasing number of sexological articles started to appear, which discussed homosexuality still within the required framework of deviance and disease, but also fitted in claims for equal treatment and full respect for homosexual people. Sexologists also actively defended the privacy of their patients against random raids by the StB and worked around censorship to make information about diverse sexuality more open and accessible to the general public. Still, being queer, and moreover a queer woman, was an arduous experience in Socialist Czechoslovakia. The next chapter takes us on a journey searching for queer identities.

CHAPTER 4
SEARCHING FOR IDENTITY

In the repressive context of East European Communist regimes, how did young girls and boys realize that they were not heterosexual, given their lack of information about other sexualities and the absence of positive role models? And after that realization, what did they do with that self-awareness and knowledge? How did they negotiate their queer identities in a social environment that presented a non-heterosexual understanding of the self as sick and deviant? Despite the growing literature on the subject of homosexuality in Eastern Europe in the 20th century, historical scholarship does not offer much insight into the question of growing up queer in the prohibitive societies of the Soviet Bloc. It is as though the lives of queer people began only in their adult years. One of the reasons for this gap is the medicalization and sexualization of queer identities, according to which the subjectivity of queer people is read only through the lens of mature sexuality and thus understood as starting only in the late teenage years when young people start to date, seek out sexual relations, and have sex. But at least since Foucault's *History of Sexuality*, we know that sexuality and its regulation begins already in early childhood.[264] And from vast gender studies scholarship we know how formative early socialization to 'proper' gender roles can be for social conceptions of the heteronormative gender and individual understandings of our sexual self.[265]

Historical documents and studies investigating childhood and adolescence in Czechoslovakia before 1989 have considered a variety of aspects and topics, but queer gender and queer sexuality have not been among them. We also have recollections of childhood by many narrators in diverse oral history projects that have been published but again, none of those narrators identified as queer. Other oral history projects, which have worked with 'homosexual men,' provide us with insightful and pioneering fragments into intimate spheres of sexual subjectivity and the personal lives of such men

---

264 Foucault 1980.

265 See especially, Michael Warner, *The Trouble with Normal: Sex, Politics, and the Ethics of Queer Life* (Cambridge, MA: Harvard University Press, 1999); Katz 1995; Ann Fausto-Sterling, *Sexing the Body: Gender Politics and the Construction of Sexuality* (New York: Basic Books, 2000); Claire Renzetti and Daniel Curran, *Women, Men, and Society* (Boston: Allyn and Bacon, 1999).

but were typically quite silent on the topic of growing up. Franz Schindler in his excellent study of "The Life of Homosexual Men during socialism" meticulously maps the opportunities and meeting places of homosexual men during the Communist regime in Czechoslovakia, mainly in Prague. Schindler argues that while the heteronormative society provided and entrenched social rituals and even institutionalized opportunities for meeting and dating for its heterosexual members, on the other hand it actively obstructed and tried to prevent such opportunities for (what he calls) the "homosexual minority." According to him, the crucial difference in the lives of the "heterosexual majority" and the "homosexual minority," as he terms them, during socialism can be seen in the sphere of strategies and possibilities to meet and establish intimate romantic and sexual contacts.[266] In this sense, Schindler shares and builds on Halberstam's thesis about "queer temporality," which articulates the same points and argues that for this reason gay and lesbian (or queer) history creates a new framework for the periodization of individual experience where rituals such as weddings or childbirth do not play a role.[267]

While Schindler's study describes in impressive detail the topography of the meeting places and the hidden communal lives of a homosexual subculture, he claims to not have the time and space to focus on the topics of realizing and forming queer subjectivity, first loves, long-term partnerships or the process of coming-out.[268] A similar strategy was used also by Jiří Fanel in his well-known book *Gay historie*, in which he meticulously maps the life of "apartment salons," closed parties and "communal gay life" in public spas, clubs and restaurants during socialism. Radek Miřácký enriched this literature by six oral history narratives of gay men and their experiences with coming-out before 1989. And the same can be said about the work of Jürgen Lemke, who also mapped mainly the public lives and adult sexuality of gay men in the GDR.[269] These works share a strange proposition that the lives of their respondents begin only when the respondents 'become gay.' The entry point into the gender and sexual subjectivity of the narrators is formed only by their active sexual behavior. Before they go through their internal coming-out or have their first homo*sexual* experience, it is as though they had no life and no personal history to speak of. Interestingly, most male biographical narratives conducted by male interviewers, collected in the SfQM oral history

---

266 Schindler 2013, 5.

267 Halberstam 2005, 5–6. This argument has since been challenged by the expanding legalization of homosexual marriage / civil union and growing acceptance of gay and lesbian parenthood in many countries around the world, as well as by the possibilities of assisted reproduction and new reproductive technologies.

268 Schindler 2013, 95.

269 Fanel 2000; Miřácký 2009; Lemke 1991.

archive, share the same feature, which suggests that different constructions of male and female sexuality can affect the ways how people remember and narrate their lives.

Despite this absence of attention to, and lack of information about, the early family life of queer narrators, for example Schindler asserts that it is a "fact that homosexuals grow up in families of the majority society, or if you wish, in families, which marginalize homosexuals and consider them undesirable deviants or criminal elements." According to him, such behavior "most likely silences the existence of the homosexual family member."[270] While Schindler reiterates here Warner's arguments about the functioning of the politics of sexual shame,[271] the generalization that all homosexuals in Communist Eastern Europe grew up in homophobic and deprecating families is not evidenced. Schindler only claims that all his narrators born before 1960 came from "families where their homosexuality was never discussed."[272] There is no reason to doubt his finding and I agree that in many ways Schindler has a point. Taboos and silences about sexuality in families while growing up, were also mentioned by the narrators that I spoke to. But I see a significant difference between *not talking* on the one hand and *hostile homophobia* on the other hand, as expressed in Schindler's earlier statement about being considered "undesirable deviants" or "criminal elements." The narratives conducted in the queer oral history project, as well as some narratives from Schindler's and Miřácký's projects that I read, indicate that even if parents did not necessarily discuss questions of sexual identity with their children, many were at least open and supportive of their children's expressions of non-conformist and transgressive gender behavior. This is where gender becomes a useful category of analysis. It has the potential to reveal important nuances of acceptance, rejection and the power dynamics of sexual identity, which otherwise stays locked only in the (rather flat) concept of "sexual orientation."[273]

All the mentioned studies share another common problem of early historical scholarship on homosexuality — an exclusive attention to men. By now, we know quite a bit about the lives of homosexual men under state socialism, with the exception of their childhood memories, experiences and identity formation. But we know very little about the lives of women and young girls, who felt queer and did not understand themselves as heterosexual. Similarly, we know very little about transsexual, transgender and non-binary people and children, who grew up during the decades of state

---

270 Schindler 2013, 6.
271 Warner 1999.
272 Schindler 2013, 6.
273 Allison Better and Brandy Simula, "How and for Whom does Gender Matter? Rethinking the Concept of Sexual Orientation." *Sexualities*. 2015: 18(5–6), 665–680; Scott, J. W. 1996.

socialism. The following chapter contributes to filling this void. Based on the institutional sources, which focus on state approaches and frameworks, medical discourse, legal proceedings, and police reports, it is not possible to study the lives of queer people from a first-person perspective. These sources speak *about* "homosexuals" or "transsexuals." They piece together how the state's expert discourses constructed homosexuality or transsexuality from their points of view and how the diverse institutional players understood non-heteronormative subjectivity and behavior. Oral history and biographical narratives offer us an invaluable window into the recent past from the individual perspectives of queer people themselves. The following chapter takes us on a journey through their childhood memories and feelings growing up queer, experiences with transgressive gender and sexuality in the context of school and youth organizations, as well as through their desperate searches for information, reference points and positive role models. As noted in the introduction, the memories challenge the premise that because of the restrictive context of the Communist political regime, queer people realized their non-normative sexual identities only later in their lives, or perhaps even only after the collapse of communism in Eastern Europe in 1989. The recollections also reveal how normative discourses on sexuality were at times used by queer people for subversive purposes, both consciously and in unintended ways.

GROWING UP QUEER

My childhood was great. Those were such carefree and happy days. I grew up by myself, without any siblings, and so I had whatever I wanted. Well, we were not rich or anything but I mean I didn't have to fight for my parents' attention with anyone. We lived in a small house with a garden in Neratovice, my mom took care of the garden and I often helped her. On the weekends dad took us on hikes. He was an excited patriot and nature lover and so we went around the castles, ruins, and other cultural sights all over the country. (František)

I was a very pampered child (*vypiplaný dítě*). I was the oldest of three brothers but I was the third born [from five children total]. Two of my older brothers died early on, they were born during the war and healthcare wasn't so good yet, I suppose, and so I was the oldest. In our family, I had the authority, ever since I was little. Also at school when I didn't like something, I simply said it. The teachers usually couldn't do anything. I suffered from child epilepsy and so they were probably afraid that if they would do something, they could push me into an attack. So from very early on I felt I was important. Even though I knew I was different from my brothers, my word was always important in the family and I know my mom loved me the most. (Josef)

See, here [pulls out a photograph], I was about six. It's my birthday. The cute tomboy with ponytails and shotgun, that's me. I have red shorts, my dad took the picture. I have another one, see [pulls out another photograph], here, riding on my dad's back like a knight on a horse. It was in a park in Holešovice. Mom took the picture. We had a lot of fun there. I had such a happy childhood... [Sigh]... Of course only until my daddy went to jail. (Miriam)

František, Josef and Miriam's nostalgic recollections of their idyllic early childhood are good examples of the way narrators frequently set up a 'quiet before the storm' context for their subsequent queer identity formation. When asked to freely narrate their memories of family life and childhood, no narrators started with feelings of discomfort or tensions surrounding their gender identity. All narrators framed their early childhood and family lives as 'happy days,' claiming their parents were loving, understanding, and sweet. Even his presumably traumatic family experience, the death of two older siblings, Josef interpreted through the positive lens of the advantage he felt by suddenly becoming "the first born." Miriam's narrative was an exception, as her father was imprisoned in 1952 for political reasons, which greatly affected her later childhood experiences and memories. Perceived poverty and lack of material goods did not seem to pose obstacles for memories of 'happy times,' even though those were recollections of the war years or early postwar years in the late 1940s. Likewise, the political context of the 1950s, when Stalinist Eastern Europe was submerged in the fearful atmosphere of the budding Cold War and the political show trials, were not mentioned by the narrators as significant. If the family was not affected directly by the political circumstances, like in Miriam's case, the narrators conceptually separated their positive early childhood and family memories from their verbalized understanding of the 1950s as the "darkest" and "worst" years of recent Czechoslovak history. Besides Miriam, none of the narrators recollecting these times from a child's perspective mentioned the socio-political context of gripping fear and the paranoia of Stalinism as influencing their family lives and childhood.[274]

It was only after assuring the listener about their family happiness and joyful early childhood that the narrators opened the door to discussing the transgressive aspects of their gender identity. Regardless of historical or cultural context, the most common memories of childhood identity formation expressed by queer adults tend to be those of gender non-conformity,

---

274 For memoirs and studies focused specifically on the 1950s see, for example, Heda Margolius Kovály, *Under a Cruel Star: A Life in Prague, 1941–1968* (New York: Holmes and Meier, 1986); Kateřina Pošová, *Jsem, protože musím... napsala jsem si ve čtrnácti do lágrového deníku* (Praha: Prostor, 2003); Alena Ludvíková, *Až budu velká, napíšu román: Deník matky a dcery z doby protektorátu* (Praha: GplusG, 2006); George Hodos, *Show Trials: Stalinist Purges in Eastern Europe, 1948–1954* (New York: Greenwood Publishing Group, 1987).

whether in terms of self-perception, social expectations or performed behavior.[275] Thus, it is not surprising that the narrators interviewed in this queer oral history project recounted similar childhood experiences, articulated in terms of gender difference. In one form or another the narrators shared their memories of "being different," "feeling different," or being "strange" or "weird" already as little children. The formulation of "difference" or "otherness" was mentioned by most narrators spontaneously already in the early stages of the interviews.[276] Most of them did not feel the need to clarify such expressions any further and considered the statements to be somehow self-obvious. Heda, almost 83 years old at the time of the interview, provided an interesting exception to this trend. When asked with the broadest possible invitation to "please tell (*vyprávěj*) me about your life," she directly and bluntly started her narrative about growing up in the 1930s by saying:

> I think I was more of a transsexual [person] than anything else. I think I was transsexual from the age zero (*od věku nula*). Men were never attractive to me. I grew up only with my mom and my grandma. My mom was a very sweet, noble person. She never raised her voice, she was always meticulously dressed, and as far as I remember everyone everywhere really liked her. My grandma was mom's mom. She was the real guy (*chlap*) in the family. But she was the one trying to make sure all the time that we were three women [Laugh]. We had a great time most of the time. I was very happy that no man lived with us, I really liked this women's community of ours (*naše ženské společenství*). Here we were. My grandma the general (*babička generál*), me, and my mom like a little fragile beautiful butterfly flying around, making sure all is good and everyone is happy. But the times themselves were not so good. My grandma, especially, was very afraid of Hitler. (Heda)

Heda's recollections of the gender constellations of her family life are remarkable. On the one hand she identifies herself as "transsexual," clearly distancing herself from the expected norms of feminine gender behavior and subjectivity that would correspond with her allegedly female physical body. On the other hand, she marvels at the "women's community" formed by the household of three women. When she calls her grandmother "a general," she obviously refers to the leading role of the grandmother in family affairs, not to her physical body or demeanor. Despite her complex understanding of her own identity and body that transcends the binary conception of heteronormative gender, Heda uses the concept of traditional patriarchy to express

---

275 Suzanne Pharr, *Homophobia: A Weapon of Sexism* (New York: Chardonne Press, 1997); Warner 1999; Daniel Carragher, "Trying to Hide: A Cross-National Study of Growing up Non-Heterosexual for Non-Identified Gay and Bisexual Male Youth," *Clinical Child Psychology and Psychiatry* 7/3 (2002): 457–474.
276 In Czech they used phrases such as *"byl jsem jinej," "cítila jsem, že jsem jiná," "divná," "nezapadám."*

power relations in the family. The family needs "a guy" to take care of things and protect the "other women." The important tasks of the "guy" included not only decision making in ordinary affairs but also protection of the heteronormative gender order of things, making sure the biological women behaved in the expected "female" ways.

> … most of all, I hated skirts and dresses. My mom was very reasonable and let me be, but my grandma! My god! She always wanted to see me all done up in dresses and skirts. Yuck! [Laughing] I remember them getting in a fight over it occasionally and it was always my grandma who won. "Don't even think about it young lady," she said every time I wanted to put pants on. Sometimes I even did put them on but she would simply not let me walk out that way. She scolded my mom for sewing the pants for me in the first place but it was my fault, I begged my mom to do it and she was so sweet, she asked me what color, and if I want pockets and all those things, yes. But to school, there was no quarrel. And mom and I both knew it. (Heda)

Not surprisingly, the dress code adhered to the expected gender norms. In the private realm there was more freedom to move around those norms, but when it came to the public space Heda's grandmother did not allow any discussion. It is suggested that the grandmother used very simple but strict arguments about propriety and respectable, orderly gender behavior conforming to societal understanding of what it means to 'be a lady' and the mother yielded to it. Whether it was because she herself shared the view or because the grandmother was simply more powerful in the family remains unclear. But it is evident that Heda was supported by her mother in her desire to dress in 'boy' clothing and there was a sense of solidarity and defiance between them in 'gender matters' against the grandmother. It is also worth mentioning that those memories took place during the last decade of the First Republic, which was heralded as the era of the 'modern emancipated woman' and fashion in many ways reflected that.[277]

More relevant to our topic is Heda's understanding and depiction of the roles in the family during her childhood and what role models those represented for a queer child, trying to make sense of the world around her. On the one hand, it was a family of three 'biological women' (of three generations) living together. As expressed, they needed a 'man' in the family and the grandma filled that role. At the same time, it was clear to Heda that it is not necessary to have a 'biological man' in the family in order to have one. It was enough to possess 'him' in a symbolic way. While Heda still read the family constellation through a patriarchal matrix (the grandmother was "the guy in the family" because she possessed power — masculinity is defined here

---

277 *Móda: Z dějin odívání 18., 19. a 20. století* (Praha: Slovart, 2011).

not by biological manhood but by exercised power), her own queer sense of the self was from her early childhood years reinforced by the idea that both biological sexes can easily and interchangeably fill and perform both social genders.

Even though she was married during the early 1950s, quickly divorced, and spent the rest of her life in self-defined "lesbian relationships," until her very old age Heda expressed comfortable uncertainty about her gender identity. And clearly, despite all the structural and ideological restrictions of the Communist system, she was able to live that gender-transgressive queer identity her entire life. She never studied queer theory or Judith Butler's concept of gender performativity nor was she familiar with any works on the politics of identity[278] but intuitively she expressed those processes as relevant for her life during state socialism:

> I do not know if I am a man or a woman. But everyone else around me does! I don't see it that way. A body is just a body, nothing else. It depends how you dress it and how you act. If people want to see you as a woman, they will. I don't think they even think about it. They just see the shell and think they know all of you. But inside, you can be anything you want. (Heda)

Miriam similarly recalled an open family environment when it came to the expression of gender identity and dress code. Her father Pavel had the whole family including both his daughters call him the female version of the name "Pavla." Nobody in the wider family saw anything wrong or strange with that and Miriam insisted that "it had absolutely no connection to being feminine... Pavla was very open minded and moved a lot in the bohemian artistic circles." Miriam's parents allowed Miriam to dress very much like a tomboy, which she proudly showed me in several photographs during our interviews. Even though Miriam never told her parents that she was queer ("even though they must have known") and regrets it until this day, she remembers her parents during her early childhood as being "exceptionally accepting of my tomboyism. I felt like a boy, played like a boy, and they let me be. They never tried to change me or push me in any way into something I didn't like." (Miriam)

---

278 Judith Butler, *Gender Trouble: Feminism and the Subversion of Identity* (New York: Routledge, 1990); Helana Darwin, "Doing Gender Beyond the Binary." *Symbolic Interaction* 2017, 2–18; Patrick R. Miller, Andrew R. Flores, Donald P. Haider-Markel, Daniel C. Lewis, Barry L. Tadlock & Jami K. Taylor, "Transgender Politics as Body Politics: Effects of Disgust, Sensitivity, and Authoritarianism on Transgender Rights Attitudes," *Politics, Groups, and Identities*, 5:1, 4–24; Anamarie Jagose, "Limity Identity," in *Lesby-by-by: Aspekty polititiky identít*, edited by Hanna Hacker (Bratislava: Aspekt, 2004).

Like Heda, however, most narrators recalled conflicts over their appearance and behavior, clothing, toys and games as the most formative experiences of their childhood. Such heteronormative pressures, especially during early childhood, play a decisive role in a child's sense of the self. These processes have been extensively analyzed in 'free' democratic societies but rarely admitted, let alone discussed, as existing in Socialist countries of Eastern Europe. Studies of childhood under communism do not mention or study heteronormativity and studies focused on queer sexuality during state socialism are not concerned with the childhood period. It is, however this automatic presumption that non-heterosexuality somehow starts only later in one's life that significantly shapes the identity formation of queer children in the first place, regardless whether it occurred before or after 1989. Studies and media often debate what might happen to (presumably heterosexual) children if adopted by homosexual parents,[279] but the opposite concerns are rarely voiced: what is happening in the minds and souls of queer children, who are growing up with the implicit expectations and pressures of their parents, relatives, and peers that it is 'normal' to feel heterosexual and in congruence with one's physical body.

American historian Michael Warner persuasively argued that a crucial aspect of the societal control of sexuality is what he called "the politics of sexual shame."[280] Warner argued that sexual shame is not just some banal aspect of our life that all people have because everyone is sometimes shy. He pointed out that sexual shame has a significant political dimension because while we all feel occasionally shy, embarrassed or nervous, others are overexposed to intense pressures of sexual shame. Warner argued that if our gender or sexual identity is not compatible with the normative mainstream one, since early childhood we are exposed not only to outward dismissal and humiliation of our self but we also face the tremendous inner pressure of self-hatred and homophobia towards ourselves. The politics of sexual shame, according to Warner, functions as a very effective regulatory mechanism of our (not only sexual) behavior because it contains unspoken and unstudied consequences of isolation and internalized self-rejection, which queer children continually face.[281]

One of the great myths, Warner asserted, is that "children themselves decide who they are, who they want to be, and what they desire." All these perceptions are carefully and firmly guided by the process of early childhood socialization in their families and schools. With sexual identity, it is not any

---

279 Judith Stacey and Timothy Biblarz, "(How) Does the Sexual Orientation of Parents Matter?" *American Sociological Review*, 2001: 66/2, 159–83; Eva Polášková, *Plánovaná lesbická rodina: klíčové aspekty přechodu k rodičovství* (Brno: Masaryk University Press, 2009); Kateřina Nedbálková, *Matky kuráže: lesbické rodiny v pozdně moderní společnosti* (Praha: SLON, 2012).
280 Warner 1999, especially chapter one.
281 Ibid.

different. Almost all children grow up with the implicit conviction of their parents that they are automatically heterosexual. Very few children grow up in an environment of real gender and sexual openness when parents and extended relatives create a space of sexual neutrality. It is thus not surprising that many queer children feel and understand this discrepancy and grow up with feelings of distance, strangeness, lack of understanding, and carry the specific burden of silence and shame. The ways, in which families and society in general do not speak about certain feelings, desires or behavior, make those feelings, desires and behavior not only unacceptable but, more importantly, unthinkable. It is then understandable, Warner continued, that queer children grow up considering themselves weird and perverse on the one hand, and try to explain their strangeness through familiar gender and sexual stereotypes and heteronormative codes on the other hand. So while searching for the reasons and agents of *who* or *what* caused the "repressing of homosexuals" during the period of state socialism in Czechoslovakia, moreover in the absence of criminalization of homosexuality or direct state persecution, these are the pressures that should be recognized, named and accounted for.[282]

As Warner theorized, the narrators shared not only feelings of recognized and accepted difference but also a deep sense of inadequacy, experienced usually in interaction with peers and at school. While the period of childhood in general was described by most narrators as "free" and "happy," the articulations of the first problems and unhappiness in childhood were in many narratives linked to gender nonconformity. This trend was most prevalent in the autobiographies of queer people who later in their lives identified as transsexual. Their memories give us a lucid sense of the heteronormative and gender pressures that all boys and girls, regardless of their gender identity and sexual orientation, were exposed to:

I would situate my first childhood memories probably into the period when I was about four and started to attend preschool [1965]. Not realizing at all that I was doing something outside of the deeply rooted norm, I mostly played in the preschool with other girls. I remember that once we were sitting on the benches in the garden and playing with yarn and suddenly the teacher came up to us and scolded me — What am I doing, why am I not playing with cars and diggers in the nearby sandbox with the boys? I really liked the teacher and felt sad that she was mad at me. I didn't understand why I should play with the boys some stupid games with cars when I liked different games. I didn't understand why girls can play with yarn and braid wreaths from dandelions and I can't. But I wanted to make the teacher happy so I went and tried to participate in the games, which I was completely indifferent to... Situations like this repeated almost

---

282 Ibid.

daily. I felt that no one understood me, including my own parents, and no one even cared to. I became more and more lonely, which made me ever weirder to the others. I became a freak, while my brother was the loved one because he was normal, liked cars and played football. (Martina)

From a certain age, usually around the sixth grade in elementary school, but at the onset of puberty at the latest, all transsexual narrators recalled that their lives turned to hell. They started to get physically harassed and verbally abused by classmates and often also teachers for "being queer" (*teplý, buzny* or *buzíci*). This type of torment was typically aimed at boys. Their perceived lack of masculinity was identified and articulated as a 'homosexual quality.' Řídký, who analyzed the sexological constructions of the "male homosexual subject" in popular advisory books published in Czechoslovakia between 1930 and 1990, came to similar conclusions. The "male homosexual," Řídký argues, was constructed and represented by the medical discourse as a deviant subject precisely for his lack of masculinity, which was instead replaced by an inadequate femininity. For these feminine qualities, a 'gay' was, according to Řídký, understood by the Czech sexological discourse and by association by the overall mainstream social discourse during state socialism, as a "defective, incomplete, deformed man."[283] This context allows us to imagine the larger context of heteronormative pressures that queer children faced. Needless to say, these pressures were experienced by all children regardless their gender and sexual identity but, for the reasons already discussed, for queer children such pressures, reactions and behavior, often by their loved ones, had severe consequences.

Warner's arguments were reiterated by many extensive and comparative research studies about the harassment and victimization of queer children and youth who do not conform to stereotypical gender roles and behavior.[284] But peer harassment and aggression, whether ethnic, social, or sexual, were not researched (and often even admitted) during state socialism. In my previous work, I documented cases of racist stereotyping and behavior towards Romani children during Czechoslovak communism, which were all interpreted by contemporary texts as behavioral and educational problems provoked by the Romani children themselves.[285] So far, there has been no such research carried in the context of sexuality and gender-nonconformity.

---

283 Řídký 2013.

284 Caitlin Ryan and Ian Rivers, "Lesbian, Gay, Bisexual and Transgender Youth: Victimization and Its Correlates in the USA and UK," *Culture, Health and Sexuality* 5:2 (2003) 103–119; *Homophobic Bullying. Safe to Learn: Embedding anti-Bullying Work in Schools*, Nottingham, DCSF Publications, 2007; Russell B. Toomey, Caitlin Ryan, Rafael Diaz, Noel A. Card and Stephen T. Rusell, "Gender-Nonconforming Lesbian, Gay, Bisexual, and Transgender Youth: School Victimization and Young Adult Psychosocial Adjustment," *Developmental Psychology*, Advance online publication. doi: 10.1037/a0020705 (2010): 1–11.

285 Sokolova 2008, especially 187–207.

The queer oral history narratives, however, reveal similar grievances. When the narrators recall that they were being harassed and punished for being different in gender and sexual terms, they also add that the situations were perceived and evaluated by the adults around them as something they caused or even provoked themselves.

While an objection could be raised that there is nothing specific about the historical context of the Communist regime in all these recollections and arguments, these accounts are powerful and revealing in terms of the pervasiveness of heteronormative pressures on people's lives across historical periods and political regimes. They expose how important gender and sexuality are as organizational principles and regulatory tools of human behavior, as well as how intrinsic and cross-culturally relevant unconscious or implicit homophobic bias is.[286] Another way to understand the process of rejecting queerness during the Communist period is, rather than through the study of discrimination, through the concepts of stigma and 'decency.' The dehumanization of the stigmatized can take a variety of forms but the central aspect of stigma is the problem of acceptance and self-acceptance. In his classic work on stigma, sociologist Erwin Goffman argued that the stigmatized understand very well the reason why others perceive them as inadequate and that "it is very hard not to agree, even if only shortly, that they are right," that the stigmatized really does not fulfill the requirements of who they should be.[287] Such a process leads to the internalization of the stigma and internalized feelings of self-rejection and homophobia, processes subsequently described by many scholars of sexuality.

Analyzing the deep and long-lasting impact of the homogenous nature of Czechoslovakia after the Second World War, sociologist Jan Průcha argued that the Communist past produced a certain paradox. Current middle-age and older generations of Czechs and Slovaks grew up in an artificially homogenous society where various kinds of diversity — racial, ethnic, cultural, and sexual — were presented as matters distant in time and place. Despite its overbearing ideological component, social education under communism

---

286 For the concept of "unconscious (or implicit) bias" see, for example, Rosalind Chou and Joe Feagin, *The Myth of the Model Minority*. 2nd edition. (Boulder, CO: Paradigm Publishers, 2015); Joe Feagin, *The White Racial Frame: Centuries of Racial Framing and Counter-Framing*. 2nd edition. (New York: Routledge, 2013); Sue Wing, *Microaggressions in Everyday Life: Race, Gender, and Sexual Orientation* (Hoboken, New Jersey: Wiley, 2010).

287 Erwin Goffman, *Stigma. Poznámky o způsobech zvládání narušené identity* (Praha: SLON, 2003), 15–16. Goffman, however, very problematically argues that the "stigmatized" should be positive and work diligently to fulfill the normative societal requirements. According to him, the "stigmatized" should not "get bitter," should not "be sad or self-pitying," and should generously overlook marginalization because the "normal" usually are not mean, they just lack proper information. Goffman thus places enormous burden and responsibility on the "stigmatized" themselves to offer a "helping hand" to the normative society to accept them. The result is then a double victimization.

was based on ideas of humanism and equality that instilled in many Czechs and Slovaks the belief that racism and other forms of discrimination are wrong, detestable and foreign.[288] At the same time, in the aftermath of the Second World War people rarely encountered difference and diversity, and when they did, they were generally taught to understand such differences as social pathologies. The paradox is that while explicit gender and sexual discrimination and violence were virtually absent in the official public sphere under communism, today's sexism, latent homophobia and implicit sexual discrimination have in fact deep historical roots in the Communist society. Průcha aptly expressed the essence of the problem when he argued that "for millions of Czechs and Slovaks the only standard of humanity was and still is 'decency' (*slušnost*) — behavior appropriate to generally accepted norms. At the same time, since childhood we are taught that there exists only one decency. To dehumanize the 'indecent' then is very easy."[289]

Childhood memories of the narrators also revealed concrete ways in which normative prescriptions of mandatory heterosexuality permeated into identity building, both within the family and at school. Despite the generally shared view that 'homosexuality was taboo' during state socialism it was apparently not so. We can learn a greal deal about state socialism, for example, through the terminology of sexually-based insults that were a part of family and school experiences of queer people as they recalled them in the articulated fears of their classmates, friends, and parents. We can also read what concrete forms homophobic harassment and humiliation of queer children and adolescents took in some individual cases during the Socialist times, things we might have suspected but until the queer oral history project did not have access to. The two accounts below are both from written autobiographical narratives of MtF transsexual women:

> I was convinced that by the time I was in high school, I had learned to mask the incompatibility of my physical and mental self very well. How much deeper then was my disappointment and sadness when I came home one day, I think I was in my third year of high school [in 1975], from the hair dresser with my new haircut. I was very happy about it. But my dad immediately started to yell at me: 'My god! What the hell do you look like? You look like a faggot! (*vypadáš jako buzík*) Great! You always wanted to look like a woman so now you added a crown to that! (*nasadils tomu korunu*).' And without any other word he slammed the door. It was such a terrible blow for me. I loved my dad so much. I started to cry, put my done-up hair under a water faucet and immediately went to another hair dresser and ordered him to give me a crew cut (*aby mě ostříhal na ježka*). I felt terrible when I saw in the mirror how I was losing my hair. (Alena)

---

288 Jan Průcha, *Multikulturní výchova: Teorie, praxe, výzkum.* (Praha: nakladatelství ISV, 2001).
289 Průcha 2001, 11.

Elementary school [1971–1980] is the period that I don't like to recall. It was a time of stress, feelings of inferiority, a time of humiliation. I was never good at writing. I'm left-handed. I think I was, or am, dyslexic, I don't know, back then there were no tests for that kind of disorder. In any case, writing was a problem for me. I'm glad I'm an adult now and can write in whatever way I want… At school, I was seated in the back with the impossible-to-educate kids (*s nevzdělatelnými dětmi*). I was perceived as a stupid child. All nine years. When I came home, I was beaten for my bad writing and bad grades. Always by dad. Mom never hit me. But I know now that dad regrets every blow that he gave me. He apologized to me for that when I grew up… When I was in the seventh grade, it all started. I wanted to be among girls, because I felt like one of them. So, logically, I started to be perceived as a homosexual. Because I was with the girls, I was perceived as a boy who is after the boys. But it wasn't like that. I was an adolescent girl who liked boys. Sometimes they yelled insults at me in the hallways, like that I'm queer and a faggot (*buzerant a teplouš*) and things like that, and looked down on me, and I felt like I'm drifting further and further from all my male friends. The teachers were okay and let me be. That is except one of them, a thick-skulled PE teacher with the features of an australopithicus (*tupý tělocvikář s rysy australopitéka*), who perpetually laughed at me and humiliated me in front of others for lacking muscles in my arms. (Lucie)

In the mid 1970s, during the grim Normalization period, explicit homophobic verbal insults were apparently a part of the everyday experience of queer youth. The question is, where did the children get this pejorative vocabulary and homophobic terminology from? Official terminology in legislative documents relating to the decriminalization efforts, as well as medical discourse, were strict and correct, speaking only of "homosexuality" and "homosexuals." So were the few sparse mentions of homosexuality in media and culture. Despite the official efforts to make this topic taboo in public discourse, however, latent homophobia and conjoining pejorative vocabulary were a part of societal understanding of sexuality and were transmitted through generations as shared and accepted, even if undiscussed, values.[290] For example, one of the first mentions of the word "faggot" in popular literature comes already from 1932, when it was used in the novel *A Golden Cloud* (*Zlatý oblak*) by the well-known Czech writer S. K. Neumann. When Neumann describes in the book a dialog of the two main male characters about their friend's homosexuality, he writes:

"Oh, so that's how it is then! In dirty talk it's called 'faggot,' right? Poor him! (*Ach, takové je to tedy! Po sprostu se tomu říká teplej, viď. Chudák!*)"[291]

---

290 Putna and Bartlová, 2011.
291 Stanislav Kostka Neumann, *Zlatý oblak* (Praha: František Borový, 1932), 216.

At the same time, however, Lucie's tendency to express her frustration with homophobia through implicit racist stereotyping should also not escape one's attention. Even though the physical appearance of the PE teacher is not relevant to the point she is making, in order to articulate his gender insensitive behavior as insulting and stupid, Lucie describes him as a "primitive." Similarly, she was seated among the "impossible-to-educate" children, presumably Roma. The adjectives hard-to-educate, impossible-to-educate or un-adaptible are all modifiers that started to appear in Czechoslovak anthropological, social and educational literature *en masse* in the mid-1970s as euphemisms to describe the 'socially backward' Roma.[292] It is a common empowering strategy of the marginalized and ridiculed individuals and groups to look around for *others*, whom they perceive to be in an even less desirable position, to strengthen their own sense of superiority through distancing from the "even less fortunate."[293]

From the personal recollections of queer youth during state socialism we learn two important insights. First, the awareness of their gender and sexual difference and the realization of their queer identity was an integral part of the process of early childhood identity building and socialization, independent of and preceeding their active sexual behavior. And second, they provide us with explicit articulations of trauma caused by homophobic remarks and treatment by both family members and school peers and teachers. Both of these findings remind us again how important oral history is as a method for excavating the complexity of the history of sexuality during state socialism. The study of medical discourse and official Communist Party documents is not enough to learn what it was like to be queer before 1989. Moreover, it is clear that the starting point for narrating queer lives during state socialism should be located not in the moments of first dates and the topography of sexual enounters in bars and public toilets, as Schindler suggests, but in the locus of early childhood, as Warner argues. It was not 'the Communist regime' that through its institutional repression instilled in queer people feelings of guilt, self-hatred and inadequacy, but rather the complex web of compulsory heterosexuality and latent homophobia saturating both private and public realms.

This is an appropriate moment to revisit Eva's personal narrative, introduced in the prologue of the book. Her narrative revealed how unexpected and intimate the struggles with one's queer identity could be during the Communist regime. She shared that at the age of 11 she was visited by Jesus and that "during communism [she] always felt more discriminated for [her]

---

292 Sokolova, 2008.

293 Gerlinda Šmausová, „Rasa jako rasistická konstrukce," in *Sociologický časopis* 1999, 35/4: 433–446; Kiczková 2006; Goffman 2003.

religion than sexuality." In her narrative, Eva used the term "lesbian" (*lesba*) and "gay" spontaneously, both when she was speaking about herself and when she was referring to her friends, male and female, before 1989. When asked about the terms, she paused and recollected, "right, back then we didn't know these terms... we didn't use them." While she openly enjoyed same-sex encounters in public places, "being religious was very fragile and intimate." Eva's negotiations of the religious and sexual aspects of her identity was very private and very painful:

> When I was a teenager, I regularly went up to the attic [of their family house]. I had a little kneeler there and a leather cat-o'-nine-tails (*důtky*). I stripped myself half-naked and whipped my back bloody for being a lesbian. It really hurt. It was not pleasurable or anything, I'm not a masochist but I felt it was the right thing to do... I never discussed it [that I'm a lesbian] with my parents or family, who probably wouldn't even care, but I knew very clearly that I like women and it was not compatible with my belief in God... But men always repulsed me, perhaps because I always felt more like a man than a woman to begin with. I never wanted to have any sexual relationship with a guy and I never did. (Eva)

Significantly, Eva mentally tormented and physically hurt herself to the point of self-mutilation and self-hatred not due to persecution or discrimination from the 'state' or not even because of heteronormative pressures placed on her by her immediate surroundings in the family and school but due to the incompatibility of her religious and sexual beliefs. Her family was not religious but from "reading literature and the Bible, [Eva] knew that it is the one way to redeem one's sins." It is remarkable that Eva felt that her parents would be indifferent to her queer identity but she did not care about that parental support because since her early age, her "highest authority" was God. At the same time, Eva did not have a problem to express her sexual identity at school or in the public space. As she recalls in other places of this book, she was not afraid to engage in public anonymous sex with other women or attend same-sex parties with people who were clearly watched by the Secret Police. At school, "everyone knew I loved girls and no one had problem with it." Clearly, Eva lived a complicated personal life before 1989. But notably, her queer sexual identity was only one of the forces responsible for that and arguably not the most important one. While her sexuality was open and adventurous, until the very end of the Communist regime, when she was almost 40 years old, Eva would not dare to be openly religious. The pressures of the repressive Communist apparatus undeniably played an important role in her life. But it is not insignificant that those pressures manifested themselves quite differently than one would likely expect when thinking about a 'lesbian woman' living in a 'Communist society.'

CHILDREN AND YOUTH IN COMMUNIST IDEOLOGY

Historical scholarship already researched how important children and youth were to the ideological goals of the Communist Party during the Socialist regime in all countries of the Soviet Bloc and analyzed pressures that burdened children and youth during state socialism.[294] Children and youth were, of course, always in the forefront of the declared interest, concern and care for the future of socialism, especially at the onset of Normalization in the early 1970s.[295] In July 1973, the Central Committee of the Communist Party of Czechoslovakia devoted its entire convention to discussing the "complex questions of contemporary children and youth in developed Socialist countries."[296] The convention came to the conclusion that it was crucial to impress upon the young generation the importance of Communist ideology and to make young people understand their responsibility for carrying out the task of "further building and cementing socialism." This task was to be carried out through family, school, and children's and youth's organizations, the most important and influential of which were the Czechoslovak Organization of Youth (PO ČSM, *Pionýrské organizace Československého svazu mládeže* 1950 — 1969), which in 1970 transformed into the Socialist Union of Youth Pionýr (PO SSM — *Pionýrské organizace Socialistického svazu mládeže*, 1970 — 1989). The articles talk about "social reproduction of youth" and "ideological socialization of children and youth." In 1981, the Central Committee of the party reiterated that "the healthy development of the youth will remain in the forefront of the attention of the Communists, the Party and societal organs, and the social organizations of our entire state."[297]

In 1985, probably because the United Nations declared that particular year "the year of youth" (*rok mládeže*), the academic journal *Sociologický časopis (Czech Sociological Review)* published an extensive monothematic issue about "youth in Socialist society," which concentrated on questions about the role of the state in the socialization of children and youth.[298] The Communist

---

294 Harriette Kevill-Davies, "Children Crusading against Communism: Mobilizing Boys as Citizen Soldiers in the Early Cold War State." *Rhetoric and Public Affairs* 21/2 (2018): 235–78; Irina Rodríguez, *My Soviet Youth: A Memoir of Ukrainian Life in the Final Years of Communism* (Jefferson, North Carolina: McFarland & Co., 2019); Michal Pullmann, *Konec Experimentu. Přestavba a pád komunismu v Československu* (Praha: Scriptorium, 2011), 124-128; Kolářová 2013; Herzog 2011.

295 Ladislav Podmele, *Komunistická morálka a výchova nového člověka* (Praha: SPN, 1971) and *Učení o společnosti a státu* (Praha: SPN, 1972); Eva Syřišťová et al., *Normalita osobnosti* (Praha: Avicenum, 1972).

296 Juraj Himal, "Mládež a společnost," *Sociologický Časopis / Czech Sociological Review* 10:4 (1974): 339–343.

297 XVI. Sjezd KSC, 1981:40.

298 *Sociologický Časopis / Czech Sociological Review* 21:5 (1985).

ideologues in this issue defined the formative experiences of the youth in squarely ideological terms, arguing that

> the individual generations of children and young people grew up in the course of forty years since the liberation of our country by the Soviet Army in qualitatively distinct conditions. Their socialization and identity development was intimately connected with the defeat of fascism, the fight for the victory of socialism, with the phase of building the foundations of socialism, with solving the problems of its further development, and with the years of building a developed Socialist society until the present.[299]

In his contribution, the chairman of the Central Committee of the Socialist Union of Youth (*ÚV SSM*) Jaroslav Jenerál argued that the goal of "all governments of the world" must be to "concentrate their main attention on solving the complex questions of economic, social, health, educational, pedagogical, psychological, cultural and other nature on the behalf of children and youth."[300] Obviously, the empty proclamations had mainly ideological goals but their broadness and repetition testified to the importance of children and youth for the ideological agenda of the Communist Party. Historians studying the pressures exerted on children and youth in Communist Eastern Europe point out precisely this ideological burden and sentiment.[301] Gender historians have extended their research to analyze how gender stereotypes affected all women and men, including early gender socialization of children.[302] However, rarely does the argumentation extend to ask what it means in terms of heteronormative pressures and what this meant for queer children growing up during the state socialism.

While the discussion on the issues of harassment, aggression and victimization among children in Czech schools slowly began already in mid-1990s,[303] the first studies directly discussing the questions of unconscious bias,

---

299 Dalibor Holda, "Čtyřicet let společenského rozvoje mládeže," *Sociologický Časopis / Czech Sociological Review* 21:5 (1985): 452–469, 452.

300 Jaroslav Jenerál, "Mládež a společnost," *Sociologický Časopis / Czech Sociological Review* 21:5 (1985): 446–451. Jenerál titled his essay after Himal's 1974 article of the same name to demonstrate the continuity and importance of the topic.

301 Dorothee Wierling, "Youth as Internal Enemy: Conflicts in Education Dictatorship in the 1960s," in *Socialist Modern: East German Everyday Culture and Politics*, edited by Katherine Pence and Paul Betts (Ann Arbor: University of Michigan Press, 2008), 157–182; Renata Salecl, *The Spoils of Freedom: Psychoanalysis and Feminism after the fall of Socialism* (New York: Routledge, 1994), especially chapter 3, "Normalization in Czechoslovakia," 38–57; Kolářová 2013; Herzog 2011.

302 Ghodsee and Mead, 2019.

303 Pavel Říčan, *Agresivita a šikana mezi dětmi* (Praha: Portál, 1995); Jean Parry and Gillian Carrington. *Čelíme šikanování. Metodický materiál* (Praha: IPPP ČR, 1995); Michal Kolář, *Skrytý svět šikanování ve školách* (Praha: Portál, 1997), and Michal Kolář, *Bolest šikanování* (Praha: Portál, 2001).

homophobia in childhood, and victimization of children for gender-non-conformity by their school peers were published only in 2009.[304] It is also not surprising that it was boys who were under greater pressure to conform to expected masculine behavior. The guiding role of sexology was seen as crucial not only by sexologists themselves, but also by parents. None of the female narrators was ever taken to a sexological office for 'consultation' by her parents. Kamila and Eva, however, found their way there later in their adult lives — Kamila because she "was friends with one of the sexologists and so [she] sometimes went to visit him"; Eva because she "had problems with drinking and wanted to ask some questions about sexuality." They both recalled seeing young boys with their mothers in the waiting rooms of the sexological offices.

> The hallway was full of anxious, dramatic-looking mothers with their teenage sons with terrified expressions on their faces. It was a horrible sight... No, I never saw any girls with their mothers. (Kamila)

> It was only guys. I went there for about a year, I moved from [Doctor] Raboch to [Doctor] Zemek because Raboch liked women and so when he saw me, a beautiful young woman, he immediately told me "Oh, come in, come to my office." Well, when he realized what my "problem"[305] was, that I was attracted to girls, he immediately shipped me off to Zemek. In front of his office, there were often one or two young boys, always with mothers, never alone, also waiting for a session. (Eva)

It is also quite telling that it was mothers who accompanied their sons to the sexological office. Even though it was usually mothers who assumed responsibility for the children and thus it was women who most often took children to pediatricians, dentists, and stayed at home with them in case of illness, it is possible that fathers did not want to be present in this context. While we know from the oral testimonies that it was usually fathers who were concerned with their son's proper sexual and gender development, it is possible they did not want to get engaged in the discussions with the sexologists because it would mean to articulate their concerns and fears openly, which would be "unmanly."

Besides the negative heteronormative pressures that queer children were most commonly exposed to, the narratives unraveled some positive stories

---

304 Irena Smetáčková and Richard Braun, *Homofobie v žákovských kolektivech: homofobní obtěžování a šikana na základních a středních školách* (Praha, Úřad vlády ČR, 2009); Olga Pechová, "Diskriminace na základě sexuální orientace," *E-psychologie* 3:3 (2009): 1–16.

305 The word *problem* is in quotation marks here because in the interview the narrator herself made a hand gesture with which she drew parentheses around the word "problem" with four fingers in the air as she spoke.

as well. An extraordinary experience of both parental acceptance and sexological intervention into family life was shared by Petra, a MtF transsexual woman.

Feelings of rejection, difference, and lack of understanding. That's what forced me to confront it. When I was sixteen [1983] I wanted to tell my parents and my friends that I like boys. I considered it so natural and normal. But even so I was afraid. But I went into it (*šla jsem do toho*). I found a sexology office and went to see a doctor there. I was shy but I told her my life story. Mainly I was telling her that since I was very small, about four years old, I felt like I'm a girl and that I like boys. The term "transsexuality" did not come out of the doctor's mouth then. We did not talk about that at all. I had no idea that something like that existed. She said that it would be best if she explained everything to my parents by herself. It was my task to tell my parents to come to see her. I remember very well how my mom was cooking spinach in the kitchen and I said I had to tell her something important. She looked at me, sat down and listened. I told her everything. She was silent and then only said: 'And are you sure that you are a homosexual? When is the meeting with the doctor? Don't say anything to dad yet.' And she went to the bedroom. She probably cried but nothing at all changed in her behavior towards me. I did not expect such a reaction! A week later dad bought a new car and my parents and I went for the first ride. I see it like it were today. Dad is driving, during the ride he didn't say anything, sometimes he looked at me. I was sitting next to him. And then he suddenly hit the brakes, stopped the car on the side of the road and started screaming at me. That this is impossible, it is caused by my friendships (*je to z toho, s kým se kamarádím*), that certainly it's the fault of the school,[306] and that one day I'll die of AIDS anyway (*jednou stejně umřu na AIDS*). I said that I'm not going to discuss it with him and that a doctor will explain it all to them. The time of the appointment was in fourteen days. During that time I avoided dad and I did not speak with him. Mom didn't say anything about the situation. Towards me she acted as though nothing ever happened. D-Day arrived. I was full of expectations and fear. When my parents came back [from the meeting with the sexologist] they held a bottle of champagne in their hands and told me between the doors: "The doctor stressed that we should be proud of you (*paní doktorka nám kladla na srdce, že máme být na tebe pyšní*). She has not seen such a well-adjusted homosexual for a long time and that you will surely be able to handle it." This really happened! I swear! I stared at them (*koukala jsem jako blázen*) and it was the last time we spoke about the topic of homosexuality. (Petra)

A few things are remarkable about Petra's recollection. One is the active and very prominent role of the sexologist in this particular narrative. What is striking in the first place is the fact that, as a sixteen-year-old, Petra easily

---

306 Petra attended a so-called *konzervatoř*, a highly competitive art high school, where she studied acting.

found a sexologist and went to see her. Despite the expressed fear, this decision and action testifies to the confidence and trust she had towards the Socialist medical establishment. At the very least, Petra expected to find understanding and help there — no small expectation in the early 1980s. A sexological office was obviously seen by the narrator as a source of authority but also of solace and hope. The active role immediately assumed by the sexologist also merits attention. The doctor's suggestion that she will be the one to speak to the parents can be interpreted both as an assertion of her medical authority and as willingly acting as a shield for a potential lack of understanding on the parents' side. From the development of the story we know that the sexologist acted on behalf of the narrator in a positive and assuring way towards the parents.

Obviously, the doctor was aware of her own positive stand prior to her visit and knew very well that such an approach would be beneficial for parental acceptance. Contrary to Řídký's assertion that "there is no such thing as a happy and well-adjusted homosexual," in Petra's recollection the sexologist used (most likely by pure coincidence) the same precise formulation to encourage the parents in their acceptance of their (allegedly homosexual) son. At the same time, the doctor acted from the position of the sole authority that should be disseminating the "correct knowledge" to the ignorant population. It is quite significant then, that in 1983 the sexologist misdiagnoses the narrator as a homosexual and does not recognize Petra's transsexuality (or at least does not question whether it is a possibility.) By 1980, transsexuality was a well-discussed issue in the expert sexological discourse, as the first successful sex-change surgeries happened in Socialist Czechoslovakia already in 1967 and 1974 respectively.[307]

Second, the father's screaming at his son that he will "die of AIDS" shows how quickly the information and fears of AIDS and its intrinsic connection with homosexuality spread through the media discourse and society at large. It is convincingly documented from the pioneering work of Kateřina Kolářová that the very first mentions of AIDS in Czechoslovak popular press came out in the very same year, 1983, in the popular magazines *Vesmír* (*The Universe*) and *Mladý Svět* (*The Young World*). The father's concern over his son's inevitable death also suggests that from the very beginning AIDS was understood in the public discourse as integrally linked with (male) homosexuality. Kolářová demonstrates in her analysis that the first descriptions and discussions of HIV/AIDS in the Czechoslovak media were quite hysterical and adopted from abroad the view that AIDS is a 'homosexual disease,' threatening through

---

307 Fifková, et al. 2002. 6.

homosexual men the whole of Czechoslovak society.[308] The argument that Kolářová puts forth through her meticulous analysis of the press is echoed and supported by this individual biographical narrative.

Lastly, the parental acceptance is itself noteworthy. While it is not possible to ignore the first instance of rejection, it is also important to acknowledge the subsequent moment of recognition. It is not important whether the parents said exactly those words or whether they even held the bottle of champagne. The significant thing is how Petra remembers this moment, the meaning she assigns to it and how she interprets it for her queer identity building and her relationship with her parents. It provides rare, first-hand evidence that at least in some cases (presumed) homosexuals were accepted in warm and positive terms by their closest family. We have many accounts of rejection, trauma, and struggle when it comes to the coming out process, especially during the Communist period.[309] Older literature, which does not work with oral history or interviews, often works with this assumption of an almost universal experience shared by young 'gays' and 'lesbians' during state socialism.[310] Capturing an account of such enthusiastic parental response of a child's coming out before 1989 is perhaps rare. But clearly, and importantly, at least in some families queer children were warmly accepted by their parents.

It is also important to mention, however, that ever since Petra fully realized that she was not a homosexual man but a transsexual heterosexual woman (which happened well after 1989), she has been afraid to tell her parents about that. She calls it "her biggest fear — parents. They are clueless." Petra's fears to tell her parents that she is transsexual suggest that there is, at least in her mind, an abyss between homosexuality and transsexuality in her parents' understanding of "her problem." While they fully accept their son's presumed homosexuality, Petra feels transsexuality would be a whole new and qualitatively different matter. Her fears support scholarly arguments that homosexuality is by far the most accepted form of 'deviance' from the heterosexual norm.[311] Its acceptance rests precisely in that it is compatible

---

308 Kateřina Kolářová, "AIDS sem, AIDS tam aneb: Hroutíme se z tempa doby. Role genderového diskurzu ve vyjednávání ideologického konsenzu v pozdně socialistickém Československu," in *Proměny genderové kultury v české společnosti, 1948-1989*, edited by Hana Havelková and Libora Oates-Indruchová (Praha: SLON, 2013); Kateřina Kolářová, "Homosexuální *asociál* a jeho zavirované tělo: vir HIV a nemoc AIDS v socialistickém diskurzu (Československo 1983-89," in '*Miluji tvory svého pohlaví': Homosexualita v dějinách a společnosti českých zemí*, edited by Pavel Himl, Jan Seidl and Franz Schindler (Praha: Academia, 2013).

309 Miřácký 2009; Schindler 2013.

310 Stehlíková, Procházka and Hromada 1995; Janošová 2000; Fanel 2000.

311 Christopher Craft, *Another Kind of Love: Male Homosexual Desire in English Discourse, 1850-1920* (Berkeley: University of California Press, 1994); Jagose 2004; Rupp 1999; Eve Kosofsky Sedgwick, *Epistemology of the Closet* (Berkeley: University of California Press, 1990); Pat Califia, *Speaking Sex to Power: The Politics of Queer Sex* (San Francisco: Cleis Press, 2002).

with the heteronormative gender order and dual understanding of homosexuality as a simple inversion of heterosexuality, which does not challenge
the stable categories of man and woman. Transsexuality, with its confusing
dimensions of both gender and sexuality is unacceptable for many people,
even though we have seen that Czech and Slovak Socialist sexologists treated
it with unexpected empathy and complexity.

GENDER ANIMOSITY IN FEMALE NARRATIVES

Self-awareness of gender non-conformity is one of the most common ways
to articulate feelings of 'difference' in early childhood years. Next to ethnic
and racial otherness, non-conformity to gender stereotypes and transgressive gender norms of expected male and female behavior is the primary
reason to ostracize, exclude and humiliate those who 'do not belong.'[312] As
with race and ethnicity, a binary gender affiliation is also commonly seen as
an outward expression of the natural order. Gerlinda Šmausová speaks of
a two-fold process of mental socialization of nature and the naturalization
of society: we first project our social understanding of the world into the
nature and animal realm and in turn utilize our observations of the natural
world as 'objective evidence' for our essentialized and stereotypical interpretations of social reality.[313] Following this logic, all narrators articulated
their gender non-conformity as "weird," "different," "unexpected," and
"strange." We have already seen that for transsexual youth, documenting the
"mistake of nature" is an essential part of identity formation. For queer men
and women, who do no identify as transsexual, the realization of 'out-of-
the-ordinary' gender difference seemed to be more articulated by men. Both
Schindler and Miřácký documented these recollections in the memories of
their male narrators.[314]

Women narrators in this oral history project shared similar sentiments,
in which they expressed classic gender stereotypes of transgressive gender
behavior. Following Warner's theorizing, they identified with those stereotypes in efforts to understand and capture their unnamed feelings of
incongruence.

---

312 Nieves Moyano, Maria del Mar Sánchez-Fuentes, " Homophobic Bullying at Schools: A System-
     atic Review of Research, Prevalence, School-related Predictors and Consequences," *Aggression
     and Violent Behavior* 2020, Vol. 53. Article 101441; Stephen T. Russell and Stacey S. Horn, eds., *Sex-
     ual Orientation, Gender Identity, and Schooling: the Nexus of Research, Practice, and Policy* (Oxford
     Univresity Press, 2017); Ryan and Rivers, 2003.
313 Gerlinda Šmausová, "Rasa jako rasistická konstrukce," *Sociologický časopis*, 35/4 (1999): 433–446.
314 Schindler 2013; Miřácký 2009.

I was a tomboy. Climbing trees, scraped knees, that was my world (*Šplhání po stromech, rozbitá kolena, to bylo moje*). Fortunately, I had enough boy friends with whom we had the same interests. My mom also encouraged me to have some nice friend who was a girl but for some reason, it never really worked out. I don't know if it was my fault or whatever because I was such a tomboy but that was just the world I really liked to be in. I don't know, maybe it's different now but back in those days girls even went to play outside in the park in a skirt. It was like skirt to school, skirt to the playground, skirt everywhere. And when you think about it, what can you do in a skirt? Really not much. All you can do is watch that no one can see between your legs. (Tamara)

Of course I liked my female teachers, that's clear. I always liked older women, even my Greta [long-term girlfriend] was sixteen years older than me. But I was always surrounded by boys — we played games, went rafting, girls were not interesting at all. Since I was little I didn't really like being around them because they were too passive ("*to byly takový buchty*"). But since the guys didn't mean anything to me either, I mean emotionally, to the contrary, I was more and more repulsed by them, it was the first time that I paused and thought about it. (Kamila)

What I found particularly striking in female oral history narratives of gender non-conformity was their explicitly expressed childhood dislike, sometimes even hate, for other girls, as expressed by Kamila. In other words, as little and young girls, who later in their lives came to love women and share their most intimate lives and passions with them, many women narrators frequently hated other girls. I found this to be one of the most extraordinary characteristics of the female narratives. There was no such trend to be found anywhere in the male homosexual oral history narratives. None of Schindler's, Miřácký's, Kloidová's, Lemke's or SfQM male narrators mentioned disliking or despising other boys in figuring out and negotiating their own identities. With many women narrators, however, negative feelings for other girls were quite strong:

Since I was a little girl, I knew I loved women. No doubt about that... But I didn't like girls my own age. I had nothing to say to my female classmates. We were so different. I hated skirts but not only that. They [girls] were always so nice and good and obedient. I was never like that at all. I liked to be wild and play hard and not to sit around and rock a doll... It always seemed boring to me. I remember the garden in our preschool. It was a big garden with a grass lawn in the middle and this paved track around it, almost like a stadium. Behind the track, there were bushes and trees and then a long fence. On the lawn there were a few benches and the teachers always sat there and suntanned or talked. And the other girls, I remember, always muddled around those benches with their strollers and dolls. The guys had priority for scooters and tricycles. I always found that so unfair. No matter how much I wanted a scooter to ride around the track when we got outside, I always had to wait for some boy to finish with it first and only then could I have it. But I would rather wait for the scooter than comb the hair of some stupid doll. (Vlasta)

Girls irritated me. It was only later that I realized I am into them but when I was little, I preferred to play with boys. Our games were full of adventure and action but the girls just sat at the bench or did gymnastics on that, what do you call it, hmm, the carpet stand (*klepadlo na koberce*) and talked or pushed their strollers. I had one very good girl friend in the building next door, we would always meet after school in the inner bloc (*na dvoře*) and played "Fast Arrows" (*Rychlé šípy*).[315] For that, it would be ideal to have five of us, of course, but we were only two. We wanted to play the Foglar games with the boys but they didn't want to include us. We played other cool games together [with the boys] but when it came to Foglar, we had to do it on our own. (Dana)

While boys and young men, who later in their lives identified as gay, always seemed to admire and desire peers of their own sex,[316] by contrast, queer women explicitly formulated their dislike for other girls in the formative years of childhood. In the female accounts, the women were enchanted by their boy peers or by their fathers. "Being a girl" was remembered and defined by them by passivity, lack of interest, and obedience, as well as by constrictive dresses and skirts, which limited free play.

Without generalizing the oral history accounts, which should be read in their own individual contexts, the consistency of the testimonies tells us something important about social values and hierarchies assigned to 'girls' and 'boys' and the hierarchy of 'female' and 'male' activities. The narratives reveal a disdain for perceived normative femininity, which does not have an equal status with perceived normative masculinity. As Vlasta demonstrated with the example of scooters in her preschool, boys seemed to get preferential treatment or the right to access desired toys that were considered 'natually male,' promoting 'male realm of action.' This is not to say that boys were seen

---

315 *Fast Arrows* (*Rychlé šípy*) was a legendary fictional private club of teenage boys from the comics and books written by Jaroslav Foglar (1907–1999), who created it as an alternative to the Boy Scouts, prohibited during both the Nazi and Communist periods. *Fast Arrows*, who experienced endless adventures in more than 317 episodes and stories, were universally known, loved, and imitated by generations of children in Czechoslovakia. The comics started in 1938 and continued with a variety of interruptions by Nazi and Communist regimes until the beginning of Normalization in 1971, when it was officially stopped by Communist censorship. During most of the Communist period, Foglar was under the surveillance of the StB and could not publish. After 1989, *Fast Arrows* (and Foglar as an author and person) witnessed a huge resurrection and boom. An important dimension of *Fast Arrows* is the fact that it was a boys' world only. There were no girls in the stories, discounting moms and the ocassional girl who passed a message from the boys to their parents, as they were running after yet another adventure. The stories were so exciting and captivating, however, that many girls identified with *Fast Arrows* regardless of their gender blindness and the absence of female characters.

316 Ibid.

as more worthy or better than girls during state socialism, but rather that despite the officially promoted ideology of equality between men and women, this equality was seen in biologically complementary and horizontally segregated ways. This is nothing new and gender scholarship has analyzed in detail the way hierarchical understandings of masculinity and femininity work in social discourse.[317] But it is illuminating to see these experiences and recollections at work in terms of the formations of lesbian and queer identities during the Communist regime.

> Since childhood I was probably certain that I was [avoids the word]... I knew very early on [that I am a lesbian]. Wait, I can show you a picture!... Other girls were always all done up and I wore sweatpants, rubber boots and a cap, and so probably 'it' was always a part of me. I was a part of the "boy's club" and I liked it that way. (Miriam)

> I started to realize my identity, which unfortunately did not correspond with my body, very early. When I was about seven. I was not at all interested in dolls and strollers, I just wanted to run around with the boys. And I knew I was into girls. (Karen)

> V.S.: How did you know that?

> Karen: You just know. You feel it. I was just like the boys, but the body... [short silence]. Not that I would want to be a boy, I mean physically, not at all, but I was one of them. And I knew that I was attracted to girls but I could never say it or show it, I mean I didn't know how, and plus they were so stupid anyway, so I laughed at them [the girls] and harassed them along with the boys (*tak jsem se jim posmívala a votravovala je s klukama*). (Karen)

> V.S.: And what about at home?

> Karen: It was great. My mom was very loving and she didn't mind at all what I wore or how I played, even though at times she did tell me that I should look more girly, I mean like wear a skirt, you know, or that I should not play with the boys so much. I think my dad was even proud of me at times, especially in front of the neighbors at our country house (*chata*) when I was helping him build [things]. But we never talked about it [Karen's non-heterosexuality]. I know they would not approve. Not even after the revolution. I never told them. There was no reason. It's a private thing. (Karen)

Like other recollections, Karen's and Miriam's testimonies are similar in their ways of associating lesbian identity with female masculinity and

---

317 Havelková and Oates-Indruchová, eds., 2013; Ann Oakley, *Sex, Gender and Society* (New York: Maurice Temple Smith, Ltd, 1972).

tomboy behavior. Neither of the two women, however, was able to articulate *how* their knowledge of lesbian identity manifested itself. What did it mean to "be attracted to girls"? Karen came close when she said that in elementary school it basically meant to harass other girls with the rest of the boys. Moreover, "feeling like a boy" also had its positive dimensions, which again supported stereotypical views of male and female potential (or the lack thereof). In this respect, their memories fulfil the stereotypical perceptions of young lesbians as boys locked in female bodies. It is striking to see how often lesbian narrators in their recollections naturalize the heteronormative pressures into adopting the 19ᵗʰ-century sexological dictum that being attracted to women equals having a man's mind. As Miriam put it, "I attended an industrial high school. *Naturally*, I was very good at technical subjects."[318] At the end of the 19ᵗʰ century, sexology on both sides of the Atlantic built its first inversion theories on this belief,[319] which still resonated with mainstream sexological views in the postwar period, especially in the Soviet Union.[320]

These recollections are very much in sync with scholarship on the politics of gender identity and transgressing gender borders. Analyzing numerous cultural productions in Anglo-American context, Judith Halberstam argued that female tomboyism is much more accepted than male femininity — but only up to a certain age. According to her, because of the "hysterical responses" to moments when boys behave "like girls" we have a tendency to believe that "female gender deviance is in general much more tolerated than male gender deviance."[321] Halberstam points out, however, that tomboyism in girls is accepted only because we have a tendency to associate it with a "natural" desire for freedom, independence and mobility. Such a tendency is often enjoyed much more by boys but Halberstam argues that it is often encouraged by parents in girls as well (as Karen recalled). That is, as long as it does not appear to grow into perceived "extreme male identification" or does not threaten to extend beyond the age of childhood and continue into proper female adolescence. Then it tends to be scorned, rejected and punished.[322] This is an interesting discrepancy in the memories of queer female and male narrators: most women narrators remembered acceptance for their gender non-conformity continuing all the way to puberty, while male narrators recollected being rejected and humiliated for transgressing the expected gender borders and roles as one their first remembered experiences of their gender subjectivity.

---

318 Italics mine.
319 Krafft-Ebbing 1886; Ellis 1901.
320 Essig 1999, 33–35.
321 Halberstam 1998, 5.
322 Ibid., 6.

SEARCHING FOR QUEER REFERENCE POINTS

In the post-WWII period, there are several dates that are widely considered pivotal moments or important turning points in the national history of Czechoslovakia: 1948, when the Communist Party officially seized power in the so-called 'Victorious February' and the country set out on the irreversible path towards state socialism; 1953, when Joseph Stalin and Klement Gottwald, the first Communist president of Czechoslovakia, both died, ending the worst years of rigid, cruel Stalinism, enabling the whole East European region to breathe more; 1968, when Czechoslovakia experienced the exciting Prague Spring under the leadership of the reformist Prime Minister Alexander Dubček and the subsequent invasion of Czechoslovakia by the "brotherly" armies of the Warsaw Pact led by the Soviet Union, which crushed all hopes for reform; 1969, when Jan Palach immolated himself on Wenceslas Square to protest the passivity and resignation that was settling over society after the invasion; 1977, when Charter 77 was formulated to protest the abuse of human rights in Eastern Europe and bolster the dissident movement of active resistance against the oppressive regime; 1985, when Mikhail Gorbachev came to power in the Soviet Union and gradually introduced his policies of *glasnost* and *perestroika*; and, of course, 1989, the year of the downfall of all Communist regimes in Eastern Europe — in Czechoslovakia starting with a student demonstration to commemorate the twentieth anniversary of Palach's death and continuing with numerous other demonstrations and strikes, culminating in the abolition of the leading role of the Communist party from the constitution and ushering in Václav Havel as the tenth president of Czechoslovakia on December 29.[323]

These milestones are important for understanding the continuities and discontinuities of the Communist regime and political and social conditions in the country. For understanding the history of sexuality and the lives of queer people living in Czechoslovakia after World War II, however, additional historical periodization is significant as well: 1950, when the long-awaited revision of the criminal code was issued. (Yet, because it did not bring the expected decriminalization of homosexuality, the year was described by many scholars, medical experts, and homosexual people at the time as well, as a year of lost chance); 1961, which remedied the expectations and decriminalized homosexuality, making Czechoslovakia one of the first countries in the world to do so; 1974, when the first successful sex-reassignment surgery in Czechoslovakia took place; 1992, which finally removed homosexuality

---

323 Mary Heimann, *Czechoslovakia: The State that Failed* (New Haven and London: Yale University Press, 2011).

from the list of diseases in Czechoslovakia; and 2006, which witnessed the legalization of registered partnership for gay men and lesbian women.[324]

Recent oral histories of queer people and research of public and medical discourses revealed that besides the above-mentioned dates, recited repeatedly in most scholarship on the subject, there were additional dates, significant from the point of view of queer people in Czechoslovakia, that have been so far eluding attention. One such date is the year 1973, when the sexologist Pavel Zemek published his ground-breaking article "They Live among Us," (*Žijí mezi námi*). Zemek's article, which appeared in the popular and widely read weekly magazine *Mladý Svět*, was the first officially published text in Socialist Czechoslovakia, which rejected the definition of homosexuality as a disease.[325] Zemek argued that homosexuality is a "variation of human sexuality in otherwise healthy individuals" and strongly criticized any attempts to cure it. Without naming homophobia, he also directly pointed out that the main problem of homosexuals is not their sexual orientation, but the intolerant attitudes of mainstream society. On the other hand, his text discussed only male homosexuality and the black-and-white photograph, accompanying the article, sported five men's pants (focused on their crotches) in a row.

The article caused an uproar among queer people and *Mladý Svět* even faced the threat of being closed down for a while, as the Soviet embassy protested the tolerant and encouraging tone of this particular article.[326] The appearance of such a text, moreover published in a major weekly for younger generations, indicates that censorship during the Normalization period was far from uniform.[327] Once again, the text documents the complex and often positive role played by Czech sexologists, many of whom clearly espoused tolerant views towards homosexuality and were not afraid to publically articulate them. Such moments were important not only because they increased the visibility of non-normative sexuality but also because they were written by medical experts, on whose widespread authority the party relied when making its claims about normality and social order. They were also written in plain, comprehensible language understandable to ordinary people. For that reason, according to Procházka, Hromada and other LGBT activists after 1989, Zemek's article provided an important reference point for positive

---

324 Seidl, 2012; Fifková, et al., 2008.

325 Procházka, 1997: 248; Pavel Zemek, "Žijí mezi námi." *Mladý svět* 15/4 (1973): 20.

326 Hromada 2000.

327 After the commotion caused by this text, no other articles about homosexuality appeared in anything other than strictly medical journals until 1987. The only exception was the popular weekly *Zdraví* (*Health*). Since it was a medically oriented magazine, homosexuality was occasionally mentioned there, including several important sexological polemics in the mid-1980s, mentioned in the previous chapter.

self-identification and for a sense of imagined queer community during the Normalization period.[328]

A number of narrators, both in Schindler's oral history project as well as my own, referred to this article as a very important text that traveled by word of mouth among queer people.[329] This article also turned the attention of queer people toward Czechoslovak sexology and encouraged them to look there for allies rather than oppressors.

Zemek's article was great. When I read it, I could not believe my own eyes. I was a bit pissed off that it was only about boys but I understood it. It was probably better that it didn't talk about girls, at least no one cared about us in relation to that article... I befriended Petr [one of the sexologists], for totally unrelated purposes, and went to visit him sometimes at Apolinářská [where the Sexological Institute was located]. He was gay himself but at that time no one knew this, it became open only after the revolution. Until then, no one spoke about it aloud, but it was clear that we understood each other. (Kamila)

I remember how touched I was when my boyfriend brought that issue of *Mladý Svět* home. I remember it like today. It was snowing outside and so he had to take off his heavy boots and coat and hat but already since the hallway he was yelling at me, "you must read this, you won't believe this." At first I thought something terrible happened but then I understood that he was excited. It was the first time that I read about myself that I'm worthy. I still didn't like much that it said so openly that we are homosexuals, I felt kind of naked in a way, but I felt the regime finally recognized we are normal people like anyone else. (Josef)

It is noteworthy that Josef credited "the regime" with the positive assessment of homosexuality, but given the fact that the article appeared in an official weekly, which everyone knew was censored like the rest of the media, it makes sense. Paradoxically, the 'regime' thus got credit from an ordinary person (Josef) for what was later perceived from higher positions of power, namely the Soviet embassy, which protested against the article, as a failure of censorship.[330] But undoubtedly, the article played an important role for the self-understanding and identity formation of queer people.

It was incredible what people like Zemek, Brzek, and Zvěřina wrote. I admired them for their courage. What they wrote remains unparalleled here. (*Obdivovala jsem [je] za statečnost, to co tady psali, to nemělo obdoby*)." (Heda)

---

328 Seidl 2012; Hromada 2000.
329 Schindler 2013; Hromada 2000; Seidl 2012.
330 Ibid.

Looking for role models to admire, look up to and identify with was a difficult task for all queer people in the context of the authoritarian regime and omnipresent ideological censorship. When recollecting these moments, a specific work of fiction kept repeatedly coming up in many interviews as having played an important role in the narrators' searches for queer reference points and in the processes of forming their sexual identities:

> How did I realize that I am into girls?[331] Of course not by myself [laugh]. Somehow I got my hands on *The Well of Loneliness* — a friend of mine loaned it to me. I read it and everything was absolutely clear to me. I recognized myself in it... It was the only book describing something like this but it [the book] was impossible to officially find anywhere. (Karen)

> When I was young, I read the *Well of Loneliness*. I got it from my first platonic love. I remember the confusion and thrill. I wanted to share my feelings so much with the whole world about it but no one else around me knew the book and I was afraid to talk about it. (Dana)

There are clear parallels between the identity challenges faced by the main character of the *Well of Loneliness*, the 1928 lesbian classic by British writer Radclyffe Hall, a girl named Stephen, and the feelings of gender tensions, transgressions, and subversions, shared by the female narrators in the interviews. To my surprise, they *all* read the book. During their adolescent or young adult years, in the depth of Czechoslovak Socialist censorship, they all managed to find a copy somewhere and they all read it. I have to admit that it was an unexpected and memorable moment for me during the interviews, when narrator after narrator all mentioned this particular book as their great source of inspiration, affection and queer identity formation.

At the same time, the narrators read the Czech translation of the book, which deliberately translated the heroine's male name as *Štěpa*, instead of the Czech equivalent of the male name Stephen, used in the original, which should translate as *Štěpán*. Using the female version of the name of the main heroine in the Czech translation instead of the male one does not provoke the same ambiguity and complexity intended in the original.[332] It is not in-

---

331 Being "into girls" (*být "na holky"*) or "into women" (*být na ženský*) are Czech colloquial phrases, still commonly used today, to describe lesbian identity or sexual affinity of women towards women. All narrators repeatedly used these phrases in various parts of their interviews. Indeed, they were the most commonly used ways to identify queerness in the female interviews. The narrators also agreed that while the term 'lesbian' was not used at all before 1989, being "into girls" and "into women" was generally used and understood in both heterosexual mainstream and queer (imagined) communities.

332 Despite its negative reception in Great Britain, *The Well of Loneliness* was translated into Czech and published in Czechoslovakia already in 1933, with a cover design by the world-renowned

significant, however, that the lesbian heroine of the book espouses clear transgender characteristics, both self-identified and perceived by her family and surroundings. If many Czech queer teenage girls saw Štěpa as their main positive role model and reference point, then the story also likely contributed to a gender stereotype, which connects lesbian women with masculinity and male characteristics.

The fact that after its first Czech publication in 1933, the second publication appeared in 1969, suggests the open atmosphere that prevailed in the country in the late 1960s. The *Well of Loneliness* was an internationally acclaimed lesbian classic with an unambiguous, transgressive gender identity of the main heroine and a story of tragic love between two women. As such, it could not have been published by mistake or coincidentally. Its appearance in 1969 can be interpreted in several interconnected ways: first, it is plausible that the editors of the publishing house *Práce* wanted to reinforce the newly obtained press freedoms by publishing a sexually controversial book that clearly undermined the heteronormative morality of the time and could not appear under strict censorship. Second, it is possible that it was a purposeful and calculated, even if implicit, effort to support homosexuality and queer people, whose identities were invisible and marginalized by the officially sanctioned discourse.

While the narrators agreed that by the early 1970s the book was no longer freely available on the shelves of bookstores and also disappeared from public libraries, apparently there existed enough copies among people that it was possible to obtain it through friendly loans.

> I got it from my beloved singer.[333] She asked me if I read it, and when I said no, she smiled and said 'you have to' and passed it to me. I devoured it in one sitting… But I have to admit that I, how would you say it, well, I kind of forgot to return it [laughs]. Once I had it, I didn't want to let go of the book and of course you couldn't get it normally in a library or a place like that. (Kamila)

Despite its absence in official public places but thanks to such private circulations, it is plausible to argue that Hall's novel helped many young queer women in Socialist Czechoslovakia to realize and shape their 'lesbian'

Czech transgender surrealist artist Toyen (Praha: Symposion). It was republished during the Socialist era in 1969 (Praha: Práce and ROH) and again after the collapse of the Communist regime in 1991 and 2002. From a linguistic perspective, it is noteworthy that in 1933 and 1969, the name of the author on the book cover appeared as Radclyffe *Hall*, while in 1992 and 2002 as Radclyffe *Hallová*. In March 2006, the state-owned Czech Radio 3 broadcast a three-part dramatization of the novel by Petra Ušelová.

333 The narrator worked at that time for a famous Czech singer, whom she mentioned by name during the interview, but did not authorize me to reveal her name publicly in this book.

identity at times, when the term 'lesbian' was non-existent and homosexual tendencies were addressed by the state only in terms of medical diagnosis. In this context, the oral interviews disclosed a significant moment, which enables us to know that Czech and Slovak queer women *had* at least one book and one heroine to privately identify with in their individualized processes of forming their queer identities.

Gay men might have found similar reference points in the Czech translation of Allen Ginsberg's 1956 poem *Howl*, which was published in Czechoslovakia already in 1959 as a part of the literary journal *Světová literatura* (World Literature) in an excellent translation by Jan Zábrana.[334] According to translator Josef Rauvolf, writer Jáchym Topol, and editor Jan Šulc, this particular issue of *Světová literatura* was extraordinary, as it introduced the Beat writers and the context of their works. The most sexually explicit passages of *Howl* were not published in the journal but "it was enough for the reader to understand what kind of poem it was."[335] Rauvolf argues that while the poem celebrates free sexuality and male homosexual love and sex, for many it was primarily a call for freedom, desire for individuality, and freedom of expression, which attracted its audience. Nonetheless, Schindler argues in his book that the male narrators in his oral history project discussed not only the publication of *Howl* itself but mainly Ginsberg's visit in Prague in 1965, as an important reference point and inspiration in their lives.[336] Czech historian Petr Blažek, who analyzed Ginsberg's visit from the point of view of the Secret Police (*StB*), additionally pointed out that Ginsberg, who was already openly gay at that time, was actively seeking contact with Czech homosexual men in Prague during his visit, which was one of the reasons subsequently used by the Czechoslovak state to deport him from Czechoslovakia.[337]

It was not only fiction, however, that helped introduce young queer people in Socialist Czechoslovakia to the topic of sex and sexuality. Interestingly, even officially sanctioned books, which were published for a completely different purpose and audience, helped with figuring out queer identities as well:

One day, I think I must had been about fifteen at that time, I was travelling on a tram and it stopped at a red light near Masaryk train station. And as I was looking out of the tram, in a shop window of a bookstore I saw a book in a red cover and I glimpsed the

---

334 Allen Ginsberg, *Kvílení* (Praha: Světová literatura, 1959, translated by Jan Zábrana). Zábrana himself was from an exceptionally persecuted family (both of his parents were jailed for many years).

335 Josef Rauvolf, "Viděl jsem nejlepší hlavy…," *Lidové noviny* 8.1. 2011: 28.

336 Schindler 2013, 24.

337 Petr Blažek, "Vyhoštění krále majálesu. Allen Ginsberg a Státní bezpečnost," *Paměť a dějiny* 5:2(2011): 28–43. Ginsberg's contacts with Czech homosexual men during his visit of Prague were recorded also in Fanel 2000, 435–436.

word "sex" written on it. I continued riding the tram, but my heart was pounding. I got home on time as expected but told my parents that I needed to take care of something and took the tram back to the bookshop. I bought the book. The seller looked at me kind of funny but I didn't care. I brought it home and read it all that night. It was a handbook for marital sex (*manželská příručka*) with plenty of colored pictures and there I fully realized for the first time that here it is. I am gay.[338] (Josef)

Josef's story is important from a reception point of view, as it reminds us to be cautious when interpreting historical sources. It indicates that regardless of the targeted heterosexual audience, the officially sanctioned marital guide, which was designed to reinforce heteronormativity and the awareness of "innate" gender differences between women and men, could have been (and indeed was in Josef's case) resignified in completely different ways by a queer readership. In other words, the same book, which laid on a nightstand in one bedroom as a guide to healthy heterosexual marriage, could have been hidden under a pillow in another bedroom as 'gay porn.'

Sometimes, the crucial reference points for self-realization for one's queer identity were unintended encounters with other 'gays' and 'lesbians.'

[My husband] was fifteen years older, we met in 1961 in [the town of] Písek, which we visited with the drama club of my high school at the theater competition "Šrámkův Písek."[339] We stayed there for a week and he worked as a waiter in a hotel where we were going for meals. So we immediately fell for each other (*zakoukali jsme se do sebe*). You know, those people, well, I think that we simply mutually recognize each other (*víte, ty lidi, prostě, já myslím, že my se mezi sebou poznáme*). He was totally obvious, even though I didn't know anything about these things, I was sixteen. All I knew was that I occasionally fell platonically in love with women and that I was not interested in guys. But that was all I knew. But meeting him I think I finally realized 'it' fully… So I fell in love with him. (Miriam)

In this recollection, Miriam shares a remarkable moment of full internal coming out based on the recognition of homosexuality of someone else. Since it was not possible, according to Miriam, to live out one's non-heterosexuality openly, she translated her same-sex desire into an attraction for someone, who shared the same desire, despite the fact that they did not necessarily attract each other. But their mutual recognition and understanding of their homosexuality, which Miriam openly admitted was the basis for their

---

338 Josef himself used the term 'gay' in the interview.

339 *Šrámkův Písek* is an annual cultural festival of theater companies and drama clubs with a long tradition, dating back to the 1950s and continuing without interruption to the present. The festival is held in summer, in the town of Písek in Southern Bohemia, where the Czech writer and poet Fráňa Šrámek (1877–1952) lived and worked for many years of his life.

relationship, was what triggered the 'attraction' and ultimately "love" for each other. Miriam's interpretation echoes the argument of queer theorist Pat Califia, who similarly argued that she likes having sex with gay men because of the "queer atmosphere" in that act of intimacy.[340] It is not the biological body of the person, with whom Califia has sex, but rather their 'gay' or 'queer' sexual identity and desire that creates the attraction for both sides. Miriam's recollection and understanding of the situation is thus reminiscent of this argument of "queer sociability," which can function as an underlying basis for queer relationships of people of 'opposite sexes.'

In other words, what Miriam articulated as foundational in her and her husband's relationship was not their physical bodies but their sexual identity. They did not have a conventional heterosexual relationship and marriage based on the fact that they were a man and a woman. Rather, they had a queer relationship based on the fact that they both understood themselves as non-heterosexuals. Miriam's story also reminds us how deceiving it might be to pass heteronormative judgments on people and relationships around us. Even though relationships like theirs were perhaps exceptional, they did happen during the Socialist times. Unless explicitly discussed, there is no certainty in who could had been involved in similar life situations. Miriam's love and her interpretation of why she fell in love with a man, further demonstrates why it is complicated to try to fit the narrators into clear-cut identity categories and why the broad-based term 'queer' might be most suitable identity to use, when discussing their lives.

The women's oral history narratives brought up another remarkable reference point and significant historical moment relevant for queer people during the Normalization era. Apparently, the 1981 coming-out of the Czech-American tennis player Martina Navrátilová, who announced her lesbian sexual orientation publicly, shortly after receiving her permanent United States citizenship, was an immensely important moment of recognition and validation for many Czech and Slovak women, who were not able to live their queer identities in visible ways in the then-Communist Czechoslovakia. It might seem obvious when considered in hindsight, but in 1981 it was far from evident. Navrátilová emigrated from Czechoslovakia in 1975 at the age of 18, and since that point she was completely erased from the official media. Even though between 1978 and 1987 Navrátilová was consistently the top-seated female tennis player in the world, the Czechoslovak Communist media got around her success by never mentioning her name.

In the quarterfinals of tournaments [the media] mentioned seven players — without Martina, in semifinals three players — without Martina. If Martina won, the result was

---

340 Califia 2002, 57.

ignored, if she lost the final, our sources mentioned only the winner. With whom the winner played and with what results was never mentioned anywhere. But the sports fans knew anyway. It was enough to tune into Voice of America, Radio Free Europe, BBC or Deutsche Welle and we got it firsthand. The idiom that radio and TV broadcast lies as the newspaper *Red Justice* prints (*radio a televise lže, jak když Rudé Právo tiskne*) became a household saying precisely in these times.[341]

When Navrátilová publicly came out, after being pressured to confirm or deny rumors that she was a lesbian, the Communist media reported the news. It begs the question, of course, why then and why that particular piece of information, when otherwise Czechoslovak media was silent on Navrátilová. The only logical interpretation seems that the point was to discredit Navrátilová in the eyes of the Czechoslovak public and to perhaps also hint at the allegedly decadent influence of the West. There is no information about the reception of this news among the general public but the queer oral history narratives revealed that the news of Navrátilová's self-declared lesbian identity was noticed and celebrated by the narrators, for most of whom Navrátilová became a positive and beloved role model.

I remember when Martina came out, it was early 80s and it was in the paper. It was so great. We talked about it endlessly with other girls, mainly we couldn't believe that she announced it, just like that, to the whole world. (Olina)

By some miracle I got tickets to the Fed Cup in 1986 when she [Navrátilová] played against [Hana] Mandlíková [the number one Czech player]. It was hopelessly sold out, plus I don't really care about tennis at all but I really wanted to see her with my own eyes. A friend of mine, Victor, worked at Čedok[342] at that time and was able to get two tickets for me. I must say, it was the experience of a lifetime. She was so strong and determined. The great thing was that the whole stadium cheered for Martina as though she were playing for us [our country]… I think that only we [Dana and her girlfriend] were so excited because she was a lesbian (*lesbička*). We knew that for several years by then. But still, I think everyone else knew it, too, and so it felt really good that people rooted for her despite that. (Dana)

I think that Navrátilová had a huge impact on us [gays and lesbians]. Especially for us girls, it was such a huge encouragement (*to byla taková vzpruha*). I'm sure the commies wanted to just smear her (*komouši ji jen chtěli očernit*) but for us she was a hero… I think

---

341 Zdeněk Valenta and Vladimír Zápotočný, "Martina Navrátilová Američankou," *Radio Praha*, *Český rozhlas* 7, January 27, 2001.

342 Čedok (*Československá dopravní kancelář*) was the official Czechoslovak travel agency, which had a monopoly on all international travel.

that it [Navrátilová's homosexuality] was also very important for young girls at that time. We, the older ones, already knew how things are but the young ones still couldn't get much information. But that Navrátilová was a lesbian was no secret and was encouraging because she was so great and famous. So she was one of us in all senses of the word. [laugh] (Kamila)

The coming out of Martina Navrátilová was spontaneously mentioned by most female narrators, and the knowledge of her coming out was confirmed by the rest of the women when asked about it specifically. Navrátilová's coming out, a fitting example of 'queer temporality,' demonstrates how important it is to approach historical periodization from a variety of perspectives, the lens of sexuality included. It is also notable that Navrátilová's coming out functioned as a source of cohesion. As Kamila described it, Navrátilová was at least by some women perceived as "one of us," helping to create a sense of a virtual 'lesbian community' through the shared knowledge of her lesbian identity. Clearly, Navrátilová served for many queer women as a role model and a source of empowerment.[343]

The recollections examined in this chapter reveal that despite censorship and state pressures at homogenization of societal opinions and values, queer youth in Communist Czechoslovakia grew up in diverse families that were different in their degree of hostility and/or acceptance of the gender and sexual identities of the narrators at the time. Even if parents were silent or non-inquisitive about the sexual orientation of their children, this did not necessarily mean that those children were raised in hostile family environments or that they were seen as 'undesirable deviants.' The censorship of the Communist regime, however, did play an important role in determining what kinds of resources and information were available for queer children and youth to realize and form their own sexuality and reflect upon it. The general absence of information, caused by the ideological censorship, meant that relatively small topics and moments, such as the existence of the *Well of Loneliness, Howl* or the sexological essay in *Mladý svět*, as well as the mere announcement of Navrátilová's coming out, had a fundamental and far-reaching impact on the lives of many queer people. It also suggests, however, that no matter how robust the system of censorship was, queer people were able to find and create their own artefacts and moments, which they could use as reference points for navigating the unfamiliar terrain of their own sexuality.

---

343 In 1996, Navrátilová herself acknowledged her importance and role model position for Czech lesbian women and community, when she provided financial assistance for the purchase of basement space for the lesbian community center called Nora. (Seidl 2012, 357–358).

CHAPTER 5
THE SUBVERSIVE POTENTIAL OF EVERYDAY LIVES

PROPER GENDER AS CAMOUFLAGE FOR IMPROPER SEXUALITY

One day, I was sitting in the Library of the Czech Academy of Sciences, leafing through the 1973 volume of the popular weekly magazine *Mladý Svět*. I was searching for the iconic article about homosexuality called "They Live among Us" (*Žijí mezi námi*), mentioned in the previous chapter, which came out in January of that year and according to many of the narrators caused uproar, both among queer people and in high official places. All of a sudden, I came across a full-page black-and-white photograph of Kamila whom I met in the late-1990s as, an open and outspoken lesbian woman. Immersed in my topic and aware of her active presence in the contemporary LGBT community, at first I thought she was featured in the paper *as* a lesbian, shocked and confused how that was possible in 1973. Quickly, however, I realized that the big photograph of a smiling beautiful young woman was showing the winner of the Prague regional round of the nationwide competition for "The Perfect Girl" (*Správná dívka*).[344]

Amazed, I read about the competition and Kamila's success in it. The aim of the popular event, which was broadcast for twelve Saturdays in row during evening primetime on state TV, was to introduce ten selected girls from each region of Socialist Czechoslovakia to compete in front of the cameras in a variety of disciplines, such as cooking, singing, sewing, applying make-up, but also speed-typing on a typewriter, ring throwing, balancing an egg on a spoon, knowledge of geography, and camping activities (such as building a tent on the stage).[345] The age span for the contestants was 16–25 so Kamila, 25-years-old at the time, just barely made the cut. The contestants were judged not only by a panel of then-famous celebrities but also by TV viewers who watched the show at home and either called or sent letters to the TV station, indicating their desired winners. Shows of this kind were actually

---

344 The Czech word *správná* can be translated in several ways, it could mean "perfect," "proper" or "cool." As a title of this competition, I would argue it was trying to combine all three meanings of the English translations together.

345 "Televizní soutěž Správná dívka." *Mladý svět* 15/4 (1973): 4.

quite popular on Czechoslovak TV during the Normalization period as they provided a sense of national community and "collective amnesia" about the uncomfortable past, attempting to entertain the public into forgetting the current political situation.[346]

After winning the Prague round, Kamila advanced into the national round, where she placed second. Because Kamila also happened to be one of the narrators in my queer oral history project, in which she had already unraveled to me, as she said, her "entire lesbian life under communism," without ever mentioning this event, I set up another interview with her to ask her about this peculiar competition. "Wow, you found that? I totally forgot all about it!" she laughed, when I mentioned running across her photograph. I asked her why she decided to participate in the event:

> To hide, of course! [She laughed heartily]. Anything with a stupid title like that was a perfect opportunity to disguise that I'm into girls. When something had a "perfect girl" or anything similar in the title, I thought to myself, hurry up, that's great, again you'll have an alibi. I'm all for fun and anything bad so I didn't mind doing it. The whole nation watched it. Well, ok, what else could they watch, right? But it was just funny how seriously the other girls took it... They kind of pushed me into it at work, the guys. At work [the City Hall in Prague] they were pressuring me to join the [Communist] Party all the time, so I was looking for any excuses I could find, my sport, taking care of my mom, whatever. But I had to join the SSM (*Union of Socialist Youth*). And it was officially the SSM that ordered me to compete and registered me. They were saying that I should go for it, that it would be fun. At that time I already knew for a long time who I was and so any chance to demonstrate that I'm normal, I said to myself, ok, what the hell, why not? The guys at work had fun with it and I had peace and quiet [*měla jsem klid*] for a while. But then, for two more years I had no peace! At the bus stop, on a tram, all the time someone was addressing me, perfect girl this and perfect girl that, so for two years I was a big celebrity. [Laugh... Pause...] But you know, I should really have won the whole show, not to finish only second. But one of the jury members, Petr Novotný — I hate the guy, you know, he is such a fat pig — he pushed for this chick from Bratislava. I don't know why, but he really wanted her to win, and she did. (Kamila)

In an interesting twist in the end of her recollection, Kamila revealed that perhaps she did care a little bit, at least about her final placement in the competition if not about the content of the event. What is evident from her narrative, however, is that participating in a show like this was a conscious and active camouflaging strategy on her part. At work, no one knew about Kamila's sexual orientation. As she explained, she presumed that "any woman with ambition to become the perfect girl," with all the associated

---

346 Bren 2010.

connotations in Socialist Czechoslovakia, presenting in front of the whole nation her culinary abilities and make-up skills, would "automatically pass as heterosexual." Or better put, her sexual orientation or gender identity would not even be put into a question. The outer manifestation of 'proper gender' was more important than the 'truth' beneath it.

As with other areas of social reality and engagement in public space, the state cared much less about the inner beliefs of people than about the manifestations of their loyalty to the status quo, be it the rule of the Communist Party or the heteronormative gender order. As Czechoslovak sexologists stressed on numerous occasions, it was not the homosexual disposition that was important but how one worked with it. As the sexology chapter revealed, given the constraints of prescriptive heterosexuality, Czechoslovak sexologists encouraged non-heterosexuals to pick within this framework whatever the queer people found most suitable for their particular state of mind and being, as long as this "choice" was compatible and compliant with the status quo. Despite the sexological benevolence, however, societal and public attitudes towards sexuality were saturated with homophobic stereotypes.

It is also noteworthy that Kamila used the "The Perfect Girl" competition as another piece of camouflage as well, to divert attention and lessen the pressures to join the Communist Party she repeatedly faced. These pressures, which forced her into the youth Communist organization against her will, also might have been the reason why Kamila pushed the whole competition out of her memory and never mentioned it in the first interview. In the second interview, she talked, with apparent joy, about the fact that for two years she was somewhat of a celebrity in the public space (at least in the Prague public transportation system) so it is remarkable that she did not remember, or chose not to remember, the story in the first place. The ease, with which Kamila blended together the two distinctly different dimensions of the camouflaging motivation for the competition suggests that living a 'double life' was a part of her everyday routine. Moreover, living a 'double life,' according to her, was a reality that not only many other people at her work lived as well, albeit for different reasons, but also a strategy that often went far beyond dressing and fashion. Sexual harassment of women in the work place Kamila naturalized as an expected form of subordination and a commonplace demonstration of secretarial professional "competence," which was tolerated (for men) and used as a reward or punishment (for women). For her, voluntarily yielding to sexual advances had the additional benefit of protecting her from questions about her sexual orientation.

Either you had sex with your boss and then you had a good salary and conditions or you didn't and then you were fired for the smallest thing. Everyone watched this [sexual orientation] extremely carefully at work. So at work, I preferred to have the reputation of a whore than to have anyone know this [that I am into girls] about me... All the time, I was in the chauffeurs' laps, flirting with the [Communist] Party bosses, yeah, the biggest coquette in town. But it worked. (Kamila)

In their own recollections, the willingness to publicly display stereotypical gender characteristics and expected normative gender behavior was a component of the everyday routine performed by all the narrators. Constraints formed by gender stereotypes undoubtedly bothered many people in Czechoslovakia, regardless of their sexual orientation and gender identity. For the queer narrators, however, removing any potential doubts about their sexual orientation or gender identity was directly tied to the 'correct' performance of male or female gender roles, corresponding with their physical bodies.

At work we had a dress code, you know. Women, pants? No way, all women had to wear skirts or dresses. It was not possible at all that you would come dressed in pants. When my mom died, I had nothing black to wear other than this two-piece pants-suit but immediately it was a problem (*okamžitě průser*), that very day! She was not even buried yet and immediately I was called in, you are not going to wear this here! Such harassment from all sides! I hated skirts, dresses even more, but at least it helped me pass [as a heterosexual]... I was also lucky that my Austrian [lesbian lover] was a seamstress, so I always looked like I came out of a fashion magazine. All the other women at work envied me [my fashion style] and who would dare to question my sexuality when I looked the best of them all! (Kamila)

Even when there was no dress code involved, some narrators felt that performing a feminine gender identity through appropriate clothing was advantageous in their efforts to hide their sexual orientation. Their testimonies also revealed that, at least presumably, the predominant understanding of homosexuality was strictly gender based, that homosexual women were 'butch' and homosexual men 'effeminate.' Since homosexuality was not discussed in the public discourse and was not admitted as a visible presence in Socialist society, it created a logical presumption that one would see 'it' and recognize 'it' when confronted with 'it.' Sexual orientation was thus constructed as simultaneously invisible yet outwardly visible and recognizable, which explains why so many narrators put such emphasis on 'correct' clothing.

At work I always wore a skirt. Not because I would have to but it was simply easier. Even though I worked at the drawing board (*u rýsovacího prkna*) among all men, no one there suspected anything because I was always very well dressed. (Miriam)

These reflections reveal not only the importance of adopting a proper dress code to hide one's sexual orientation, but also the degree to which assumptions about gender and sexual identity were based on superficial visual markers. In a social environment that ostensibly equates dress codes and sexual identity, it is easier to hide a trangressive identity. Taking definitions of womanhood or homosexuality as given or self-evident often conceals the complexities and ambiguities of lived identities. Since gender and sexual discourses during the Communist era lacked the ability to both name and go beyond the obvious normative expectations, it became relatively easy for queer women to mask their identities behind those expectations, preventing further scrutiny.

CHALLENGING MYTHS ABOUT FEMALE SEXUALITY

Even though the narrators upheld certain gender stereotypes, it does not mean that they necessarily behaved in gender-stereotypical or expected ways. If nothing else, their gradually realized desires for same-sex intimacy and queer sexuality let them into transgressive realms. Some historians and sexologists have argued that women (regardless of their sexual orientation) are naturally passive and indirect, and based on this argument suggested that in the context of the Communist period it was very difficult for lesbian women to meet partners of the same sex.[347] For most female narrators, however, finding other women interested in women during the Socialist period was not a problem:

> When I was sixteen [in 1964] I was in Austria with the Czechoslovak national junior table tennis team and during our last dinner, the coach of the Austrian team came into the dining room with the most beautiful woman I had ever seen. I stopped eating, our eyes met and it was like lightening. She was sixteen years older than me but we spent together twelve wonderful years… It was never a problem to see each other. Through the sport, I always got a visa to go [abroad] and she could also travel to Czechoslovakia. Also, I worked at the mayor's office of Prague… and of course that helped me a lot to be able to travel… And to hide my Austrian [lover] also was not a big problem, everything was happening under the code word "sport." (Kamila)

Traditionally, male sexuality has been connected with sex, and female sexuality with love and feelings.[348] Also in the eyes of Czech and Slovak sexologists, as was evident in the previous chapter, women (regardless of their

---

347 Pondělíček and Pondělíčková-Mašlová 1971; Fanel 2000; Brzek and Hubálek 1988.
348 Rupp, 2013 and 1999; Faderman 1981; Smith-Rosenberg 1975.

sexual orientation) were 'naturally' passive, shy and private, which then determined the overall sexological interpretations of women's and men's (homo)sexual behavior during the Communist period.[349] Such stereotypes play into different historical constructions of male and female sexuality, which then also determines interpretative approaches to sexuality historians use. Additionally, such arguments enter into perceptions and interpretations of public manifestations of gay and lesbian sexualities as well. Because information about 'homosexual men' was readily available in archival sources (police reports, court proceedings, and medical files), while information about 'homosexual women' was sparse, male sexuality was subsequently interpreted by many influential historians as more active, visible, frequent, and thus also as more significant than female sexuality.[350] Such myths have been challenged by recent queer and feminist studies and projects, which exposed that women as well have historically enjoyed same-sex sexual encounters in public places, including in the restrictive environment of state socialism behind the Iron Curtain.[351]

Socialist Czechoslovakia was not an exception in this regard. Contrary to the mainstream accounts of the history of (homo)sexuality in the Czech lands and Czechoslovakia, which without much investigation pronounced women's sexuality in public as non-existent, some female narrators in the queer oral history project did recall their own sexual encounters in public spaces. Their valuable memories broaden our understanding of public sex during state socialism far beyond the well-documented history of gay men's sexuality, which covered the salon and club scene in the urban context, as well as the topography of anonymous gay sex in public restrooms, parks, and other places in Prague and other large Czech cities.[352] Importantly, these memories also challenge stereotypes about female sexual passivity and show how important it is for historical interpretations *what* questions are asked and *who* has the opportunity to answer them.

> In Karel's salon in Vinohrady, there was a great terrace and on nice days everyone was walking around naked. Women, men, everyone. If you wanted to have sex, you could simply do so. People changed, you could meet new people there and simply enjoy yourself in whatever way you needed. (Ludmila)

---

349 Pondělíček, Pondělíčková-Mašlová 1971; Brzek, Hubálek 1988; Brzek, Pondělíčková-Mašlová 1992; Fanel 2000.

350 Chauncey, Jr. 1994; Katz 1995.

351 Basiuk and Burszta 2020; Stella 2015; Rupp 2013 and 1999; Halberstam 1998; Faderman 1981.

352 Jan Seidl, ed. *Teplá Praha: průvodce po queer historii hlavního města 1380–2000* (Brno: Černé pole, 2014); Schindler 2013.

I love sex. Okay? It's fun, relaxing, and in a relationship it tends to get a bit boring... With girls who were strangers (*s neznámýma holkama*) you could do whatever your wanted. It depended on, of course, what kind of sex you wanted and how one wanted to do it but it was no problem to do it. Outside, or in the toilets... And I never had a problem to find other girls who would be into it as well. (Eva)

My favorite place was Špejchar. There was a nice, big outdoor beer garden with long wooden tables at the corner of Letná. It wasn't anything fancy but in the back there were public toilets and I loved to go there with girls... to have sex, of course. My friend Jindra found them [the girls] for me. He was handicapped, walking with French crutches and when I was coming to the garden he was yelling at me already from afar, "Come on, come on, she is already waiting for you!" So I would go ahead and buy them [the women] sausage and beer, sometimes also other things and then we would have sex. Or, on other occasions, they would host me. (Tamara)

Tamara said that she knew other women who shared her passion for public sex. In her recollections, she never looked for any relationships in these sexual encounters. It was "only for sex." Often, she did not even know the names of these girls and sometimes she "never even saw them again." This statement seems a bit exaggerated, given how small Prague is and how relatively small the 'community' of similarly minded women likely was. But evidently, after their sexual adventures, Tamara was not looking for the girls again. Perhaps, she did not want to see them ever again in order to enjoy her sense of having anonymous sex and so the belief that she never saw them again could express her desire to perceive the experiences that way.

Women's accounts of their own public sex encounters during socialism, similar to the memories of Tamara, Ludmila, and Eva shared above, were not frequent among the female narratives. But they should not be ignored. They challenge the understanding of female sexuality as passive and 'lesbian love' as primarily an emotional and private desire. They also undermine perceptions of women's same-sex desire and sexual behavior as hidden in long-term, stable, monogamous partnerships behind bedroom walls. Additionally, we cannot be sure that other women simply chose not to share such memories during the interviews. Similar to previous 'Western' research findings, also this 'Eastern' queer oral history project exposed that, at least for some women, same-sex sex was an activity that offered noncommittal relaxation and fun and was not necessarily connected to long-term relationships.

During the 1970s, Eva had a long-term relationship with a well-known "underground personality," Nina, with whom she shared "the excitement of sex and deep belief in God." Nina organized home sex parties for self-identified queer people. They would meet together in Nina's apartment in the Lesser Town in Prague. "Nina was not a dissident but she knew a lot of underground people and so she was even in prison, but certainly not because she was a lesbian," claimed Eva, who participated in many of the parties. On other days, they would take their passion out to the streets.

> We lived only for sex — it was something that completely devoured me. We didn't care at all who saw us. It was nice to be outside in the open. And to tell the truth, people didn't care much even if they saw us. (Eva)

Ultimately, the relationship between Nina and Eva ended in 1980, "because Nina wanted only sex and I wanted something more. Nina couldn't understand that and couldn't reconcile herself with the fact that I no longer wanted to be with her. Our relationship was very intense and stormy, actually with a lot of violence, and it also ended in a fight (*bitka*)". (Eva). Eva's words indicate that she and Nina were enjoying sex not only outside the surrounding heteronormativity, but literally out in the streets. In addition, her candid confession of the violence present in their relationship resonates with scholarship that argues that contraty to stereotypes that lesbian relationships are devoid of domestic violence, same-sex partnersthips are not immune to it. Regardless of the gender and sexual identities of the partners, all relationships may need to negotiate power dynamics, personal ambitions, unhealthy egos, insecurities or jealousy.[353]

Eva and Nina's story also reveals that despite the restrictive context of criminalized "public indignity" of homosexual sexual encounters during the Socialist era, punishable by prison sentences, some people were not deterred by it. While some historians interpret the presence of anti-homosexual legislation as automatic evidence of the lack of public sexual behavior, Eva's and Tamara's experiences indicate that not all queer people were deterred by police attention but rather accepted it as a part of the "normality" of the authoritarian state.

> Oh yes, they [the police] were bugging us when they caught us, once they even took us to the station but very soon they let us go again. It was a nuisance but never anything really serious. After all, everyone was under the watchful eye of the police — that was just reality, it didn't matter if you were queer (*teplej*) or not. (Eva)

Quite remarkably, Eva herself articulated that homosexuality was only one "otherness" in a long list of diverse undesired identities and suspicious types of behavior during Czechoslovak socialism. Moreover, she felt that

---

353 Janice Ristock, *No More Secrets: Violence in Lesbian Relationships* (New York, NY: Routledge Press, 2002); Claire Renzetti and Charles Harvey Miley, eds., *Violence in Gay and Lesbian Domestic Partnerships* (New York: Harrington Park Press, 1996).

because 'everyone' was scrutinized by the Communist state, in the end one's sexual orientation was not even that important.

An important twist in Eva's life happened in 1980, after breaking up with Nina. Through placing a personal ad in the daily newspaper *Lidová demokracie* Eva met her "most significant lover before 1989," a chemical engineer Helen. Helen was her "femme fatale" and they had a wonderful, loving, beautiful relationship "full of love and sex" that lasted close to five years. They lived together, Helen "looked all day long into the microscope" and Eva painted. In their free time, they visited exhibitions, art shows, and walked the two German shepherd dogs that Helen brought into the relationship. The only problem was that Helen did not believe in God, which, over time, proved an insurmountable problem for Eva, who was deeply religious. In 1984, Eva secretly joined the Jehovah's Witnesses and decided to leave Helen because she "felt it was more important to get closer to God." Even though retrospectively she concluded that she "gave up too much" and deeply regretted the decision to break up with Helen over the issue of religion, Eva's participation in the community of Jehovah's Witnesses was short-lived.

> I felt inseparable from the community of Jehovah's Witnesses. All the time I heard that one day I will also find a brother, whom I will marry and have children with. But I didn't need a man and I certainly didn't want any children. Nobody there knew about my sexual orientation... After a few years, I finally decided to leave them for good. The one thing I could not stand was their absolute insistence that all women must wear long skirts and only skirts. I never wore skirts before and I hated skirts. I could bear the talk about my marriage and kids and all that but I couldn't stand the skirt. I fought with it inside myself for a few years but finally I couldn't do it anymore. (Eva)

Eva's dramatic personal story provides an invaluable glimpse into negotiating strategies and decision-making processes of someone, whose sexual and religious dimensions of her identity were both disapproved of by the Communist state. Her narrative unravels a life full of unanticipated details and turns, but most importantly it exposes how unexpected and surprising the moments can be when the proverbial glass gets too full and spills over. After a while, Eva's inner belief in God became an obstacle and limit for her ability to live out her queer identity. Deliberately, she decided to end a satisfying, loving relationship with another woman, which certainly was not an easy relationship to find in Socialist Czechoslovakia. On the other hand, Eva was able to gradually withstand the pressures for gender conformity and refused to submit to a rigidly enforced feminine dress code in her clandestine religious community. But that does not mean that it could not have worked the other way around. Both her same-sex relationship and wearing pants were wrong in the eyes of her religious community because they both violated what was conceived as proper womanhood. Instead of breaking up with Helen, Eva could just as likely have concluded that it was okay to wear a skirt because it effectively protected her relationship with a woman, which was more important for her sense of identity and personal well-being than wearing pants.[354]

During the Communist period, restrictions took many forms. Other forces besides homosexuality, such as religion, or cultural and political activities, for example, posed insurmountable dilemmas and barriers in the personal decisions and actions of many people. The lack of open public debate about either religion or sexuality meant that everyone had to struggle with these challenges in very individual ways. Paradoxically, despite its emphasis on collectivism, Communist restrictions led to massive individualization and the atomization of society. Surprisingly, however, when asked what the end of the Communist regime meant for her, Eva resolutely denied that it had any significant impact on her life. "1989 meant absolutely nothing to me. It didn't change my life at all. Much more important for me was breaking up with Helen." Eva's story and her reluctance to interpret the Velvet Revolution as a great moment in her life, resonates with an important point of theorist Jiřina Šmejkalová, who argued that "women's narratives from the era of socialism perhaps most obviously break the myths of a direct relationship between the 'totalitarian' regime and the 'discrimination' of women" that is often disseminated in 'Western' publications about 'Eastern' women.[355]

SAME-SEX PERSONAL ADS – READING BETWEEN THE LINES

The ability to place same-sex personal ads on the pages of censored Socialist newspapers and magazines seems to be a matter of historical controversy. Fanel and Janošová broadly assert that because of censorship, it was not possible to place same-sex personal ads in the state media during the Socialist period. Janošová even adds that "editors-in-chief and their deputies faced punishment for doing so."[356] However, neither of them cites any reliable sources or evidence for such an assertion. Rather, it seems that their argument is an expected conclusion built on their general interpretation of

---

354 From a more general gendered perspective, it is also interesting how obvious the choice of pants became for women in the atheist socialist society. Until the late 1960s, women in Czechoslovakia wore predominantly skirts, both to work and in leisure times, and girls were required to wear skirts to school. Women and girls in Czechoslovakia started to wear pants only as part of the "unisex" fashion which came to the country from the West in the culturally relaxed late-1960s. (I am grateful to Hana Havelková for this insight).

355 Jiřina Šmejkalová, "Zpráva o knihách zapomnění," *Aspekt* 1/1999, 193.

356 Fanel 2000; Janošová 2000, 48.

the Socialist period in Czechoslovakia as 'repressive for gay culture.' While sharing their view of the general difficulty to place same-sex personal ads during state socialism, Seidl nonetheless concedes that based on the "memory of the homosexual subculture" it seems that such prohibition did not concern the whole country and that "in Brno or Ústí nad Labem, for example, newspapers *Lidová demokracie* and *Průboj* published same-sex ads."[357] He still asserts, however, that "in Prague it was not possible." Seidl draws this conclusion from "several interviews with eyewitnesses," as well as from two short opinion pieces, entitled "…How about Ads?" and "I'm Looking for a Partner," published in 1989 in *Lambda* magazine. Moreover, Seidl argues, permission to legally place same-sex personal ads in newspapers and magazines was one of the first concrete goals of the newly emerged homosexual movement in 1989.[358] Like with many other issues in the history of (homo)sexuality, however, this argument holds only when applied to and based on the memories and experiences of gay men.

Women's memories, as well as official statements from the publishing houses and relevant state institutions, offer a different picture of the existence of same-sex ads in the Socialist media. According to all the female narrators, personal same-sex ads placed in selected newspapers and magazines were one of the most important and common ways to meet other women during the Socialist period. The narrators mentioned that the daily or weekly periodicals *Lidová demokracie, Ahoj na sobotu, Svobodné slovo, Vlasta, Mladá fronta* and *Mladý svět* all accepted same-sex ads in their personal classifieds sections since the late 1960s. Procházka supports their recollections, arguing that "of course there were never any *Male Seeking Male* and *Female Seeking Female* sections but during the 1960s and 1970s certain newspapers accepted such ads into the *Miscellaneous* section."[359] During her interview, Soňa supported Procházka's claim about the presence of explicitly open same-sex ads during this time. She recounted that in 1969, when she lived for almost a year in Vienna after the Soviet invasion in 1968 (she returned back to Czechoslovakia in the summer of 1969, thus receiving amnesty for her emigration), "My mother regularly sent me some magazines there, and also *Mladý svět*, which had personal ads in it. There was a female-seeking-female ad so I answered it" (Soňa). Upon her return to Prague in summer 1969, she went on a date from this ad and that was how she found her way into the world of Prague's queer community, meeting in the Šroubek restaurant in Hotel Evropa.

There is no simple "yes or no" answer to the question of the existence of same-sex personal ads in the Socialist media but it is evident that narrators in

---

357 Seidl 2012, 311.
358 Ibid.
359 Procházka 1997.

different oral history projects varied in their success in placing same-sex ads during state socialism. Some narrators were rejected and told, when trying to place their ad, that "we don't publish such ads," while others managed to place their personal ads without problems, even in the very same times. For example, Dana claimed that "in 1986 and 1987, I was still reading those ads and occasionally even placed one, but without much response." On the other hand, Josef's effort to place a same-sex ad in *Svobodné slovo* in December 1985 failed. His ensuing complaint to the highest state authorities about the newspaper's rejection of his same-sex ad, which resulted in Josef's year-and-half long correspondence with the *Czech and Federal Offices for Press and Information (ČÚTI and FÚTI)*, is fascinating and merits separate attention, especially in the context of an individual's negotiations with state power during the late Socialist period. The unexpected story of the open confrontation between Josef and the state supervisory organs about his same-sex ad is discussed in detail in the last chapter.

When studying personal ads as an important aspect of queer subjectivity during state socialism, several important points should be considered. First, the Communist regime did not allow personal ads in the printed media in all years of its rule but, perhaps surprisingly, this was true for heterosexual personal ads as well. Throughout the Communist period, the state applied varying degrees of censorship and control over its printed media, which changed significantly from era to era. More to the point, the degree of control and censorship in media was not based on and related to sexuality but rather to the changing political constellations. Immediately after the accession to power in 1948, the Communist leadership issued a prohibition of all personal ads, which were seen as vestiges of bourgeois society. This ban was lifted only in 1964, most likely because Stalinist emphasis on heavy industry and sex segregation in certain professions gradually made searching for life partners in some regions of the country unreasonably difficult for young people.[360]

Second, there were only several periodicals, well-known among queer people, which accepted same-sex ads. Moreover, as both Procházka and the narrators themselves indicated, the same-sex ads could not be worded as explicitly seeking same-sex relationships. If one tried to place a same-sex ad without this knowledge in some different paper, the attempt was unlikely to succeed. And third, even in magazines and newspapers that accepted covert same-sex ads, success of placing such ads often depended on the personal attitudes of editors-in-chief and other journalists working in the given media.

---

360 Karel Kaplan, *O cenzuře v Československu v letech 1945-1956* (Praha: Ústav soudobých dějin, 1994); Jana Hoffmannová, "Seznamovací inzeráty mladých lidí." *Naše řeč* 68 (1985): 113–124; Josef Staněk, Zn. *"Jen Upřímně a vážně." Hierarchie hodnot v seznamovacím inzerátu* (Praha: Mladá fronta, 1977).

Even though censorship was one of the most centralized and powerful dimensions of authoritarian state control, its everyday practice rested in the hands of individual workers and their willingness and ability to apply it.[361]

There is an interesting paradox when it comes to same-sex ads during the Socialist period. Since homosexuality was officially considered a medical diagnosis listed among sexual disorders, logically the state printed media were not officially supporting and promoting same-sex ads; at the same time, since homosexuality was considered a medical diagnosis and not a legitimate social identity, there was no need for explicit prohibition of same-sex ads either. Before 1989, only once, in November 1985, was there a written central command, issued by the *ČÚTI* and *FÚTI*, not to publish same-sex personal ads — this was connected to a Prague murder case and explained by *ČÚTI* as a security issue.[362] This directive, issued in a very particular context and time, however, does not serve as evidence for arguments about a same-sex ban in other time periods.

This flexible terrain, as queer women narrators shared, provided a potential for creative ways to formulate same-sex ads and then submit them in a variety of formats in certain papers. The final placement of same-sex ads depended on the openness and willingness of individual editors to publish such ads, usually prepared skillfully by those who placed them. It is not surprising then that different individuals, living in the same time period and even the same city, had different experiences with their attempts to place same-sex ads during Czechoslovak socialism. While some queer people recalled that their same-sex ad "wasn't accepted anywhere, nor did I ever get a proper explanation from anyone why it was so, not even when I personally came to the editor's office,"[363] other queer narrators insisted that placing a same-sex ad during socialism was not a problem.

In the 1960s, I regularly read *Mladý Svět* because it was full of such ads. I don't know why it was possible but I always found some and sometimes even answered… I don't know about men's ads, didn't see those, I only looked for girls' ads. (Heda)

I never read much, but one exception was *Mladý Svět*. I didn't have much money but every Thursday, it was published on Thursday, I ran to the newspaper stand to get the new issue. The personals section was the first thing I read, looking for something interesting. You could always tell when it was one of 'our' ads. (Ludmila)

---

361 Oates-Indruchová 2020. Her book provides an excellent account of the diverse application of censorship and surveillance in the comparative context of Czechoslovak and Hungarian social sciences and humanities.

362 Schindler 2013, 24. The context of the central command to ban same-sex ads, issued by *ČÚTI a FÚTI* on November 19, 1985, is discussed in detail in the last chapter, along with Josef's case.

363 "Hledám partnera…," *Lambda* 1/4 (1989): 8–9. (Cited in Seidl 2012, 311).

Sometimes, covert same-sex ads appeared directly among heterosexual personal ads, most commonly disguised as ads looking for friendship, or pals for hiking in nature or theater visits. Zuzana argued that queer people could recognize 'their ads' without much trouble, even though the ads were written in ways as to not raise any suspicions. The success of such an endeavor depended on the creativity of those who placed the ads, as well as on the perception of those who read them.

In those times, it was impossible to get to know someone in normal ways. Fortunately, girls always found me, I didn't need ads. But I know how it went because I read them. The most common way was "language teaching." [364] Get it? 'I will teach a female friend a tongue.' [laughing]. Such ads were written in ways that you always knew that's 'ours.' Teaching a "tongue." German, not English, that was already suspicious, but the GDR was ok so German was totally fine. Languages, those were completely unambiguous. I don't know anyone who would have problems placing such an ad and I know it was common. We joked about it even long after the revolution. Even in bars when the commies were long gone it was one of the famous meeting lines, 'How is your knowledge of languages?' 'Want to learn a new tongue?'[365] [laughing]... And then, also 'spend a vacation together.' That was another favorite. I am looking for a female friend to spend the summer vacation together (*hledám kamarádku pro společně strávenou dovolenou*). (Zuzana)

Oh, yeah, ads. Of course I did that. 'I'm looking for a female friend to enjoy cultural experiences together' (*Hledám přítelkyni pro společné sdílení kulturních zážitků*), that was usually what I used and also looked for. I met two of my long-term girlfriends that way. I know that a lot of people say that it was a taboo but I don't know, we met this way and also regularly read the paper together just for fun to see what's there. (Olina)

These recollections provide valuable testimonies about queer women's ability to move within the constraints of presumed censorship during the Socialist times. They also testify to the creativity and cunning of the women, who placed such ads. It is interesting that while men, mentioned in the works of Seidl, Schindler and Miřácký, complained about their inability to place same-sex ads in the state-controlled papers, queer women simply went around and through these hurdles by subverting the meanings of other phrases and formulations, commonly used in standard (heterosexual)

---

364 In the Czech language, the phrase "teaching language" (*učit jazyk*) has a double meaning because Czech has only one term for both "language" and "tongue." "Teaching tongue," which is expressed identically as "teaching language," then gains a covert sexual meaning. It makes sense that an ad, in which a woman offered "I will teach tongue" (*naučím jazyk*), was understood differently by queer and heterosexual readers.
365 The closest English joke to these phrases would be: "How cunning a linguist are you?"

ads. Moreover, queer women used rhetoric that would be hard to censor as problematic from an ideological point of view, such as "sharing cultural experiences" (*sdílení kulturních zážitků*), which was completely verbally compliant with the regime's proclaimed goal of "building a Socialist society." The queer women narrators did not interpret the necessity of carefully reading between the lines, which searching for same-sex ads required, as a nuisance or hardship but as additional fun and adventure, one shared only by a virtual community of the privy ones.

Clearly, the ads created and placed by queer women in state-controlled papers during Socialist times simultaneously were and were not "same-sex" ads. While many of such ads probably escaped editors' attention because the editors were not able to read the codes or would not even suspect that the ads contained some subversive coding, it does not follow that the editors were only dupes who would never understand or speculate over the covert meaning of such ads. Some likely knew but for a variety of reasons took the opportunity and exercised their individual agency to help and support queer people's ability to meet each other through same-sex ads. Moreover, since all narrators worked in a variety of jobs without ever revealing their sexual identities, it is quite possible that some editors were queer themselves and forwarded such ads through the print machines with a sense of satisfaction and pleasure. Especially since some narrators said that they used coded language, which could be considered borderline:

> All ads had a "sign" (*značka*)[366] at the end. A very common sign in our ads was "Sign: *Well of Loneliness* (*Značka: Studna osamění*)." Even for gay ads. (Standa)

> Mentioning the *Well of Loneliness* was frequent. It could be a "sign" [at the end] or somehow worked into the text of the ad. But you know these ads were quite short so you had to think it through carefully... So I always enjoyed looking for how other girls went about it. I remember one, for example, that said something like 'In the well there is wisdom, but a lonely person cannot discover it' (*ve studni je moudrost, ale osamocen ji člověk neobjeví*) or something like that. I remember thinking that it was really clever and wanted to meet that girl but I had my partner at that time and read it only for fun. (Zuzana)

Mentioning the *Well of Loneliness* as one of the code words in same-sex personal ads is remarkable precisely because many female narrators

---

366 *Značka*, placed at the end of all ads under the abbreviation "Zn." was a word or phrase, which summarized the most important point of the ad or emphasized, what was considered the most important aspect from the point of view of the person, who was placing the ad. Frequent "signs" in personal adds were "Zn. serious only," "Zn. kindred soul," "Zn. weekends," etc.

mentioned this book as one of the most important reference points while searching for their own queer identities. The lesbian classic thus functioned on several different levels, in both individual and collective senses: as a real story, a narrative of queer growing up and sexual maturing, as well as code language in virtual meeting spaces. The narrators' recollections also convey a sense of a mutually shared virtual community and collective conscious-ness among queer women who participated in the process of placing and reading the covert same-sex ads. Even if the women did not answer the ads or did not act upon them in any practical way, the simple act of reading and feeling a sense of participation contributed to a sense of shared queer community. The narratives suggest that it was comforting and formative to have such space, even if only imaginary, because it enabled queer wom-en to know that there were other women as well, who loved and desired other women.

At the same time, being able to decode the intended meaning between the lines of the ads did not require only knowledge of the codes and creativity of those placing the ads, but also the same knowledge and perceptive skills of those who read the ads. And the two sides did not always meet.

In 1980 I met another musician, whom I went to visit in Havlíčkův Brod, where she lived. I placed an ad in *Lidová demokracie*, I was looking for a 'kindred soul' (*hledala jsem 'spřízněnou duši'*). My ad was answered by six women, from those I chose two whom I felt were interesting, and replied to them. In those days, everything went by regu-lar snail mail, no cell phones, no internet. Not even a phone. So we exchanged a few letters... The woman from Brod was an amateur pianist, she had a real grand piano, which was cool, and so I started to go there [to Brod], played her piano and drank. She cooked for me. She was quite fat, had heavy diabetes, and was alone. I think that she was most probably heterosexual (*myslím, že byla nejspíš heterosexuální*) and genuinely was looking for a friendship. (Vlasta)

While Vlasta was looking for a "lesbian lover," as she herself said in the interview, obviously she was not able to satisfactorily decode and interpret the replies. Her account also suggests that the real intentions of her same-sex ad were unspoken even in the private mail correspondence between the two women and were not discussed even once they met outside of the supervisory eye of the media/post and started their relationship. Remarkably, even after having about a year-long intimate relationship with this woman, Vlasta still was not sure whether her girlfriend was heterosexual or queer. Vlasta ex-plained that "we were intimate but never really talked about it. I don't know what she thought or didn't think. All I know is that I felt rather sorry for her and that it was no love affair." Clearly, the intended meaning and reading of the ad that brought these two women together was never discussed between them. Strikingly, Vlasta concluded from this that since she never fell in love with the woman herself and since they apparently never openly talked about their sexual identities, this must have meant that her girlfriend was "most probably heterosexual."

Of course, we don't know anything about the other woman's sexual self-understanding or her interpretation of her relationship with Vlasta, but this story is a good reminder of the ambiguities of sexual identities and the dangers of trying to assign clear hetero-homo qualities to queer relationships during Czechoslovak socialism. Once again, it echoes the important question that historian Leila Rupp asked about her own aunt: do we have the right to call 'lesbian' (or 'heterosexual' for that matter) women who do not see themselves in these categories?[367] What do we gain by pushing such women (or men) into a clear-cut and pre-fabricated category of 'homosexual'? Does it help us to better understand the past? We should be careful not to settle for a comforting illusion that by categorizing women, their identities and behavior into definite categories, we have mastered some certainty and finally know what 'really' happened. The deeper one moves into the source materials, the more elusive some clear-cut 'lesbian history' of Communist Czechoslovakia becomes.

QUEER FAMILY CONSTELLATIONS

As was discussed in the third chapter, from a sexological point of view, homosexuality (and transsexuality), and marriage were quite compatible during state socialism. Marriage of homosexuals and transsexuals, when open and consented to by their (presumably heterosexual) partners, was even considered by the sexologists to be one of the best methods for "adjusting" homosexuals and transsexuals to responsible and normative Socialist intimate behavior. As sexologists explained, the point was not to "cure" homosexuals and transsexuals out of their "sexual disorders." Rather, through their responsibility towards their husbands and wives, family and children, the goal was to help them to be monogamous, responsible, proper, and orderly citizens contributing to the building of the Socialist society. In other words, if transsexual and homosexual individuals agreed to outwardly follow the rules by playing the façade of an orderly heterosexual couple and family, they were encouraged by the state to do so and no one really seemed to care much what kinds of gender and sexual identities people took on and performed in the privacy of their homes. According to sexological writings, in such family constellations both sexologists and queer people together agreed that it was

---

367 Rupp 1999, 9.

in everyone's best interest if the queer people simply performed heterosexuality and did not disclose or discuss the inner workings of such relationships.[368] That, however, presumed a partnership (and marriage), in which one partner was heterosexual. Otherwise, sexologists argued that a "marriage of two homosexual persons is a wholly different matter" and neither approved nor discussed the point of such unions.[369]

Early post-Socialist accounts of homosexuality in Czechoslovakia during the Socialist period did not anticipate or integrate the notions of intent and consent into their argumentation. Instead, the institution of marriage was interpreted by these authors as a repressive tool used by the 'Communist regime' to persecute homosexuals. They acknowledged that "marriage was quite common among homosexuals" during state socialism, but they categorized 'gays and lesbians' married before 1989 as 'victims' of an oppressive regime that forced them to both marry and suppress their 'true' sexual identities. Married queer people were treated by these historians as either passive and ignorant of their own sexuality, or as conformist participants in some higher 'system,' in which they had no choice. Either they had no clue about their homosexuality, which manifested itself only later on in their lives, or, if they were aware of the fact that they were 'gay' (or 'lesbian'), they must have been forced into the marital unions against their will. [370] In these accounts, sexual identity was approached in simple binary and essentialist terms to narrate the following fairy tale: a person is *either* heterosexual *or* homosexual; not knowing *yet* about one's homosexuality means that a person is *truly, innately* homosexual and only lacks the external knowledge in order to realize it; that revelation was *en masse* provided by the collapse of the Communist regime in 1989, and ever since, 'gays and lesbians' do not marry 'heterosexuals' anymore against their will.

Sexual identity, however, is unstable, flexible, and complex. And so were the negotiations of queer family constellations in the context of Communist power. Since most of the queer women narrators shared that they were also married during the Communist period, I was curious what their reasons for marriage were and in what kinds of family constellations they lived their lives. What became immediately apparent and challenged previous historical interpretations of 'homosexual' marriages during state socialism, was the degree of conscious decision-making and active planning that went into those acts of marriage. Whether they took place in the 1950s or 1980s, many narrators articulated remarkable marriage stories. Contrary to arguments about their passivity or ignorance, many women narrators married with

---

368 Šípová 1980; Myšková and Mocek 1980; Brzek and Šípová 1979.
369 Brzek 1981, 18.
370 Fanel 2000; Seidl 2012; Miřácký 2009; Janošová 2000.

a full knowledge of their queer identity, as well as with a clear motive and strategy.

I got married to a mathematician in 1952 to make my mom happy. He was completely madly in love with me so I said, Ok, why not. He was an intellectual from university circles like me, so we had a lot in common. We didn't have any sexual contact before the marriage and when we tried to sleep together on our wedding night, it was a fiasco. He was trying some heterosexual mating rituals on me but it just seemed terribly funny to me, so I kept laughing and laughing. You know, as I told you, I always felt more like a guy myself and so it seemed utterly ridiculous to me that he was approaching me like a woman. It felt really awkward and strange to me that basically two men were trying to have sex together and so it didn't really work... Nonetheless, we had a fine marriage for a few years, my mom was really happy about it and kept saying, What a bummer that grandma didn't live to see it. (Heda)

Heda divorced her husband in 1954 and ever since lived in 'lesbian' relationships with other women until her death in 2012 at the age of 83. Clearly, already when marrying her husband, she was quite sure that she was not heterosexual. During the interview, Heda identified herself quite openly as a 'lesbian' but also argued that since early childhood she feels much more "transsexual" than anything else. Her identity could be simplified as 'butch lesbian' but that is not how she saw herself. More importantly, Heda's choice to get married had a clear purpose and strategy, "to make [her] mom happy." The marriage both provided camouflage and facilitated a sense of proper social belonging. Heda performed heterosexuality for her mother, for her husband and for society, with a clear understanding that it was just that, a performance. Rather than hiding herself, Heda's priority seemed to be to satisfy her mother and demonstrate that her social upbringing towards being a "proper lady," which her grandma used to be so fervent about during her childhood and adolescence, worked. Dana articulated similar reasons and concerns, when talking about her marriage:

I've known that I am into girls since I was about seventeen or so. There was no information around, it wasn't like you could get on the internet and browse a million pages... I felt that men were not as attractive for me as women were. Still, I started to date men and I have to say it wasn't totally unpleasant. I dated one for about a year and a half and then he asked me if I wanted to get married. So I thought about it and then decided, why not? My parents, especially my mom, kept saying all the time how every woman gets married, you can't stay single, etc... Two years after we got married we got divorced but that was mainly because we were just too different and started to argue about silly things. And also, I did not want to get pregnant with him so I thought it's time to get out... My parents were satisfied because I was divorced and not single. My mom always said that no one cares whether the marriage lasts but being single is what makes people's talk. I think that she cared most about her own reputation because she suspected I was into women so I pleased her and everything was fine. (Dana)

Like Heda, Dana knew very well that she was not heterosexual when she decided to get married. And similarly, she seems to have done it much more for her parents and surroundings than for herself. She says that heterosexual dating wasn't "totally unpleasant," which however can be read that it was not all that pleasant either. It is also quite interesting that despite understanding her identity as 'being into girls,' Dana interpreted her marital conflicts as not being primarily connected to the question of sexual orientation. 'Being different' from her husband and arguing "about silly things" in her narrative did not equate with being different in their sexual preferences but rather as having different interests and worldviews: "I was much more interested in an active lifestyle than he was. On the weekend, I wanted to go biking or hiking, I was really into cross country skiing. When the river would freeze over I would immediately take out my ice skates. Gradually, he got lazier and lazier, preferring to just be." While not being opposed to having children, Dana did not "want to get pregnant with him." She regreted not having any children but saw that as "bad decision making" (*špatné rozhodování*) during her adult life rather than a consequence of being a 'lesbian.'

In Heda's and Dana's narratives, marriage fulfills yet another important function. Clearly, marriage was a desired status not only for camouflaging purposes. Even for heterosexuals, being married increased their social status, not only for the sake of material benefits but also in a purely symbolic sense. Marriage, as an essential constitutive element of the family was highly regarded by Communist ideology. As a privileged form of union it functioned as a building block of the heteronormative order, giving one prestige, maturity, *gravitas*, and refuge — a concept frequently mentioned in connection with the Socialist family.[371] At the same time, divorce was common during Socialist times and did not carry social stigma, which resonates in the remarkably frivolous responses of both Heda and Dana to the marriage proposals by their partners: "I said, ok, why not" (Heda) and "So I thought about it and then decided, why not?" (Dana).

Getting married had an additional benefit for women; they finally became *women* even in the linguistic sense. Unlike men, who qualified to the title "sir" or "Mr." (*pan*) by simply growing up and becoming an adult, women were addressed as "Miss" (*slečna*) until they got married. Only through marriage did they earn the social right to be addressed as "Mrs." (*paní*). Addressing an adult, mature or even older woman as "miss" was humiliating,

---

371 Einhorn 1983; Heitlinger 1979.

often carrying the pejorative connotation of "old maid." Unfortunately, as the title *paní* depended solely on a woman's marital status and not her age, level of education or professional position, it was difficult to acquire that form of address in ways other than getting married (not only in formal social and professional settings but also in personal forms and other identification materials). As a social symbol and symbolic act, marriage was an important marker of proper and expected gender positioning within broader society. Dana's mother was right. From a social point of view, regardless of one's sexual orientation or gender identity, her daughter was far better off divorced than single.

For many queer people, marriage functioned as a convenient camouflage for a variety of reasons. To please one's parents or to hide one's sexual orientation are not surprising but rather expected motivations. To help a friend to emigrate to the West, or to get an apartment, which was an item in short supply during state socialism, were much more creative ways to utilize the institution of marriage.

I got married because my husband needed to be married in order to get a visa to travel to West Germany so that he could emigrate. He was gay and I knew about the plan all along, since I myself was terribly in love with one beautiful woman, unfortunately a married one, with a little daughter. So it made a lot of sense for both of us... He got some invitation to West Germany but in order to get the visa, he needed to be married. As for me, after he left, I would get the apartment, which was a terrible hole in the Lesser Town (*Malá Strana*), a horrible place but at least something to be in. I really needed the apartment so that my girlfriend with her little daughter could move in together with me... So in July 1967, we married and already in September [of that year] he left. I think my parents knew all along that he was gay as well but they didn't dare to speak about my relationship because a year earlier they interfered in my sister's relationship and [as a result] she followed her boyfriend to West Germany forever. They [the parents] really wanted my sister to break up with her boyfriend and kept bugging her about it. So she pretended she did, he emigrated and the whole time they were secretly corresponding, and finally she followed him. My mom knew it was partially her fault because she wouldn't let her be. So she didn't want to be so nosy in my relationship. My mom apparently went to talk to some priest about my marriage, and since my husband was religious, he got the green light from the priest. So we helped each other. It was normal. (Miriam)

Miriam and her husband got married without emotional attachments for mutual profit, and with a full knowledge of their queer sexual identities. Also, they were not ignorant of their sexual and emotional desires and, obviously, tended to those feelings outside of the institutional framework. Miriam and her husband were not pressured into their marriage because they were 'homosexual' but because it was the easiest way to get around the restrictive and repressive housing and visa policies in Communist Czechoslovakia.

One of the most common ways to ensure a safe return of citizens of Socialist Czechoslovakia, who were allowed to visit non-Socialist countries, back to their home country, was the 'hostage concept.' If the travelling person was not to be unconditionally trusted, like Kamila, for example, it was standard practice to not allow the whole family to travel to the West. Instead, the family was separated and only a few family members received travel visas, so that the travelers had emotional attachments to return to.[372] In terms of state housing, it was virtually impossible for young people to be assigned apartments without being married, and being pregnant or having children helped, of course. Even then, however, it was not an automatic or easy task to find a separate living. In the absence of a commertical housing market, young families were placed on long wait lists and sometimes had to live for several years with their parents or in-laws before the state granted them the coveted apartment.[373] Miriam's marriage to her gay friend thus must be read in this context as a rational, cunning decision, which enabled both of them to side-step ideological restrictions, which were faced by all Socialist citizens regardless their sexual orientation.

Moreover, Miriam interpreted the whole situation as a reflection of the political thaw and the ensuing benevolence of the state in the late 1960s, which not only allowed her to divorce smoothly after her husband's emigration and keep the apartment, but also did not result in any further negative consequences for her, even though she had the stain of being from a "family of emigrants."

> I waited for several months to file for the divorce. First, I needed some paper from the police that he was missing. So I got that and with this missing report it was actually quite easy to get the divorce. But it really was possible only because of the sixties that nothing happened to me. When you were in a situation that your sister emigrated and a year later your husband left, too […shakes her head…], if it was the same situation as in the 1950s, when my dad went to jail for six years for something completely ridiculous, the whole family would be arrested. To have two emigrants in the family was terrible but because it was 1968, it somehow fell through the cracks… He [her husband] was defended [in the divorce hearing] *ex officio* by some older female lawyer, who thought we were married for real and so she came to me and said "Please, don't be afraid of anything that I'm going to say. I must say that I disagree with the divorce

---

372   Hamplová 2010.

373   Olga Šmídová, "Vlastnictví a kvazi-vlastnictví bytů za socialismu a jejich postsocialistická mutace," In *Původní a noví vlastníci*, edited by Anne Olivier (Praha: Cahiers du CEFRES. N° 11, 2012).

but don't worry, they'll divorce you immediately. But I represent the state so officially I must say that I am against the divorce." (Miriam)

As Miriam's story shows, in Socialist state affairs form or the façade was far more important than substance. As long as form was properly upheld, often there were no more questions asked. This trend appears repeatedly in the queer narratives in a variety of circumstances. Most important was an outward loyalty and conformity to the status quo but there was little prying under the lid of things. The narratives revealed that if queer people had their professional careers or lives turned upside down by the state, it was not because of their sexual orientation or gender identity, but due to expressing their political dissent.

Even more remarkable for queer family constellations during socialism was the development of Miriam's life after her divorce in the spring of 1968. Interestingly, besides considering the influential atmosphere of the late 1960s as being responsible for the absence of any negative consequences for the emigrations in her family, Miriam did not mention the year of 1968 as a historical milestone important either for her personal life or the history of the country. Miriam remembered the year 1968 solely through the lens of her relationship with her new girlfriend, whom she deeply loved. "We had a beautiful, loving relationship for several years," Miriam reminisced about her life in that time. She had her "dirty, little" apartment but the two women actually never lived there together. Unfortunately, Miriam's lover was married. So unlike Miriam, who simply lived a "beautiful relationship" with her, her lover lived a double life; a secret one with Miriam, and another, open one with her unsuspecting husband. In this sense, this particular extramarital affair and infidelity was not any different from any other relationship, where one partner secretly cheats on the other partner.

She [the lover] did not want to break up the family, you know, they had a little child together and so she didn't want to get a divorce. It makes sense. But honestly, I was an idiot, too. I have no idea what I thought we would do in my dirty, little hole, with her and the little child — how we would get by. Well, if we could get some nice, big apartment, that would be a different story! But there? (Miriam)

Interestingly, Miriam's grievances about their inability to live together were not about two queer women living in restrictive political regime, but about the insufficient quality of Miriam's apartment that was too small and not suitable for two adults and a child. Otherwise, Miriam believed that

two women living together was ok — that was no problem. My aunt was fine living all her life openly with her girlfriend at Kampa. And her girlfriend was also totally obvious at first sight, she was really the totally male-type in all respects. And they were just fine (*byly úplně v pohodě*). Men, though, had it much worse. Because two women kissing on the street and living together, who cares. But two men, well, let's face it, that's weird. (Miriam)

According to Miriam, during state socialism men were under much more scrutiny than women when it came to personal intimacy in the public, which is more connected to deep-seated gender stereotypes than to sexual orientation alone. In her own words, however, Miriam herself never felt persecuted for her sexual identity. During both interviews, she vehemently resisted being assigned any clear identity labels. Not a single time did she use the term lesbian to identify herself. She was married twice and "loved" both of her husbands, with whom she lived together in shared apartments. She had several long-term relationships with women, from a few to eleven years, with whom she was "deeply in love," at the same time, she was never able to live with any of them in one apartment. During our interviews, conducted in her home, she proudly showed me the Colour Planet Award for outstanding contributions to the LGBT movement, which she received in a public ceremony in 2009. For over a decade, she was the vice-chairman of the first 'homosexual' organization in Czechoslovakia after 1989 and the "representative of Czech lesbians" in it. But in her narrative, she refused to stuff herself into any explicit category — during the Communist regime or after its collapse.

With my girlfriend, we never thought in any categories. We just loved each other. I was 22 or 23 and I was not thinking at all about what it means [to be with a man or a woman]. I never did. I don't care... And I'm not into any categories or labels now either. (Miriam)

Miriam's reluctance to articulate a clear identity for herself illustrates once again the complexities of working with queer narratives. What does it mean to "love" someone? If people do not identify with certain categories, can we still use them to interpret their lives? If the surrounding society or state institutions, like the women themselves, do not perceive two women living together as "lesbians," can we write about "lesbian history"?

During socialism, the contents and official meanings of social identities were defined by experts, who also assigned them to various individuals and groups. Due to censored public discourse, social identities were not subject to negotiations and reinterpretions through open public debates. Normative performances were praised and rewarded; transgressive performances, which were perceived as threatening to the social and political order of the Socialist state, were subject to expert scrutiny.[374] In terms of gender and sexuality, by presenting the definitions of womanhood, manhood, heterosexuality and homosexuality as given and self-evident, and by suppressing open discussions about them, the state did not provide opportunities to see and interpret gender and sexual identites as complex and ambiguous. The public discourse on gender and sexuality during the Socialist period lacked the ability to both name and go beyond the obvious normative expectations. It then became relatively easy, as many queer women recalled, to mask their actually-lived lives and identities behind those expectations, preventing any further scrutiny. As, for example, Kamila narrated her life, shared with her girlfriend and "their son" (as Kamila explicitly called him), in the early 1980s.

We lived together for several years, in one apartment, with the son of my girlfriend, who was five at the time. We never had any problems, either with our neighbors or our families. Well, I didn't have a family anymore but my girlfriend's family knew and accepted that she lived with her female friend. Problems started when Luke went to school and he apparently kept enthusiastically talking about me at school. He kept saying, "We did this with Kamila," and "Kamila fixed this at home," and "Mom and Kamila did this and that," and "Kamila took me here and there." He also talked about his father, who regularly took him every other weekend... So one day the director of the school called us both in to explain the situation. My girlfriend got all upset and defensive, but I told her, just calm down, what can they do? And so we went. The director said that Luke is talking about me and they don't understand what's going on, that it's confusing and asked who I was. So I said that I am just a friend, living with them and helping since the father is around only on the weekends, and asked in turn, whether there is anything wrong with that. The boy is well-fed, well-dressed, performs well academically, is happy, so is there any problem? I asked. And, of course, she said, No, of course there is no problem. What else could she say? It was unimaginable [during socialism] that anyone would ask directly if we were lesbians. Impossible! I was not afraid of this question a single bit. Who would dare to ask? And in what words?... But, of course, they sent the child welfare office to us. They (*sociálka*) came several times, checked the usual stuff, if Luke has his own room, if the place is clean, if we have enough food in the fridge and off they went. They came maybe four times and it was over. After that, no one bothered us anymore. (Kamila)

This remarkable story shows that, at least in some cases, it was possible for queer women to live a 'lesbian' relationship in one household before 1989, even together with a small child. Again, as long as the sexual nature of the relationship was denied, or at least not named. Kamila's story exhibits an interesting mixture of openness and deceit. On the one hand, it was obvious

---

374 Havelková and Oates-Indruchová, eds., 2014; Bren 2010.

to the relatives, neighbors, and the school that the two women lived together and that they raised the child together. Kamila, her girlfriend, and their son apparently functioned outside together as a family — for example they spent summer and winter vacations in state resorts together as a family. In other words, it was the two women and the child that formed and represented the family unit, while the father stood aside from the family, taking his son only every other weekend. For understanding the way in which the state and the social atmosphere of the times made it possible or impossible for queer people to live their lives, it is important that Kamila recollected her same-sex family life at that time as relatively easy and non-problematic. Contrary to our largely intuitive pressumption that it was 'impossible' for 'gays and lesbians' to breathe and live in the ways they desired during the Communist regime, we see here detailed and concrete evidence that, at least for some queer people, it was possible. Moreover, Kamila remembers her family life with her girlfriend without bitterness or sense of persecution.

A crucial dimension of any queer family experience, however, seemed to be the degree of openness and explicit naming of such family constellations. All women narrators agreed that it was the naming that was taboo, not the actual behavior and living. The prohibition of naming seemed to rest on two intertwined factors: on the one hand, the unwillingness of the Socialist state to admit or even discuss that, despite the heavy endorsement and heteronormative indoctrination of 'proper' marital and family lifestyle, queer family constellations do exist; and on the other hand, latent, unexamined homophobia of the state structures and society at large, which survived in a variety of forms into the post-Socialist period. At the same time, this is not a trend that would be specific only to Communist societies in Eastern Europe. To the contrary, the same processes have been described by historians of sexuality in the 'free' West as well. Despite the absence of a Communist dictatorship, in the post-WWII period queer people in the United States, Canada, Great Britain, France, or West Germany also did not live completely open 'gay' and 'lesbian' relationships, especially with small children. Such developments came only very gradually and were closely tied to the visibility and emancipation of the LGBT movements in the West.[375]

The gradual existence of an outspoken and successful gay and lesbian movement in the West since the late 1960s, however, provided completely different political and social circumstances for the everyday lives of queer people in those countries. It does not mean, that homophobia did not exist in 'free' democratic societies or that the state institutions in the West openly and enthusiastically supported gay and lesbian activities and demands. It means that if lesbian women and gay men in 'the West' wanted to live their

---

375 Sokolová and Fojtová 2013; D'Emilio and Freedman 1988; Seidman 1993; Weeks 1977.

same-sex relationships and families explicitly and openly, they had far great-er and better chances to find the opportunities to do so. Over the course of the 20th century, a variety of distinctly queer neighborhoods, communities and communes have developed spontaneously in urban areas and large cities across Western Europe, Canada and the United States, giving queer people space and conditions to develop their lives in relatively free and autonomous ways.[376] Prevented by the presence of the centrally run Communist regimes, such development did not take place during state socialism in Eastern Eu-rope. At the same time, most of the narratives showed that queer people *were able* to live their 'transgressive' lives even in the oppressive atmosphere of silence and absence. However, the point is not to marvel at the Socialist state's tolerance — it is a testament to the strength, creativity, and courage of the queer people themselves.

Kamila's story also shows that the state, in this encounter, formally rep-resented by the school and the child welfare office, did not have the leverage or perhaps even the interest to actually change anything regarding Kamila and her girlfriend's particular situation. Perhaps the director just wanted to let the women know that 'she knows' and to wait for their reaction. While we do not know if the school or child welfare office believed that the two women were just friends or suspected they also had a sexual relationship, it did not matter as the societal taboo about homosexuality worked in the women's fa-vor. Divorce was common during state socialism and the spectrum of post-di-vorce situations diverse.[377] Some women, especially those with very young children, went back to their parents after a divorce, many women stayed alone, while others found new men. Apparently, finding a female friend to help after a divorce was acceptable, too. Once again, a form proved more important than the content, and as long as the form did not challenge the heteronormative order or the political system, there was no need to suppress it. As Bren argues in the context of consumer culture, Communist power did not care about people's privacy as long as they publicly obeyed and expressed their loyalty, or at least apathy, to the regime.[378]

The complexity of the state approach to the question of same-sex re-lationships and parenting is further demonstrated in the developments of Miriam's relationship with her beloved girlfriend, who had a little daughter.

---

376 Chauncey 2008; Charles Kaiser, *The Gay Metropolis: The Landmark History of Gay Life in Ameri-ca* (New York: Grove Press, 2007); Elizabeth Lapovsky Kennedy and Madeleine D. Davis, *Boots of Leather, Slippers of Gold: The History of a Lesbian Community. 20th Anniversary Edition.* (New York and London: Routledge, 2014); Rupp 2010; Julie A. Podmore, "Gone 'Underground'? Lesbian Visibility and the Consolidation of Queer Space in Montréal," *Social & Cultural Geography*, 2006: 7/4, 595–625; Michael Sibalis, "Urban Space and Homosexuality: The Example of the Marais, Paris' "Gay Ghetto,"" *Urban Studies* 2004: 41/9, 1739–1758.

377 Dudová 2012.

378 Bren 2010.

The reason why Miriam and her girlfriend ultimately broke up was that the girlfriend's husband found out about their relationship.

> Of course she had to get divorced. Her husband found out about us, he even listened to our phone conversations. He was livid and filed for divorce, asking for the custody of his daughter. He argued that his wife cheated on him with another woman and thus she's not a good example for the girl. (Miriam)

> V.S.: What was not a good example for the girl? That she cheated on him or that she did so with a woman?

> Miriam: Well, I'm sure both. But it was probably more important that she was with another woman. I think that he felt terribly insulted and hurt by that. I told my girl-friend that she should let him have the girl because it would soon be clear that he is not capable of taking care of her, but she didn't want to hear it... But in the end she did get the child. I remember it was a big stressful lawsuit. She was defended by one of our best divorce attorneys of the time, the first wife of the famous psychiatrist, Dr. Plzák, Eliška Plzáková. And Eliška vigorously and shrewdly defended my girlfriend, arguing that a small child belongs with the mother. I think that Dr. Plzák would completely agree with that. And in the end she [the attorney] succeeded and got the child for her.

These two situations, Kamila's recollection of her encounter with the school and Miriam's description of the divorce lawsuit, provide us with extraordinary and illuminating insights into the state approach to homosexuality during the Communist period. In the two narratives of Kamila and Miriam, we step into family constellations of women who had small children and decided to live (or have sexual relations) with other women. In both cases, albeit for different reasons, the 'state' was asked to examine the situations and interfere. In Kamila's case, the child's welfare office was asked by the school to investigate Luke's family conditions because he lived in a household with two women; in Miriam's case the court was asked by the husband to give him custody of his child because the mother had an extramarital affair with another woman. In both cases, the state authorities and institutions decided or ruled in favor of the queer women. In other words, the fact that a mother of a small child lived in one household (as in Kamila's case) or had a document-ed sexual relationship (as in Miriam's girlfriend's case) with another woman was *not* a reason to take a child away from those women.

Interestingly, it was the children who were the center of attention in both of these cases; the lifestyles of the children's mothers were considered as auxiliary evidence, not the prime issues for investigation. In both cases the 'state' decided that it was not against the interest of the child and his or her moral and social development to continue to live with a mother who either has an explicit same-sex relationship or creates a functioning family (whether with sexual content or without it) with another woman. We should also note, however, that gender stereotypes played a crucial role in the divorce case. Stereotypes about a woman's alleged innate ability to take better care of a small child than a man can, as well as a man's alleged 'naturally' incompetent parenting, apparently proved more important and persuasive than allegations about the queer sexuality of the mother. Attitudes towards sexuality were anchored in attitudes towards gender during state socialism, and while heteronormativity was based on gender stereotypes, those paradoxically sometimes worked in favor of queer behavior, as was demonstrated in both of these cases, as well as in marriages of transsexual people, understood and supported by many sexologists as unproblematic 'heterosexual unions.'

QUEER SOLIDARITY

The most visible, active and outspoken current queer initiatives in the Czech Republic are Prague Pride; STUD Brno; PROUD: a platform for equality, recognition and diversity (*Platforma pro ROvnost, Uznání a Diverzitu*); and Mezipatra. They all identify with broadly defined LGBT politics of fluid and inclusionary gender and sexual identities, explicitly recognizing and supporting transgender people and projects.[379] Such development is fairly new, however, dating only to 2010. In the 1990s and the early 2000s, the newly emerged gay and lesbian political movements and the gay and lesbian cultural scenes in the Czech Republic were rather narrowly conceived and divided. Not only in terms of gay men and lesbian women, but also in terms of homo-hetero and homo-trans divides. A broadly-based and flexibly understood queer community was nonexistent then. The early post-Socialist Czech gay and lesbian movement, represented during the first two decades after the collapse of the Communist regime by SOHO (*Association of Citizens with Homosexual Orientation*) and later on by GLL (*Gay and Lesbian League*) generally perceived queer subjectivity as a problematic concept and it took time before queer collective

---

379 PROUD explicitly refuses to identify with 'gay' or 'lesbian' identity politics and adopts rather an emancipatory concept of sexual identity (Seidman, Steven. "Identity and Politics in a Postmodern Gay Culture: Some Historical and Conceptual Notes." In *Fear of a Queer Planet: Queer Politics and Social Theory*, edited by Michael Warner (Minneapolis: University of Minnesota Press, 1993, 110): "The fundamental basis of all PROUD's activities is the belief that people are free and equal, in both dignity and rights, without any differences. The association's vision is of a Czech society in which sexual orientation and identity are not crucial factors in determining the quality of human life." (www.proudem.cz)

organizing in the Czech Republic acquired its current inclusionary and flexible character.[380]

Most Czech scholars, including historians, writing in the 1990s and early 2000s about homosexuality in the Czech lands and Czechoslovakia before 1989, contributed to those divides by asserting a separatist view of different, distinct and mutually non-communicating 'gay' and 'lesbian' histories, explaining such characterizations as 'natural' and 'understandable.' The absence of 'lesbians' in these accounts was justified by a reasoning that since women were not a part of the "homosexual subculture" (defined as male, however), nor had they a "community" of their own, "naturally," they were not included in the narrative.[381] As a result, women were mostly missing in the historical accounts of homosexuality, not only during Czechoslovak Communist period, but in previous eras as well. When they did appear, they were relegated to separate arguments or chapters. In short, 'lesbian' women either did not exist, or, when they did, they were separated from 'gay' men. However, the ongoing queer oral history project keeps revealing that when we include different narrators, ask different questions and look in other places besides notorious cafes, bars and spas, there is a more elaborate queer world to be found. Queer men and women living through state socialism were not such strangers as some historians make us believe and, in some cases, they apparently shared a sense of solidarity together.

Early post-Socialist feminist analyses of the situation of women in Communist Eastern Europe argued that before 1989 there was absence of antagonism, competition, and hostility between (presumably heterosexual) women and men.[382] In the so-called East-West debates on the position of women in Communist Eastern Europe before 1989, Jiřina Šiklová articulated the influential thesis of "gender solidarity under Communist oppression," in which she argued that both women and men in Socialist Czechoslovakia had greater problems and priorities during the Communist era than to worry about their gender differences and animosity. She proposed that the "common enemy" of the "regime" brought women and men together as they shared together their mutual "oppression" by the Communist regime. Contrary to Western feminist claims, she argued, "Eastern" women and men rose above silly gender disputes and worked together to survive with dignity under the boot of the authoritarian regime. Šiklová based most of her argumentation on the role

---

380 Věra Sokolová and Simona Fojtová, "Strategies of Inclusion and Shifting Attitudes towards Visibility in the Gay, Lesbian, and Queer Discourse in the Czech Republic after 1989," In *Queer Visibility in Post-socialist Cultures*, eds. by Narcisz Fejes and Andrea P. Balogh (Chicago and Bristol: Intellect Books, 2013), pp. 105–129; *Analýza situace LGBT menšin v ČR* (Praha: Úřad vlády, 2007).

381 Stehlíková, Procházka and Hromada 1995; Procházka 1997; Fanel 2000; Putna and Bartlová 2011.

382 Šiklová 1994; Einhorn 1993; Alena Wagnerová, *Die Frau im Sozialismus, Beispiel ČSSR* (Hamburg: Hoffmann und Campe, 1974).

of women in dissident activities, where they performed the menial, invisible work for "their" men.[383]

Her argument was largely debunked by subsequent research, namely by the meticulous work of Hana Havelková, who challenged the solidarity thesis and convincingly argued that the relations, as well as power struggles, between men and women in Socialist Czechoslovakia were as hostile and gendered as they were in the democratic 'West.'[384] In the latest repositioning of this thesis, Kateřina Zábrodská similarly exposed the solidarity under oppression argument to be just a commonly shared myth. In her critical discourse analysis of interviews with Czech women conducted in 1994, Zábrodská identified and exposed that contrary to the common belief, Czech (heterosexual) women during socialism were actually quite unhappy with their men, acutely aware of their inferior symbolic (and real) positions and did not hesitate to articulate their negative perceptions and hostile attitudes towards their husbands and partners.[385]

Interestingly, however, queer women in the queer history oral project spontaneously narrated a similarly idealized picture of 'gay' and 'lesbian' relations and shared 'community' that Šiklová proposed about the whole society in 1990. By and large, the narrators recollected that 'homosexual' men and women knew each other and consciously worked together to help each other. The "common enemy," represented by the Communist Party for Šiklová, was the heteronormative order for these narrators. They mentioned a variety of mechanisms and strategies, in which queer women and men not only helped each other to hide their sexual orientation but also simply had a very good time together in a communal sense. This is not to deny or question the existence of the distinctly "male homosexual subculture" and spaces that Seidl, Fanel, Schindler and Miřácký document.[386] Many home parties, 'salons,' bath houses and *holandas* were designed for men only and functioned as meeting places for "gay men." As one male narrator in the queer oral history project recalled, "gay men" also managed to be creative in ways that were not

383 Jiřina Šiklová, "The Grey Zone and the Future of Dissent in Czechoslovakia." *Social Research* 57 (1990): 347–363.

384 Hana Havelková, "'Patriarchy' in Czech Society." *Hypatia*, 1993: 8(4), 89–96; Hana Havelková, "Women in and after a "Classless Society," in C. Zmroczek & P. Mahony (eds.), *Women and Social Class: International Feminist Perspectives* (London & New York: Routledge, 1999); Hana Havelková, "Abstract Citizenship? Women and Power in the Czech Republic," in A. M. Berggren & B. Hobson (eds.), *Crossing Borders: Gender and Citizenship in Transition* (Stockholm: FRN — Swedish Council for Planning and Coordination of Research, 1997).

385 Kateřina Zábrodská, "Between Femininity and Feminism: Negotiating the Identity of a 'Czech Socialist Woman' in biographical interviews." In *Proměny genderové kultury v české společnosti, 1948–1989*, edited by Hana Havelková and Libora Oates-Indruchová (Praha: SLON, 2013).

386 Seidl 2012; Schindler 2013; Fanel 2000; Miřácký 2009.

mentioned in the previous scholarship, and which were not shared by any of the female narrators either.

> What we also did was to use the opportunities of official celebration days for certain professions. You know, this was very popular under the commies. It was common to have a fireman's day, miner's day, railroad workers day, etc., a lot of professions had their special day. And so we went ahead and reserved a whole pub or cultural club house (*kulturák*) somewhere just for men and legally had our own [gay] party [laugh]. (Standa)

While celebrating a variety of gender-mixed professions was also common, in celebrating gender-segregated professions 'male' professions were recognized more during state socialism than predominantly female ones. For example, while there was a fireman's day or a miner's day, there was no day of secretaries or day of nurses.[387] That could be a part of the reason why using these holidays for creating queer public/private spaces seemed to be a strategy for men more than women. Nonetheless, transforming the state-endorsed horizontal sex segregation in certain professions through a complete subversion of its official meaning to their advantage for a "gay party" is a clever strategy, which additionally suggests a high degree of cohesion and effort to organize on the part of homosexual men. None of the female narrators mentioned, for example, that queer women would ever utilize the widely popular and always celebrated International Women's Day (*MDŽ*) for a 'lesbian party.' The idea seems inviting. On the other hand, *MDŽ* was a state holiday forced upon society by the Communist leadership as an ideological proclamation of gender equality, and as such it was not taken seriously by ordinary people. During state socialism, International Women's Day was connected to a number of forced ideological rituals and mandatory appearances, and on the whole worked as a quintessential celebration of patriarchy and heteronormativity rather than a genuine celebration of women.

In other contexts, however, 'gay' men and 'lesbian' women apparently spent their time together, recognized each other, helped each other, and shared certain coded language and signs.

> From 1958, I lived together with two other friends of mine in an apartment on Tomášská street. We did not date or anything like that, we were just friends. It was a long apartment with three bedrooms, all the way from the street to the courtyard. So we divided it into three living sections with separate door bells. The door bells were already there like that, we didn't install them, I think it was used for single living already in the times of the First Republic. For the first part of the apartment, you were supposed to ring the

---

387 Dudová 2012, 66.

bell once, for the second part twice and I lived all the way in the back, where you had to ring the bell three times. So when our boys (*naši kluci*) [queer men] came to visit me for the first time, I told them: "When you come, you must ring the bell three times." And they looked at me almost insulted and replied, 'You think we don't know that? Of course we know we should ring the bell three times!' So that's how I learned that our [queer] secret code (*poznávací znamení*) is three rings. The guys taught me that, they enlightened me. (Heda)

Also, it was proper to have at home a dark ceramic ash tray with a white bear. Not that you had to have it and could not live without it but it was considered a part of good morals (*součást dobrých mravů*) to have it, not only at home but also in cafés. This knowledge circulated among 'our' people (*mezi našima lidma*). It was not so easy to get it, in fact, I don't even know where you would buy one. I wanted it for a long time and couldn't get my hands on it but then I got it from my boyfriend at the time, which made me really happy... I still have it at home. (Standa)

The mention of a distinct 'queer' ashtray was an interesting and unexpected moment in the interviews when two narrators, who did not know each other at all, spontaneously mentioned this small detail. A few other narrators remembered this specific ashtray as well, but only after a direct question.

Yes! I remember that! It was this ceramic ash tray that our [queer-friendly] pubs had. It was black, quite beautiful, very simple, but beautiful, with a white bear. And you immediately knew that this is our place (*naše místo*)... When I went to visit Lída [a close friend, also a 'lesbian'] she had it on her table. It shocked me because she did not even smoke. So I asked her where she got it and, imagine, she stole it! Can you believe that? She simply stole it from a pub. She claimed it's no theft, she just "borrowed" it so that when we get together here we can live it out. I said, "You don't even smoke!" You know, I felt insulted or something that she took it. "No, but you do!" she said, "so please let it go, you are making such a scene because of a stupid ash tray"... (*prosím tě, ty toho naděláš kvůli blbýmu popelníku*). (Tamara)

V.S.: What exactly bothered you — do you know?

Tamara: Well, it's not like I would go crazy about the theft itself, who cares about that, everyone was stealing then, and just look around, it continues to this day, but that she took *that* ash tray. You know? To have it at home, just for herself. I know she said it's for us when we meet there and true, it was always there, but you know, she didn't even smoke, so it seemed to me [...pause, looking for words...], I don't know, selfish, I guess.

While Tamara expressly recalled the aesthetic beauty of the ashtray, it seems clear that for both Standa and Tamara the ashtray represented an important sign of a shared communal value which they could not share publicly. In Tamara's recollection, the most revealing detail is the moment of Lída's stealing the ashtray from a pub. For Tamara, the act of stealing itself did not pose a moral problem, to the contrary, she assured me that stealing during socialism was (as it is now, during capitalism) a common feature of Czech social world. What evidently bothered her was her friend's violation of the covert queer communal space, marked only by secret codes, such as the ashtray. The ashtray was a symbol of a hidden collective identity, not a mere piece of ceramics. It is as if Lída took a rainbow flag from the pub's wall. Clearly, Lída was aware of this symbolism as well, when she claimed that she doesn't smoke herself but other 'lesbian' friends do and the point of "borrowing" the ashtray was that they can "live it out," when they meet together in her apartment. By perceiving the act as selfish, Tamara implicitly suggested that in a public space, the ashtray had the symbolic power of creating an invisible but shared "queer space." This symbolism was not needed when the friends met in the privacy of their home where everyone's 'lesbian' identity was in the open and there was no need to mark the space as such.

Narrators mentioned also other codes and signs, such as certain types of clothing, that they used to identify other queer people in ways that were not conspicuous to the surrounding mainstream society. Interestingly, however, while women narrators mentioned clothing codes for recognizing (some) 'gay' men, they did not mention any similar clothing codes for queer women.

> Our boys usually wore black long coats to recognize each other. A long black coat, black hat, they were all dressed in black, usually they also had a mustache and this way they recognized each other, especially in certain places, by Dětský dům [a department store], for example. There were places, where it was clear who was who, especially when dressed certain way. (Olina)

It is also striking how often queer narrators, both women and men, used the designation "our" (*náš, našinec*) and phrases such as "our people," "our bars," "our community," and "our places." When asked to reflect on whether they felt that such a strong sense of community already existed before 1989, or if they started to gain that sense of collective identity only with the rise of the gay and lesbian movement after 1989, they all answered that they felt like being a part of "something bigger" already during the Socialist period, even though they had a hard time verbalizing this feeling in concrete terms.

> We always helped each other. Always. It was absolutely a given that when you knew it was *our* person (*náš člověk*), you would totally help them. (Dana)

That was one thing you could always count on. Once you knew one of *our* people, you knew that you could count on them. I didn't have a [work] position where I could be exactly useful but I always tried and often I got help from *our* people as well. (Ludmila)

V.S.: Can you be more specific?

Ludmila: Well, for example theater tickets. Karel [a queer friend] worked in Studio Ypsilon. He was doing lights there and so he could get tickets with a discount, sometimes even for free. And he would call up and offer it to us. Also, whenever we [Ludmila and her girlfriend, with whom she shared an apartment] needed to have something fixed at home that we couldn't do ourselves, we could always count on Viktor [another queer friend], who would come and help us. Viktor was very handy, he worked for the railways, where he also met most of his boyfriends, but he lived in the railway housing (*na drážní ubytovně*) and so when he would come to our place to help us, we would cook him a dinner, talk, and have a good time. So basically, the bad is always useful for something good (*to špatný, je vždycky k něčemu dobrý*).

As mentioned earlier, while personal interviews and biographical narratives in feminist post-Socialist projects helped to debunk the notion of an alleged mutual solidarity between heterosexual men and women during the Communist regime, the queer narratives of socialism tended to affirm such solidarity in the face of adversity among queer men and women during the same time period. While the context of the gender power dynamics is different, of course, the revelations about queer solidarity during state socialism are important as well, for debunking the notions of the alleged separation of gay men and lesbian women and their assumed lack of interest in the lives of each other.

At the same time, one should be careful not to overrate and idealize the memories of shared queer solidarity either. Feelings of retroactive empowerment, nostalgia for the times of youth, and current feelings of detachment from the contemporary LGBT movement might play a strong role in shaping the memories of older queer people in particular sentimental ways.

I don't know how but we could always tell who is *our* person (*náš člověk*). It's not like now, when you don't recognize anyone anymore. I'm often surprised to learn that someone is gay, someone you would not suspect at all. And people in [managerial] positions, they don't care at all about *our* people. We used to help each other, but now a lot of gays act very arrogant. (Standa)

It is important to remember that many narrators were quite old at the times of the interviews and all of them were already retired from their jobs. Since many of them, especially men, did not have children or other relatives, who could help them in their senior age, some of the narrators suffer not only from relative poverty but also from feelings of loneliness and lack of attention. Three female narrators died by the time this book was published. Two of them left behind their life partners of several decades, who had to move out of the apartments they used to share together because they lacked the right to stay since they were not married. Standa's bitterness about the 'arrogance' of today's (younger) gays was likely connected to the fact that he was looking for a part-time job which would help him out with his low senior pension. Most of his friendships, and thus contacts, were in 'his' (gay) community but still he could not find anything. Even though unemployment has been on the rise in the Czech Republic and especially older people have a hard time finding jobs regardless of their gender or sexual identity, Standa interpreted his inability to succeed on the job market as a failure of gay solidarity between gay men "in positions" of power with their less fortunate fellows. Nostalgia for job security during socialism, protected through the "duty to work," facilitated in Standa's recollection a tribal myth of homogenous and protective gay community during the hostile Communist times, in which "our people" always took care of their own kind.

This nostalgia, spanning the narrators' youth, strengths, jobs and active sexual lives, was formative also for their memories of state socialism as essentially good years. As one of the narrators put it, "communism was the best time of my life" (Tamara). I was struck by this repeated assertion of the overall positive evaluation of the Communist past, which was also echoed in the narratives collected by Miřácký and Schindler. Such interpretations of state socialism challenge not only mainstream historical scholarship on homosexuality during East European communism in other countries of the Soviet Bloc, but also contradict many other recollections of hardships, humiliation or lack of freedom that narrators shared during their interviews. Clearly, the collected queer narratives are complex. For a variety of reasons, many queer people remember the lives they lived during state socialism in a positive light and some of them even projected these positive sentiments on the period of the Communist rule as a whole. Such interpretations are valuable and must be respected and integrated in the historical narratives of state socialism even if they might be unsettling or hard to believe. But they also must be contextualized. While the "Communist regime" should not be demonized as the site of unequivocal evil, it is important to keep in mind the destruction of civil society, the continual violations of human rights that took place, and the systematic efforts to destroy people's individuality and diversity that characterized the Communist rule.

CHAPTER 6
QUEER CONFRONTATIONS WITH THE STATE

The 'Communist regime' consisted of a number of institutional actors, the state police being a repressive and feared one. While Czech sexology often played an enabling role, actively attempting to help queer people to enact their choices and live out their desires, not surprisingly, the state police always represented a negative threat. According to other historians, the constant presence of the police state in Czechoslovakia and other East European countries during the Communist era played a major role in restricting the degree of agency queer people actually could have had in living their individual lives.[388] The queer oral narratives in this project touched on this issue as well. However, the narrators also recounted their sense that the potential harassment and punishment often depended on the whims and personal decisions of individual police officers. Since 1961, Czechoslovak anti-homosexual legislation prosecuted only sexual acts between individuals of the same sex that did not take place voluntarily, occurred for pay, involved individuals who were younger than eighteen, and "in circumstances that created public indignation."[389]

The vastly ambiguous wording left the police a large playing field to move within when interpreting what constituted both the "circumstances" of sexual activity and "public indignation," and, as narrators recalled, police at times did not shy away from abusing their power when they felt like it.

I was never harassed myself but the boys who also came to the salon of Karel Lasto-vička in Vinohrady, which I frequently visited, often came bloody, beaten up by the police. There was this beautiful young musician, an angel, he had his hair dyed blond and played the violin and other instruments. So this boy went on the street with his boyfriend and the police came and kicked them bloody, yelling at them "you faggots!" And they hadn't done anything, they weren't even holding hands. If, for example, they kissed, then I wouldn't say anything... well, I mean I would say something... but this was for nothing, without any reason, they only walked next to each other. But some of them [gay men] were really easy to read. (Vlasta)

---

388 Seidl 2012; Schindler 2013; Healey 2001; Essig 1999; Pisankaneva 2005; Turcescu and Stan 2005.
389 §244 TrZ, 1961 Sb.

I walked in the subway with one of our boys and suddenly two police officers stopped us and carded us. And so I asked why they are carding us and they told me that I should watch out for this man because he is 'dangerous.' So I asked, if *he* is dangerous, why are they writing down *my* personal information. I thanked them for their warning but told them they had no right to write down my data. One of the policemen stood close to my face and just shouted directly into it to shut up and never to show my face with this guy again. (Josef)

Police harassment was apparently quite random, depending largely on the mood of police officers and the context of the situation. Neither historians nor historical sources mention any systematic order or motivation on the part of the police to harass specifically queer people. Available archival evidence does not provide any documents, reports, orders, meeting minutes or proposed policies that would indicate that, at any period of the Communist rule between 1948 and 1989, the state power would be specifically targetting queer people in Czechoslovakia.[390] The only documented exception was the year 1985, when the police claimed to "investigate the murder of one homosexual man by another homosexual man" and used the case as a pretext to systematically enter gay-friendly bars and known places of same-sex congregation and write down lists of names of people who frequented those places.[391] Since the early 1980s, medical experts, especially dermatovenerologists, in cooperation with the police, also started to target specifically homosexual men in order to put together lists of "potential risk subjects," in relation to an alleged rise of sexually transmitted diseases in Czechoslovakia and the onset of the HIV/AIDS era.[392]

On the whole, however, both female and male narrators interpreted the police attention and harassment as having very little or nothing to do with their sexual orientation or gender identity. Some speculated that police attention had, in fact, completely different reasons.

When I was young [in the mid-1970s], I was regularly visiting the *holanda*[393] at Palacky square. And there was always a secret police wagon parked nearby. Other guys said that they were watching us and sure, sometimes they came and talked to us. But I think they were just killing their time. They [the police officers] were never mean or nasty.

---

390 Seidl 2012.

391 Fanel 2000; Procházka 1997.

392 Kolářová 2013; Jan Janula, "Sociologický a venerologický průzkum podílu homosexuálně založených jedinců na šíření pohlavních nemocí." *Československá dermatologie* 59/3 (1984): 168–177.

393 The term "holanda" likely comes from the gay friendly neighborhood in Amsterdam, where gay men met for public sex. In the Czechoslovak context, it was a very common and popular term to refer to meeting places of homosexual men, especially in Prague and Brno. The term appears in academic scholarship, activist literature, as well as in personal memoirs of gay men (Schindler 2013; Seidl 2014).

Usually they joked with us, smoked a cigarette and off they went. Personally, I'm convinced they were there because they were watching [Václav] Havel, who lived across
the street. (Standa)

Czech historian Rudolf Vévoda, who researched the files of the Czechoslovak Secret Police (*StB*) at the Institute of the Study of Totalitarian Regimes in
Prague, came to similar results. According to his analysis, the StB decided to
"step into the picture" only in moments, when it evaluated the "moral delin-
quencies" at hand as a usable and effective tool for compromising their political opponent or when it wanted to force him or her by pressure into signing
a covert cooperation with StB. Vévoda argues that homosexuality as such was
not the prime target of potential persecution and suggests that the direction
of police attention worked rather the other way around; information about
one's homosexuality (whether male or female) was interesting to the police
only if it could be used to extract other relevant anti-state information from
the subjects in question. At the same time, Vévoda continues, when it seemed
useful, the police did not hesitate to blackmail or harass "homosexuals."[394]
The evidence collected by historians so far suggests that the lack of distinct
repressive policy of the state towards "homosexuals" was framed by the relatively tolerant law from 1961, as well as by the authority of the expert voices
in a variety of other scientific and professional fields.[395]

The interprertation of the wording of the law into practice, and thus formal state approaches to homosexuality and queer people, in effect depended
on diverse sets of individual local actors, who had the power and motivation
to apply varying degrees of understanding, leniency, regulation or harassment. It is informative to examine how some queer people themselves understood and interpreted their own encounters with state power. The previous chapters already shared a number of individual stories, in which queer
people came upon a variety of situations, in which their sexualities were in
question. Most of these confrontations were of a private nature but some recounted public clashes between individuals and the state, which exposed remarkable dimensions of queer encounters with Communist power. Namely
the stories told by Kamila, about the school investigation of the private set-up
of her queer family, and by Miriam, about the divorce lawsuit, in which her
lover was fighting for the custody of her child after their same-sex extramarital relationship had been exposed by her girlfriend's husband. Both of these
cases uncovered unexpectedly responsive and sympathazing approaches and

---

394 Rudolf Vévoda, "Státní bezpečnost a perzekuce homosexuálů v 70. a 80. Letech minulého stole-
     tí." Lecture presented during the *Queer History Month* at Society for Queer Memory, April 1, 2016.
395 Hana Havelková came to a similar conclusion in her own research of the "expert voices" during
     State Socialism, Havelková and Oates-Indruchová, eds., 2013.

formal legal decisions taken by the state toward queer people, which revev-aled how surprisingly little the Communist state cared about people's sexual identities and private arrangements.

The last chapter takes a closer look at three additional moments in queer people's lives, in which individual queer people got into confrontations with state power and negotiated their personal beliefs and identities with the state. The encounters took place in different decades, from the 1950s through the 1980s, and in different professional and personal contexts. They show how different queer people understood their relationships with the Communist state and their positions within the Socialist society, and how they interpret-ed their sexual identities within this matrix. Contrary to any simplifying and homogenizing tendencies, the stories uncover three complex historical narratives, which reveal a wide spectrum of intersectional positionalities, strategies, motivations and interpretations of queer encounters with the state in Socialist Czechoslovakia.

THE HUNGARIAN WORKING CLASS WAS RIGHT TO REVOLT

Between 1954 and 1956, Heda spent two years in Budapest, Hungary, on a post-doctoral fellowship (*aspirantura*) in Slavonic Studies. She returned home in July 1956, to continue her research position at the Slavonic Institute of the Academy of Sciences in Prague. At that time, she was already divorced from her husband, whom she married briefly in 1952 after her graduation from Charles University. In Budapest, Heda had a several-months-long romantic relationship with another woman but "unfortunately it was only a platonic one. Neither of us made the first step to make it into something more." Heda really enjoyed her time in Budapest. She even preferred it to Prague because "the atmosphere there was somehow more radical. You could smell it in the air."

She returned to Prague "just before the Hungarian uprising, so I could not even entertain the sinful thought of emigrating because I was no longer there." The Hungarian uprising lasted for a relatively short time, from Octo-ber 23 to November 10, when the Soviet Army managed to brutally suppress it. But the revolt was as influential as it was brief. It was the third significant challenge to the Soviet control of Eastern Europe, after the East German Up-rising in June 1953 and the workers' riots in the Polish town of Poznan in June of 1956, but certainly it was the strongest and most radical rejection of the Soviet-style rule in the Communist Bloc. The weekly magazine *Time* declared the Hungarian Freedom Fighter the Man of the Year 1956 and the willingness and endurance of the Hungarian people to try to depose the Communists from power was admired not only in the free West but was hard to censor even in the other countries of the Soviet Bloc.[396]

For that reason, it was very important in the satellite countries of the Communist Bloc to engage in public denunciations of the Hungarian revolution. Similar to the Stalinist Purge trials in the early 1950s, workers in factories and other state institutions were called into large public meetings and asked to either sign petitions condemning the act of the Hungarian uprising and its protagonists, or publically speak up against it.[397] The Academy of Sciences, where Heda worked, held one such mandatory public meeting in November 1956. It is worth sharing Heda's recollection's of the event in a greater length.

I wanted to go back after the summer to visit Budapest again but there was the uprising and I couldn't do it. They [the leadership of the Academy], you know the custom back then, convened one of those stupid meetings. We all had to get together and declare that we denounce, and we reject, and we condemn it. I, of course, was not only in any mood to condemn, I felt somehow edgy and sharp-tongued (*cejtila jsem se ňáká nabroušená*), so I raised my hand and said that I cannot condemn it because the Hungarian working class was right to revolt because of this and that, and I just spelled the whole story out for them (*maďarská dělnická třída povstala právem, protože a protože, tak jsem to celý jako vykecala*). Well, it was a huge upheaval. Terrible outrage. It was in the Academy, Professor Mukařovský was there and all the others. Terrible indignation, such a disgrace (*byl to děsnej průšvih, strašný pobouření, šílená vostuda*). They were dragging me all over the place, and I told myself, they will definitely kick me out, that's clear, now they are going to fire me and I'm done with. Some three comrades were interrogating me all the time, asking if I was in the Petöfi Circle[398] and I said, "Unfortunately no, that would be a great honor because it gathers the best Hungarian minds and I did not reach that level." [...laughs...] Well, of course it only made it worse. It was a horrible shame. So first I was expecting that they are going to fire me, and second that they are going to lock me up in jail. But neither happened. We had a very decent director — very decent (*velmi slušnýho*) — and he somehow covered it up. So they publicly denounced me and it was over.... Probably, as it was after the [purge] trials already, and also because in our Institute there were very decent people there, even in the [Communist] Party there. So they just simply said, Well Heda, she doesn't

---

396 Kubik 1994.

397 Hodos 1987.

398 The Petöfi Circle was a student organization formed by Young Communists of Hungary in April 1956. It was named after the famous 19th century poet Sándor Petöfi, who fought for Hungarian autonomy from the Habsburg Monarchy. The Circle, centered around student leaders and famous intellectuals, demanded more democracy and people's control over their affairs, mass meetings, published literary papers, supported the Polish Worker's uprising in Poznan and finally was a driving force behind the mass demonstrations that ultimately led to the Hungarian Revolution in the fall of 1956.

have it all right up in her head, she has an extra wheel in her head (*má o kolečko navíc*), [...laughs...] and they simply muddled it up and it was over. They flushed it down, in the end... But from that time on, I lived in permanent infamy. (*Byla jsem furt na hanbě*). The Institute was very decent towards me. They took it that I was crazy (*brali mě, jako že jsem cvok*), but they did not fire me. But in a way, I got a life-sentence for Hungary. I was being punished over and over, all the time I was in trouble. I could not be a re-searcher anymore, my salary got lowered, I could no longer travel anywhere abroad, not even to Poland. I could only visit Bulgaria, so I re-specialized on that. When the tough Normalization period came [after 1970], the director finally had to fire me. That's why I also have such a small pension now, that's my life-long punishment. Peo-ple who did not have these problems, have significantly higher pensions! So I'm being punished for the rest of my life. (Heda)

From Heda's narrative one can tangibly feel the deep sense of injustice that accompanied her professional career for the rest of her life. Even though she worked all her life in the prestigious Academy of Sciences, translated from East European languages, published linguistic studies and dictio-nary-commentaries, even though she was highly regarded as an expert in her field, professionally her career was over. She could not teach, her research possibilities were limited, she could not academically advance and intellectu-ally grow. It was her choice to speak up and she paid the price of professional destruction.

What is most significant in the context of this book, however, is the con-sequences Heda's collision with Communist power had for her personal life, and her interpretations of that. Throughout both interviews, whenever Heda would recall any interactions with the repressive apparatus of the state, such as problems with police harassment, questioning her sexual orientation, she would always come back to interpret it through the lens of 1956. She remem-bered several concrete situations when she would be on a date with another woman and the police would "for no apparent reason show up from a bush" to destroy their romantic moment:

That summer [1973] I was asked to show my I.D. three times when I was only sitting in the park with a female friend. My girlfriends were told by the police to 'watch out for me' because I am 'dangerous.' We were not even kissing or holding hands or anything but the police came and carded us and told us to leave the park. I felt very humiliated and unjustly treated then. (Heda)

Remarkably, Heda did not interpret these situations as being harassed for her queer identity. She understood these violations of her privacy and subjectivity as an act of political persecution. Even though she said, she "felt humiliated," this sense of embarrassment seemed directed towards her girlfriend, in front of whom the police singled Heda out. The police ordered Heda to leave the park, making the point that she not only symbolically, but literally as well, did not belong in the public space. The act of carding is humiliating itself, as it implicitly positions one as a suspicious person. Morever, the feelings of frustration and powerlessness that police can show up anytime, anywhere, harass her, and enter into her private world, made Heda's life miserable and unpredictable for most of her adult years. Heda was convinced, however, that the same thing would happen had she dated men. She insisted that the main reason why the police were in the same park with her in the first place was not because she was a 'lesbian' but because she was a political outcast.

> It was that Hungarian thing again, I know it. (*To bylo zase to Maďarsko, já to vím.*)... I think they used it [my alleged homosexuality] mainly as pretext. Since 1956, I was on a political black-list. I couldn't even turn in my kitchen without it becoming a reason for state attention... I don't think I was discriminated because of my sexuality during communism. I never talked about it but I think that all the people in our Institute knew about it anyway, and they didn't talk about it either. But I never felt they would look down on me for that or anything. That was not a reason for people to be interested in you (*to nebyl důvod, kterej by lidi zajímal*). Political problems though, those were a different story. Those were constantly with you. I couldn't teach, my salary was lowered, I have a small pension — that was a life sentence. (Heda)

Even though at this moment of the interview she was primarily talking about her experiences with police harassment while dating women, Heda again turned the flow of the narrative back to her professional marginalization and reiterated her grievances connected to teaching and the negative financial consequences of her courage. Unlike other narrators, who agreed at one point or another that 'the regime' did treat them badly because of their sexual orientation or gender identity, Heda never conceded to that. She stated explicitly several times during the interview that she felt she "was never discriminated against for the fact that [I] loved women." In terms of understanding her sexual identity, Heda believed that she "was open" and "it was not a problem." Being open did not necessarily mean talking about her sexuality explicitly but even that had its reason. Heda shared that she did not talk about her sexuality openly not because she would feel she had to hide her sexual orientation "because of the regime," but because, as an Evangelical Christian, she believed in moral purity, chasteness and modesty in sexual matters and expression.

Heda also very clearly distinguished between "Communists" on the one hand, and "people" on the other hand. "Communists," or alternatively the "regime," was represented in her stories by "comrades," who interrogated her in 1956, and the police officers who harassed her through the Normalization period. These elements were "bad" and destroyed Heda's life. All other "people" were "good," understanding, helpful and, Heda's favorite designation, "decent" (*slušní*). This distinction is remarkable also from the point of view that many of her colleagues at the Academy of Sciences were members of the Communist party as well. But those were "good and decent people," contrary to the "comrades," representing the repressive apparatus. Their ocassional lapses, like when they all collectively condemned her at the Institute's meeting, were excused by Heda as insignificant because "not always were they able to act on their free will." Even her firing from the Institute she understood as "the director had to kick me out." In these interpretations Heda presented a complex understanding of "Communist power," which was not universal and blind, but depended on the individual person who carried it out and how he or she worked with it.

The professional destruction and subsequent financial punishment were so traumatizing and had such far-reaching consequences for Heda that she viewed all the other negative experiences in her life through them. And probably rightly so. It might seem like a long time to be harassed in 1973 for political reasons connected to 1956 but it was a time when "the restoration of order" was being reinforced: obedience and loyalty from ordinary people was required in much stricter ways than during the 1960s and the Communist party's fear of dissent and repetition of old acts of defiance was growing. It is also well documented that it was primarily intellectuals and academics who were being squashed into silence the most during the early years of Normalization.[399] Since Heda was also fired from her job at the Academy of Sciences at this time, she was likely right that her sexual orientation had very little, if anything, to do with this and functioned only as an additional tool to torment her. Which brings us back to Vévoda's argument that homosexuality was a secondary, not a primary, reason for the attention from the repressive apparatus of the state.[400]

Additionally, Heda's recollections challenge historical accounts that focused exclusively on men's sexuality and based on that research argued that the Socialist state police harassed only 'homosexual' men in the public space. Apparently, 'homosexual' women were targeted as well. At the same time, the narrators did not know of any of their female friends who were taken into custody, sent to medical treatment or jailed for same-sex encounters (sexual or romantic) in the public. Further supporting Vévoda's findings, it seems that such queer encounters with Communist power did not result in further

---

399 Milan Šimečka, *The Restoration of Order: The Normalization of Czechoslovakia, 1969–1976* (New York: Verso, 1984); Bren 2010; Salecl 1994.
400 Vévoda 2016.

repressive consequences for queer people as the main purpose of such confrontations were the momentary harassment and discomfort of the targeted people.[401]

"A WHORE AMONG PIGS"

From 1966 to 1979, Kamila worked as a secretary in the City Hall of Prague (*Národní výbor hlavního města Prahy*).[402] It was a prestigious job in the locus of power. She got the job at the age of eighteen, fresh out of high school, young, beautiful, strong, and outspoken. It was the second half of the sixties afterall, and bold opinions were tolerated. Even so, nobody would get a job like this randomnly, without personal connections and interventions. When Kamila was still in high school, she was an excellent athlete, making it all the way to the Czechoslovak junior national table tennis team. With the national team, she was able to travel abroad to participate in various tournaments and matches, representing the country. Because she always displayed enough loyalty to her Socialist country, never openly criticized it and never considered emigrating and staying abroad, through the connections on this team she also got her first employment offer, as she was finishing high school. "One of the assistants that was moving around our team told me that he knows that there is an administrative position open at City Hall, which would be perfect for me, and that I should go there and introduce myself." So she went and got the job on the spot.

While the political and social atmosphere in City Hall changed dramatically during the Normalization period, one aspect remained steady throughout her 13 years in the job: Kamila complained bitterly about the constant harassment and inappropriate behavior of men towards women, mainly secretaries, in the workplace.

---

401 This was apparently quite different in the Soviet Union, where lesbian women were frequently sent to psychiatric treatments and hospitalized against their will for simply admitting homoerotic desires (Essig 1999). Again, these details demonstrate that the context of socialist Czechoslovakia was in many respects distinct from other East European countries and queer sexuality was not repressed and singled out like elsewhere.

402 The name *Národní výbor hlavního města Prahy* (National Committee of the Capital City of Prague) changed to *Magistrátní úřad hlavního města Prahy* (Magisterial Office of the Capital City of Prague) in the fall of 1990. In 1995 it became *Magistrát hlavního města Prahy* (Magistrate of the Capital City of Prague). The Mayor of Prague has held the title of *Primátor* since 1922 (with no changes during the Communist period). During Kamila's work at the Prague's City Hall there were two Mayors: Ludvík Černý (1964–1970) and Zdeněk Zuska (1970–1981), who controlled the Prague City Hall during the Normalization decade and resigned in 1981 to become a member of the Czechoslovak government.

Secretaries during communism were just inventory for fucking (*inventář na šukání*)…
I worked directly in Mayor's Zuska's office. The black 603s [Tatra limousines] were
everywhere… all the biggest officials and all they wanted to do was to booze and neck
with the girls. Do you know what it was like to be smothered and touched by Kapek and
other pigs like him?[403] (Kamila)

In Kamila's recollections, not much work was ever done in the City Hall.
According to her, daily routines and performances in the offices and hallways
were all about demonstrations of power and submission in diverse forms.

The younger guys, it was ass-kissing the older officials. I don't think anyone believed in
anything seriously, we were all just pretending. But, of course, it wasn't a bad job overall. But you had to know how to walk the line. When I started there, immediately after
high school, I worked from point zero (*dělala jsem od píky*), I mean I 'worked' worked,
otherwise, there were plenty of bed jobs (*postelovejch prací, těch bylo spousta*) available
for the girls. (Kamila)

Her descriptions of over a decade spent at the City Hall painted a picture of an intricate network of power, fear, favors, loyalty, obligations — and
above all, sexism and sexual favors — that one had to be involved in to work
there and keep the job. Certainly, it was Kamila's choice to get a position in
the City Hall in Prague, where she had to know, even at the young age of eighteen, that the institution was staffed either with members of the Communist
party or at least people loyal to the system. Kamila herself did not take the
job in order to challenge the regime but because "it wasn't a bad job." She
liked being at the center of attention; she enjoyed the frivolity, the parties,
the relatively high salary — in other words, as she articulated herself, she
"liked the smell of power." In her memories, however, Kamila also connected
her encounters with high politics and power with the necessity to hide her
sexual orientation.

Everyone watched this [sexual orientation] extremely carefully at work. So in my
work, I preferred to have the reputation of a whore than to have anyone know[that
I am into girls]. (Kamila)

---

403 Antonín Kapek was a highly influential Communist politician. He was considered to be one of
the architects of Normalization policies. He was the chairman of the Prague regional organization of the Communist Party, which meant that he spent a lot of time at the City Hall, where
Kamila worked. From 1958 all the way to 1989, he was also the member of the Highest Politburo
of the Czechoslovak Communist Party. In 1968, he was one of the five Communist leaders who
signed and sent to Brezhnev the so-called Letter of Invitation asking the Soviet army to "save"
Czechoslovakia. Because of this letter, he was forced to leave all his positions in the Communist
Party after 1989, and became one of few high-placed officials, who were expelled from the Communist Party after the end of the Communist regime. Shortly after the Velvet Revolution, in May
1990, he hanged himself in his country house west of Prague. (Rupnik 2002; Staar 1982.)

During her employment at the City Hall, Kamila resisted joining the Communist Party, but eventually was compelled to join the Union of Socialist Youth (*SSM*).

The craziest moment was 1968. On August 18, I came back from a 3-week vacation in Austria and Italy with Greta [her Austrian girlfriend]. That Sunday I came back, and on Wednesday I heard tanks roaring under my window. So I packed my suitcase again, as I say, visa for four days and a suitcase for life [laughs], I even packed things like my high school diploma, and went back to Austria. The first fourteen days, people were fleeing in large numbers, there was really a big opening, people went even without a passport. I had a chance to stay there [in Austria]. I could play table tennis, have an apartment, and on top of that I had the great love of my life there but... [pauses]... I came back. Because of my mom. At that time, she was already quite sick and old. Nobody could believe it when I came back, they thought I had lost my mind. When I called up the regular meeting on Monday morning (*když jsem svolávala poradu*), they all thought I was calling from Vienna. They were die-hard commies (*kovaní komouši*) and still they couldn't understand why I came back. But the truth is that after this, I had holy peace. Through the return I was somehow checked through and afterwards no one dared anything towards me. I could do and say whatever I wanted and no one questioned it. And I did speak up! Only later did I learn that everyone was afraid of me, even my bosses. They thought that I was with the Secret State Police (StB) or KGB or the counter-intelligence or I don't know what, but the more I dared the more I got away with it. (Kamila)

Obviously, Kamila had a complicated relationship with (not only Communist) power. On the one hand, she enjoyed privileges that came along with her position. She was gradually promoted all the way up to being the personal secretary of the Communist mayor Zdeněk Zuska. At the same time, she claimed to profess outward loyalty to the Communist regime "against her will" and often interpreted her demonstration of obedience and loyalty as a way to hide her sexual orientation. Clearly, she used her position and the power associated with it in very pragmatic ways. She did not have a problem promenading herself with Communist officials, which in the 1960s and 1970s brought her many advantages and privileges. She also never considered the option of leaving her job to demonstrate her disagreement with the ruling regime. At a direct question whether she ever thought of that she asked surprisingly, "Why would I do that?"

Interestingly, working close to the center of Communist power was for Kamila compatible with her disdain and scorn for the Communists. As Bren argued, during the Normalization period in Czechoslovakia, the Communist Party did not demand any revolutionary zeal from its citizens. Rather, what the party leaders wanted from ordinary people was apolitical, passive behavior, and a manifestation of outward loyalty and obedience.[404] Kamila did exactly that. She refused to join the Communist Party, and throughout the years she resisted the pressures to do so. At the same time, she seemed to use any chance possible to climb up the power ladder and have a 'good life.' As she explained, besides taking care of her mother, "being somebody" was the main reason why she decided not to stay in Vienna after the Soviet invasion afterall.

I am a vain, ambitious perfectionist (*jsem ješitná a ambicióznī*) and I wanted to be some-body. I didn't want to be an emigrant from the East. Only in Austria, those four days there, was I deciding whether I will come back or not. I will never be able to explain in words the hell I was going through in those four days. The thought that I would be an outsider — that's probably what brought me back. At that time, I already knew the [German] language but that I would be an emigrant, outsider, I didn't want that. I was exactly twenty. My boss was convinced that I was leaving for good. He was a serious comrade, but he still did not turn me in at that time (*to byl těžkej soudruh a přesto mě neprásknul*). At that time, I had no idea that Normalization would come, purges and all that shit. We all thought it [the Soviet occupation] would last just for a short while. God, I hate them so much those Russians (*panebože, já je tak nenávidím, ty Rusáky*). But it's my own fault that, as a heavy patriot, I came back on that 27th of August. (Kamila)

It's notable that Kamila talks about herself as a potential "emigrant" (from Czechoslovakia) and not a potential "immigrant" (into Austria). Obviously, the act of leaving her home country behind and being seen as an intruder and "outsider" in a new country was more significant for her than thinking about her potential stay in Austria in terms of becoming an integral part of the new country. Kamila expressed very strongly her belief that coming from "the East" would disqualify her from being "somebody" in Vienna. Back in Prague, she had a stable and influential career at Prague's City Hall, lots of friends, and a relatively good life. Clearly, heteronormative pressures and the need to hide her sexual identity in Socialist Czechoslovakia were not stronger than the potential feelings of ostracism for being a foreigner in Austria, where arguably, she could live out her sexual identity in much more open ways than she was able to back in Prague.

Kamila's complicated relationship with 'the state' exposed personal di-lemmas that were likely shared by many citizens of Communist East Europe-an countries before 1989, regardless of their sexual orientation. Her narrative cautions not to fall into the trap of interpreting questions of 'discrimination against sexual orientation' without looking at broad and individualized

---

404 Bren 2010.

pictures of multilayered identities that people have in diverse circumstances. In the context of Socialist Czechoslovakia, no one was *only* a 'homosexual,' 'heterosexual,' 'man,' 'woman,' 'Communist Party member,' 'religious believer,' or 'intellectual.' While recognizing that all of these categories are complex in themselves, every single person had a multilayered identity, encapsulating many different dimensions that were sometimes in congruence and sometimes at odds.

Many male narrators in interviews conducted by Schindler and Miřácký complained about "being discriminated against by the regime."[405] They were recounting their grievances in relation to their ability to lead open (homo) sexual lives with honesty and dignity. At the same time, their narratives were not set in wider contexts. We know where and how they met other men, what kinds of sex they had, how they could and could not live their private lives. But we know very little (or nothing) about their jobs and their professional positions within them; we do not know anything about their relationship to the Communist Party and Communist power. We have no idea if they helped to sustain the Communist regime in power through the façade of loyalty and passive resistance or challenged it through some concrete activities. Miřácký, for example, states that three of his narrators were members of the Communist Party but does not discuss the meanings and consequences of this information any further.[406] The narrated grievances should not be ignored or belittled — they are important and help us understand how people navigated their queer identities in the conditions of a political regime that did not recognize their identities as legitimate. But queer sexuality during the Communist era should be analyzed as an integral part of a larger picture, not as an isolated, self-revealing category.

As we saw in Kamila's case, job positions close to the center of power helped one achieve a convenient life. Kamila recalled that it was a struggle to "sit in chauffers' laps," which she interpreted as "gross" because she "liked girls." Such interpretation suggests the unsettling notion that heterosexual women, other young secretaries around her, did not have a problem with sexist and sexualized behavior towards them and might have even enjoyed it based on the logic that they 'liked men.' But sexual harassment and sexist abuse of power should be clearly distinguished from a discrimination based on sexual orientation. Sexism in the workplace, in the Socialist state as elsewhere, was a demonstration of power on the part of men who felt that an integral component of their privilege was the entitled and free access to young women who should gratefully attend to their desires. As Kamila noted herself, "Either you gave him [sex] and then you were completely fine and

---

405 Schindler 2013; Miřácký 2009.
406 Ibid.

had privileges, or you didn't and then you faced scrutiny, higher demands [in your job], harassment and potentially ended up with lower pay." As uncomfortable as it was for Kamila to face and deal with these unwanted sexist proposals and the lewd behavior of her bosses, such behavior should not be interpreted through the lens of her queer sexuality but clearly identified as sexism affecting all women regardless of their sexual orientation and identity.

What was clear from Kamila's narrative, however, was that unmarried women in her workplace faced greater pressures from unwanted male advances than married women did. "Of course they [the men in power] went mainly after the single ones (*jasně, že šli hlavně po nezadanejch [ženách]*). No guy in power there had a married woman as his personal secretary. The secreataries were all young gazelles, just office equipment for fucking (*byly jen šukací inventář*)." The most distinctive line of sexual harassment seemed to run between married and unmarried women, not 'heterosexual' and 'homosexual' ones. However, all women were likely assumed to be heterosexual.

[During the 1970s], I was working [also] as a manager[407] for a certain very popular singer and actress, and among artists it's normal that they kiss each other when they meet. She would call me up, "Kamila, it's Friday, I'm sure you have heavy bags, I'll give you a lift," and she zoomed in with her white Cortina among those black [Tatras] 603s. The whole thirteen years I was hiding that I like girls and she scurries up the stairs and right in the hallway in front of the office she hugs me and kisses me. And the asshole deputy (*ten hajzl náměstek*) just stood there with his mouth open and said "Oh, I see! So you can do it with her but not with me!" [laughs] And for a while I got hell from him... (Kamila)

Remarkably, Kamila's male colleague did not mind that two women kissed in front of him and perhaps shared even more intimacy outside work. What enraged him was the realization that Kamila's rejections of his advances were truly meant as rejecting *him*.

Kamila said that in her thirteen years in the Prague City Hall job, "All the time I faced questions — 'You are such a young beautiful woman, how come you are not married yet'? 'When are you going to get married?' It was endless." The fact that she could not produce a boyfriend or a husband to ward off the unwanted sexual proposals of the men around her was challenging. In this context, she was undoubtedly in a different and more difficult position than the heterosexual women around her, who could more easily point to their boyfriends for protection from such unwanted behavior. In this sense,

---

407 In the interview, Kamila herself used the word "manager," which is the same in Czech and English.

Kamila's queer identity presented a clear disadvantage. On the one hand, she felt she could not disclose her same-sex orientation because she "would lose [her] job on the spot. It was unthinkable!" On the other hand she had to face heteronormative pressures and questions. In describing, how she dealt with these situations she revealed some of the strategies that, according to her, "many of us [queer people] used."

> We [the queer people] were always hiding in one way or another. Sometimes, I was pretending to date some guy to get some break from those pigs. It was always one us (*byl to vždycky někdo od nás*). One time, I even had "a fiancé," but unfortunately he was so easy to read! He would even pick me up at work but it was worse than better because he was so obvious! [...laugh...] But, surprisingly, it worked even the other way around. My best friend Pepa owned a pub, well he was a director there, in those days of course no one owned anything, and so I was picking him up at work because all the waitresses were after him. So as soon as one of us ['gays' or 'lesbians'] needed a similar alibi, someone jumped in to help. In this context we always helped each other. (Kamila)

Kamila's recollection reveals not only a clear sense of strategy on how to get rid of an unwanted heterosexual attention by some queer people but also the sense of queer solidarity, already discussed in previous chapters, among 'homosexual' people, men and women, who faced similar heteronormative pressures. At the same time, Kamila's story is revealing more about sexist behavior and gender stereotyping than providing evidence of 'discrimination against homosexuals' by the Communist regime.

DEAR COMRADES...

Prior to the existence of electronic social networks and dating platforms, same-sex personal ads were a common way queer people used to meet partners and friends. That is, in countries, which did not exert censorship and state control over media. As already discussed in one of the previous chapters, one's ability to place a same-sex ad was ambiguous in the context of Socialist Czechoslovakia. The success of placing same-sex ads seemed to be closely tied to the wording of those ads. While women were able to place ads without much difficulty because they used carefully thought-out and creative ways to hide the real purpose of their same-sex ads, men might have been less successful perhaps because they were too direct. Apparently, some queer people, and especially women, remembered that they were able to place same-sex ads in the selected state-controlled papers, either directly and openly in the woman-seeking-woman format submitted in the *Miscellaneous* section, or in diverse covert ways in the heterosexual sections or sections offering a variety of services. Others recalled that placing same-sex ads was not possible during the Communist regime and that queer people were discouraged by this 'general knowledge' to even try it. A few narrators explicitly mentioned that their same-sex ads were rejected.[408] That could be a quick end to the story: queer people either succeeded, or they didn't even try, or they were rejected and stopped trying.

Josef, however, decided to demand an answer and explanation from the state, why his same-sex personal ad, placed in November 1985, was rejected by the daily *Svobodné slovo*. The year-and-a-half personal struggle Josef led with the *Federal Office for Press and Information* (FÚTI) and the *Czech Office for Press and Information* (ČÚTI), provides an exceptional opportunity to see and examine the negotiations between a queer individual and the Communist state over the meanings and interpretations of (unnamed) sexuality and terminological nuances of 'same-sex' and 'male friendship.' On the day of our first interview, before he ever met me, Josef already brought with him and gave me a large file of photocopied correspondence between himself and the FÚTI and ČÚTI, which documented his fight. His letters are extraordinary as they present a rare moment of open defiance and 'speaking back' from one (after 1989 self-defined gay) individual in the face of adversity. Josef's letters are remarkable not only because of the boldness with which he directly addressed the machinery of state power, but also for the discursive strategy he chose. Moreover, because the state institutions kept corresponding with Josef, the exchange exposes the conflict from both sides. Josef wrote his first letter in February 1986, and addressed it to both FÚTI and ČÚTI institutions:

Dear Comrades,

The daily *Svobodné slovo* and weekly *Ahoj na sobotu* were, at least according to my knowledge, the only periodicals where a man could place an ad (into the section "*Miscellaneous*") that he is looking for a male friend and a woman that she is looking for a female friend. I wanted to do the same thing, but instead I received a written notification from the publishing house Melantrich that: "Based on the directive of FÚTI and ČÚTI, the editor-in-chief of *Svobodné slovo* decided, effective of Nov. 11, 1985, to stop publishing all ads, in which a man seeks a man or a woman seeks a woman."

So I am asking you: Why did you formulate such a "directive"? What is wrong? What is antisocial about the fact that I want to find through a newspaper ad a male friend, who would fit my nature? Is it in some way threatening to the building of advanced socialism in our country? I am 38 and I am single. Is it somehow antisocial that I live as an "old bachelor"? I have a demanding job and work in the [Communist] Party

---

408 Seidl 2012; Schindler 2013. See also chapter 4.

and other social functions. For that reason, I don't have much time, nor it is my habit, to sit in pubs, coffee houses or [visit] various parties. And when I decided to place an ad — I ran into an obstacle.

Thank you in advance for your answer.

With Comradely Regards,

Josef F.[409]

This initial letter is significant in several respects. First, it provides an answer to the question whether same-sex ads were possible to publish before 1989. Josef cites the original letter, which spurred his inquiry, sent to him by the Melantrich publishing house as an explanation of Melantrich's rejection of Josef's same-sex ad. Melantrich states explicitly that "based on the directive" from above, "the editor-in-chief decided... *to stop* publishing all [same-sex] ads." In other words, according to the publishing house itself, until November 1985 the daily *Svobodné slovo* did publish same-sex ads. Even so, such admission does not necessarily invalidate the recollections of narrators whose same-sex ads were rejected by this daily. Likely, low-level editors had decision-making authority when dealing with all personal ads, to reject those which they deemed problematic for a variety of reasons and it could have been they who rejected specific same-sex ads.

Such a statement, however, is important in a different respect: it makes it clear that officially the Melantrich publishing house, a powerful, ideologically scrutinized and centrally-controlled media institution, did not consider publishing a same-sex ad a problem. This is a significant detail, reflecting the official state attitude towards homosexuality. The Melantrich publishing house did not stand outside of state structures or ideological pressures. Similarly, FÚTI and ČÚTI felt compelled to issue a directive prohibiting same-sex ads (the reasons for that decisions follow shortly), which suggests that without this directive same-sex ads could likely continue to be published. Second, we see that it was the editor-in-chief himself, who decided to stop the acceptance of same-sex ads. In other words, there was a central directive but the publishing house makes it clear that the final decision rested in the hands of the editor-in-chief. This is another important detail, which testifies to the dispersed authority of the 'regime.' On the other hand, this correspondence falls already into the era of *glasnost* and *perestroika* when decentralization was taking place at all levels and areas of state authority.[410]

---

409 Letter from February 3, 1986 (PAJF).
410 Havelková and Oates-Indruchová, eds., 2014; Pullman 2011.

Third, in confronting the state and its federal offices, Josef is alluding to his homosexuality as openly as he can but comes short of ever using the word 'homosexual' or any similar term directly. In this way, he is stepping forward into a presumably fragile position to speak on the behalf of people interested in same-sex relations. At the same time, Josef did not want to associate himself with "homosexuality" and formulated his protest in terms of talking about himself as "a bachelor." On the one hand, he speaks about "his nature," on the other hand, that nature can be (with some imagination) read precisely as being an unmarried bachelor. Such tiptoeing around naming and ambiguity of meaning was common during state socialism, not only in regard to sexuality, but in general discursive practices as well. It should also be noted that Josef explicitly asks "what's the problem with a woman looking for a female friend." The explicit inclusion of women in his letter is remarkable and supports the shared consensus among many queer narrators that before 1989, queer men and women lived in an atmosphere of mutual solidarity and helped each other 'in whatever way they could,' as mentioned previously.

And last, Josef's initiative also challenges views that during the late Socialist period citizens in Czechoslovakia were passive, docile, afraid and never protested against state power.[411] Josef did protest, moreover in a context that could be regarded as uncomfortable or volatile. On the other hand, one cannot overlook that Josef was a member of the Communist Party and used that fact in the letter as his shield. He presented himself as a proper Socialist citizen, dutifully fulfilling his Party obligations. Likely, he calculated that his potentially disputable reputation as a (closeted) 'homosexual' will be more than compensated by his Party membership. It is also possible that it was indeed his sense of belonging in the ring of Communist 'comradery' which provided him with the sense of entitlement in demanding some answers from 'his' party. Josef's allusion to his Party membership and through it positioning himself as a loyal citizen and regime 'insider' might be the most important reason why both FÚTI and ČÚTI corresponded with him for over a year, as Josef was never satisfied with their responses.

Because Josef was not hearing back from ČÚTI, exactly a month after sending his first letter, he addressed ČÚTI again:

Dear Comrades,

On February 3, 1986, I addressed a letter to you with a question, why there exists a directive not to publish personal ads in which a man seeks a man or a woman seeks a woman. Even though a month has passed since my intitial inquiry, I have not yet received any answer from you. Are you not bound by governmetntal decree

---

411 Bren 2010.

No. 150/1958 Sb. about attending to complaints, announcements and impetuses of the working class (*Pro Vás neplatí vládní vyhláška... o vyřizování stížností, oznámení a podnětů pracujících*)?[412]

This second letter is especially remarkable for its reproaching tone, in which Josef, again from a close-to-open 'gay' position, assertively demands answers. Fascinating is the direct accusation of breaking a specific governmental decree, which put Josef on the offensive. Not only does he not hesitate to repeat explicitly that he was trying to place a same-sex ad, now he added an allegation that the state institution was not keeping up with its own regulations. In about three weeks, Josef received his answer, signed by a "ČÚTI worker" (*Pracovník ČÚTI*) with an illegible signature. In the official answer, this unidentified worker stated that

for generally-known journalistic and other ethical reasons, no editorial office is required to publish ads which cause any doubts. Ads that you are mentioning undoubtedly fall into that category. The editorial office thus proceeded correctly when it refused [to publish] your ad. After all, as an independent legal subject, it has full right to do so. The caused delay in answering you was unintentional and we a p o l o g i z e for that.[413]

If one would expect that after this answer Josef would sheathe his weapons and stop corresponding with the press institutions, one would be wrong. Josef wrote back again, complaining about this "arrogant, ignorant and law-contradicting" answer, "which is not an answer at all," addressing his new complaint to an even higher institution, the Czech National Council (*Česká Národní Rada* — ČNR).[414]

Josef's courage and sense of pride demonstrates that there were queer people, who were not passive and afraid to stand up for their rights during the Communist regime. His correspondence is also a testament to active and resisting citizenship in the late Socialist period. Perhaps even more remarkable is the fact that not only did ČÚTI, FÚTI and ČNR keep corresponding with Josef for over a year, but that in the end, they actually apologized to him for the previous answer and the tone of the "ČÚTI worker," stating that "this particular worker was reprimanded according to §76 of the Labor Law and was moved to a new position to deal with a different agenda."[415] Whether the

---

412 Letter from March 3, 1986 (PAJF).

413 Letter from March 20, 1986. Spacing of the word "apologize," as well as all other punctuation is in the original (PAJF).

414 Letters from April 1 and July 3, 1986 (PAJF).

415 Letters of the ČNR from May 20, 29186 and from ČÚTI from July 21, 1986 (PAJF).

punishment of the "ČÚTI worker" and the apology to Josef were sincere or were just empty rhetoric, cannot be determined. Either way, it demonstrates that the state was at least rhetorically attempting to uphold the civil right of a (presumably homosexual) citizen to get answers to his questions and to be treated without discrimination.

Several successive answers of the state national press offices to Josef reveal a remarkably convoluted argumentation put together by different (and increasingly higher-placed) state officials, explaining why same-sex ads should not be published. On February 20, 1986, the chief controller of FÚTI, Dr. Richard Petrásek, sent a long letter to Josef, elaborating on those reasons.[416] The content of Petrásek's letter, strikingly different from the previous response of ČÚTI, exposes the subjectivity and individualized nature of official attitudes towards the same issue by diverse state institutions and state administrators. An excerpt from Petrásek's letter shows that arguments of state officials were far from unitary.

About the Directive of FÚTI and ČÚTI I can say the following:

… Last year, several brutal sexual murders took place in Czechoslovakia. The investigation of these crimes showed that in several cases the perpetrators placed ads in *Svobodné slovo* and *Ahoj na sobotu* with approximately this wording: "A 40-year-old man is looking for a younger male friend for the purpose of getting close (*sblížení*)." The ads were placed by homosexual men, who were looking for younger partners, who then became their victims. Based on the warning of the Ministry of Interior it was recommended to the editors-in-chief of periodicals to approach advertising of persons looking for same-sex relationships [*inzerce osob hledajících seznámení s osobou stejného pohlaví*] more carefully. However, we realize with regret that the editor-in-chief of *Svobodné slovo* understood this recommendation in his own way and greatly simplified the whole situation.

Same-sex ads are published in many more periodicals than you think — for example *Vlasta, Mladý svět, Ohníček, Pionýr, Pionýrská stezka*, etc. However, as you certainly must understand, it is in contradiction with the interests and goals of the Socialist state and society to allow homosexuals to seek out their potential victims in the form of personal advertisements. In this case, it is the duty of the editor-in-chief to protect society and citizens against the abuse of the free press, which is totally in contradiction with the above-cited press law. I hope that you understand the difficult job facing the

---

416 Petrásek's letter probably intersected with Josef's complaint to ČÚTI about not receiving any answer, as around this time there are several letters, which are answering each other in belated ways.

editor-in-chief. To distinguish such ads from a very short wording is a very demanding and serious task...

   With Comradely Regards,
   Richard Petrásek, J.D. [417]

Ohníček, *Pionýr*, and *Pionýrská stezka* were children's periodicals and so Josef with a load of irony rhetorically asked during the interview, "Whether doctor Petrásek was urging him to become a pedophile." Josef was right that mentioning the children's and youth periodicals did not make much sense. Was Petrásek suggesting that a 38-year-old man really place a same-sex ad there? Or was he mechanically pointing out periodicals that still accept same-sex ads without thinking through the consequences of such a suggestion? Clearly, in the very next sentence, he asserts that it is the duty of the Socialist state to protect its citizens against criminal elements, who abuse "free press" in order to lure victims. In other words, what do the children's magazines have to do with both Josef's and Petrásek's points? Petrásek was the only person in the correspondence who openly used the term "homosexual." At the same time, he did not use that term in relation to Josef but only to explain the context of the murder cases and warn about "homosexual murderers." While Petrásek identifies the murderers as "homosexuals," in his argumentation he, perhaps inadvertently, also lists as one of the goals and duties of the Socialist state to protect homosexual men from becoming victims of violence. Who else would be answering those same-sex ads looking to get "close"? Importantly, Petrásek's letter made it clear that, at least rhetorically, the problem was not the homosexuality of those men but their criminal behavior (or their status as a murder victim).

   Moreover, Petrásek again confirmed the independence of the editors-in-chief to interpret central directives on their own. In this case, he even went so far as to argue that the editor-in-chief of *Svobodné slovo* interpreted the central directive in an unnecessarily harsh and simplified manner. The clumsiness of Petrásek's answer shows more than anything the unease with which the state officials tried to navigate the terrain between politically correct language and the defense of ideology. At the same time, his answer (cited here in about one third of its full length), as well as the whole correspondence, reveal unexpected patience and correctness in the never-ending communication with one individual citizen. Josef wrote to several different central institutions and as the rhetoric of their repeated replies started to escalate, they also began to contradict each other. In the end, the chief of the legislative office of the Czech National Council (*Česká národní rada*), where Josef addressed one of his final, already quite angry letters, disregarded all

---

417 Letter from February 20, 1986 (PAJF).

previous explanations about murder cases and the need to protect citizens and admitted that

> the decision-making process of what to publish and not publish on the pages of a newspaper is fully and solely in the hands of the editor-in-chief. If he decided not to publish ads in which persons of the same sex are looking to meet each other (*osoby téhož pohlaví hledají seznámení*), then it is not against the law, it is his lawful decision... It is, however, necessary to agree with your objection that the form, in which [ČÚTI] dealt with your complaint, does not correspond with the standard to which a central organ of the Czech Socialist Republic should be upheld. (František Fremund, J.D.)[418]

In a surprising twist, and contradicting Petrásek's previous answers, the chief of the legislative office of the Czech National Council suddenly claimed in 1986 that there was no censorship in the Czechoslovak media at all and that all decisions were made on the local level of editors-in-chief of individual newspapers.[419] Inadvertently, however, Fremund's answer is perhaps closest to how the translation of policy to practice worked in reality. Directives or orders written in the central offices and institutions of 'the regime' were rarely practiced in the precisely intended ways. Even if local officials were ordered to follow directives from above, they still had the discursive freedom to invest their interpretations and applications of laws with their own attitudes, prejudices and stereotypes. This does not mean that local officials were free to do what they wanted or that they were not monitored by their superiors. Rather, it means that such officials, simply as interpretive beings, could have applied policies in ways that more directly related to popular consciousness and culture than according to the ideological straightjacket of the letter of the law.[420]

In the case of (homo)sexuality, it is important to keep in mind that there never was any special directive or policy on how to treat or behave towards homosexual or queer people. These attitudes, by both the state institutions and ordinary people, were governed mostly by silence and thus based on the prejudices or openness of those involved. Fremund's official answer, as well as the whole correspondence for that matter, showed the level of subjectivity and decision-making power that the editors-in-chief possessed and suggested that with regards to homosexuality, levels of censorship rested in

---

418 Letter from May 20, 1986 (PAJF).

419 It is important to note in this context that Socialist censorship after 1968 relied mainly on auto-censorship (for example of such editors), which in turn granted the superiors alibis to distance themselves from such individuals in case of problem or need. (Oates-Indruchová 2008).

420 For an insightful discussion of discourse and agency in context, see also Pierre Bourdieu's concept of "habitus," in *Language & Symbolic Power* (Cambridge, MA: Harvard University Press, 1991).

the hands of individual people in different positions of power.[421] This also explains the differences in various periodicals and magazines and supports the memories of narrators, who allegedly had "their allied editors," who applied their vested powers in subjective, and sometimes subversive, ways.

In the interview, Josef disclosed that during his entire correspondence with state institutions, he did not feel afraid that he might start getting harassed or discriminated for his sexual orientation, which he alluded to in his first letter and which then got discussed on a general level by the state officials. His confidence proved right and he faced no negative consequences for this exchange. Unlike Heda, however, he was not criticizing the Communist regime. To the contrary, he was openly professing his loyalty to the Socialist state and exercising his Party membership and given that, his (presumed) homosexuality was of no interest to the state police. Perhaps the very idea that a Party member was also an outspoken 'homosexual' seemed so unsettling to the corresponding officials, that no one pursued it any further. In this regard, the correspondence only further unmasked how much the discourse on homosexuality (and queerness in general) of Socialist Czechoslovakia was burdened with fear of explicit naming by all people involved. Josef's homosexuality — and thus also the true nature of the same-sex ads — was never directly addressed by either side. This inability or fear of naming had both negative and positive effects in different situations during the Socialist regime. But in the general context of authoritarian one-party rule, what is not said and named is much harder to prohibit or repress, so the lack of naming often opened doors for finding and creating subversive spaces even within officially sanctioned contexts.

The selected stories unraveled three different contexts, in which queer individuals collided with state power during different moments of Communist rule, and discussed how the particular individual people reacted in those life situations, what strategies they used, and how they interpreted what happened. The point is not to place those three life moments in direct discussion or comparion. But rather to show how uniquely different queer people could experience their sexual identities in relation to state power and why it is important not to treat the queer narratives in homogenizing ways. Heda believed that throughout her entire adult life she had to pay for her refusal to denounce the Hungarian Uprising in 1956. Whenever state organs and institutions would interfere with her sense of freedom, including her sexual identity, she would interpret it as a 'logical' consequence and punishment for her open political stance, which happened decades ago. Even though at times she might have been harassed in public spaces by the plain-clothed

---

421 For similar arguments in the context of Czechoslovak Normalization humanities and social sciences, see Oates-Indruchová 2008.

secret police officers for her sexuality, she never interpreted it that way. She believed she was monitored by the police for much of her life because of her open critique of the regime in 1956, and that her queer identity was always used only as pretense to harass her for political reasons. Even though her repression by the machinery of Communist power was far-reaching with life-long consequences, Heda did not draw a causal link between her sexual orientation and political persecution. In fact, she kept distinquishing her "private life" (*osobní život*) from her "life" in general. When evaluating her "private life," she called it "calm and uneventful. I had a good life. And I was very lucky with my [female] partners."

Kamila, on the other hand, enjoyed her time at the center of (Communist) power, always looking for ways to reconcile her declared dislike of the regime and her 'lesbian' identity with her desire to keep a lucrative, fun, and useful job at Prague City Hall. While she felt that she had to hide her sexual orientation and was forced to face continual sexual harassment, while working at City Hall, her work "for the Communist officials" paid some big rewards. She was able to get visas and regularly visit her lesbian lover in Austria, with whom she had a twelve-year-long relationship, a travel privilege other Czechoslovak citizens (regardless of their sexual orientation) could only dream of during the Normalization period. She liked the privileges that came with her job and was willing to play the game in pragmatic ways. In this sense, she exerted a lot of personal agency and autonomy. Unlike Heda's, however, Kamila's interpretation of the influence of the Communist regime on her sexual identity was deeply negative. During both interviews, she repeatedly stated how much she "hates Russians" and understood communism as a clearly bad political regime, but did not reflect on her own positionality and complicity within this 'regime.' On the contrary, she explained her active involvement in the center of Communist power by her need to hide her lesbian identity.

Josef directly confronted state power, even though he used his Party membership as a defensive shield. He did not criticize the political situation like Heda did in 1956, but he was also acting within an entirely different historical context. In 1986, Mikhail Gorbachev was already in power in the Soviet Union and the political and social atmosphere began to loosen up modestly even in Czechoslovakia, as the concepts of *glasnost* and *perestroika* began to be discussed more openly. Josef was clearly not afraid to confront and criticize state institutions, in writing, and from an implicitly gay position. His act certainly required not only courage to make a stand but also a sense of courage and pride in his sexual identity. The reactions of FÚTI and ČÚTI then made it clear that, at least rhetorically, the Communist state professed tolerance of same-sex relationships. That is a remarkable finding. It does not mean that all people in the positions of power in Socialist Czechoslovakia shared this view or that there was no homophobia present in society. It does not diminish the consequences of homosexuality being defined as a sexual disorder. But such findings do indicate that the relationships between individuals and state/society, as well as between the state and sexuality, were far more complex than we have considered thus far.

CHAPTER 7
EPILOGUE

On Saturday, Sept. 9, 1989, the main Communist daily *Rudé právo* published in its weekend edition *Haló na sobotu* an extensive, two-page article entitled "Openly about One Hidden Problem" ("Otevřeně o jednom skrytém problému").[422] It featured a long letter which *Rudé právo* had received from Petr P., and an ensuing discussion of homosexuality and the situation of homosexuals in Socialist Czechoslovakia with three invited experts: the lawyer Vítězslav Květenský, as well as sexologist Ivo Procházka and psychologist Slavomil Hubálek — both from the Sexological Institute in Prague. The article and the expert interviews were prepared by Jiří Janouškovec, a journalist employed in *Rudé právo*'s department of letters (*oddělení dopisů*). The title page of the weekend edition featured a short preview entitled Homosexuality (in visible, bold letters), which encouraged readers to turn to pages 8–9 and read the whole article, stating that "Homosexuality is a fact of nature and it will not disappear if only we keep shamefully silent about it (*nezmizí jen proto, že bychom o ní stydlivě mlčeli*). According to estimates, it concerns 3.5 percent of all men. We share a letter from one of them, as well as expert opinions by a lawyer, sexologist, and psychologist."[423]

In his letter, Petr P. laid out a crushing critique of the Socialist state's and society's approach to homosexuality and homosexual people. He criticized the inadequate state of sexual education in Socialist Czechoslovakia, which did not provide children and youth with enough information about various forms of sexuality and failed to distinquish homosexuality from promiscuity and prostitution; he pointed out that the Czechoslovak state was "lagging behind the world" (*zaostává za světem*) in its approach to homosexuality, both in terms of framing homosexuality as a medical issue, as well as in the discriminatory legislature embodied in paragraph 244 of the penal code, which set different ages of consent for heterosexual and homosexual encounters. In his letter, Petr P. repeatedly used Western countries, namely the United States and Denmark, as examples of good practice, launching into various

---

422 "Otevřeně o jednom skrytém problému" ("Openly about One Hidden Problem"), *Rudé právo* Sept. 9, 1989, edition *Haló na sobotu* 36/1989, 8–9. Digitized archive of the Institute for Czech Literature of the Academy of Sciences (Digitalizovaný archiv časopisů, Ústav pro českou literaturu AV ČR, v.v.i.).

423 "Homosexualita," *Rudé právo* Sept. 9, 1989, edition *Haló na sobotu* 36/1989, 1.

Czechoslovak institutions for their inability to provide proper conditions for homosexuals to lead dignified and open lives. Additionally, he criticized deep-seated and pervasive homophobia, which he diagnosed as a "product of silence" and the incompetent approach of the state. Petr P. identified himself as a university-educated intellectual, who graduated with honors but ended up as a manual worker in an undefined profession, because his "sexual orientation was evaluated as inappropriate" (*moje pohlavní orientace byla vyhodnocena jako nevhodná*). He concluded that because of the homophobic prejudices permeating both state institutional and societeal attitudes, the absence of meeting places for homosexuals and their inability to live their lives openly, homosexuals in Czechoslovakia were forced to meet in anonymous places, such as public toilets and parks, were ashamed of their sexual identities, and in the end were resigned to passively accept the dismal conditions set by the state.[424]

The fact that a letter like this was published with all its vocal criticisms demonstrates that in the early fall of 1989, the political and social situation in Eastern Europe was indeed dramatically changing and even places like *Rudé právo* were susceptive to critical voices. Nonetheless, it is astounding that *Rudé právo* agreed to publish such a sharp, detailed analysis of the failing state approach to homosexuality and wide-spread homophobia in the country –moreover, one written by a self-identitified homosexual. In his reaction to Petr P. lawyer Vítězslav Květenský dismissed Petr P.'s grievances, defended the standing discriminatory legal code as "appropriate" and rejected Petr P.'s call for the legalization of same-sex unions. Květenský argued that "in the foreseeable future, I don't consider legalization of such unions as realistic or meaningful (*reálný ani účelný*)."[425] Sexologists Ivo Procházka and Slavomil Hubálek, on the other hand, in a discussion led by Jiří Janouškovec, sided with Petr P., confirmed or supported all his criticisms, dispelled myths about homosexuality, and argued for the extension of civil rights for homosexual people. Procházka informed readers that "for seven years now, there is a functioning psychotherapeutic group at the Sexological Institute [for homosexual people], and for the past two years, we have a homosexual club (*klub homosexuálů*)." Hubálek added that because "meeting options are very limited" for homosexuals, "the club was created out of our own initiative to provide them with such an opportunity." Procházka ended with a plea that

---

424 Letter of Petr P., published in "Otevřeně o jednom skrytém problému," *Rudé právo* Sept. 9, 1989, edition *Haló na sobotu* 36/1989, 8.

425 "A lawyer's opinion" (*Vyjádření právníka*), a part of "Otevřeně o jednom skrytém problému," *Rudé právo* Sept. 9, 1989, edition *Haló na sobotu* 36/1989, 8.

"it is vital to create [other] contexts and places where homosexual people can meet."[426]

A month later, on Saturday, Oct. 7, 1989, *Haló na sobotu* published readers' responses, which arrived in the editorial office of *Rudé právo* after the appearance of the original article.[427] In a generous space of a full page, *Haló na sobotu* featured fifteen reader responses, ranging from very short ones to quite long excerpts. Janouškovec did not comment or interpret the reactions in any way, he simply stated that they arrived and here they were. Only three, moreover very short, reactions expressed negative sentiments towards homosexuality and homosexuals. The twelve longer responses, while sharing Petr P.'s criticisms of inadequate state support of homosexuals, conveyed respect, understanding, empathy, and solidarity with homosexual people. Half of the supportive letters featured were from self-identified heterosexual readers, half of them shared personal coming-outs and the experiences of six self-identified homosexual people, five men and one woman. The overall tone of the readers' responses, as well as the general picture of homosexuality and homosexual people, was thus very positive and supportive.

The publication of this article, as well as the published responses from readers, intrigued me because together they deeply resonated with many points and arguments presented in this book. My sense of resonance only intensified when historian Jan Seidl told me about and showed me a slim file in the Archive of the Society of Queer Memory in Prague, which contained *all* of the letters from readers, which in the fall of 1989 arrived in the editorial office of *Rudé právo* in reaction to the mentioned article about homosexuality. The cover letter of the archival collection, addressed to Ivo Procházka, reads:

Dear Comrade Doctor,

Enclosed, as promised, I'm sending the photocopies of all the letters which I received in reaction to our article. Some of them were edited and are ready to be published. Please respect the anonymity of the writers. I am sending the letters only for your information, I answered all of them personally.

I am looking forward to continuing our cooperation.

Sincerely,

Jiří Janouškovec[428]

---

426 "What We Know and Don't Know about Homosexuals" (*Co víme a nevíme o homosexuálech*), a part of "Otevřeně o jednom skrytém problému," *Rudé právo* Sept. 9, 1989, edition *Haló na sobotu* 36/1989, 9.

427 "Letters from Readers: Reactions to the Article Openly about One Hidden Problem" (*Dopisy čtenářů: Z ohlasů na článek Otevřeně o jednom skrytém problému*), *Rudé právo* Oct. 7, 1989, edition *Haló na sobotu* 40/1989, 2.

428 Archive of the Society for Queer Memory (SfQM), Fond č. 16, karton 15. "Jiří Hromada." Cover letter from Jiří Janouškovec, Oct. 4, 1989. I would like to express my deep thanks and gratitude to Jan Seidl for telling me about and showing me this collection.

The file contained 39 letters. About a third of the letters were typed on a typewriter, but most were handwritten. Some of them were very long, five-to-seven-page single-spaced letters were not uncommon. Only a few letters did not contain the full name and home address of the writer; most writers shared this personal information, even if they asked the newspaper to keep it confidential. A surprising dimension of the collection was that a full half of the incoming letters were written by self-identified homosexual people, overwhelmingly by men. Among the twenty letters from homosexuals, there was only one written by a woman, the remaining nineteen were from men. Like the selection of responses, which were ultimately published, the great majority of the letters that arrived were supportive and positive. Only five letters expressed negative sentiments towards homosexuality and homosexuals, and only one was vulgar. Interestingly, the responses came from all over the country, only two were from Prague, the others were from 22 different towns and villages of Czechoslovakia. Remarkable also was the objectivity of the selection process for the publication. In both tone and proportion, the published selection reflected almost exactly the actual letters that arrived. Last, but not least, the exact wordings of the published responses were to be found in the actual letters. No words or expressions were changed or their meanings manipulated.

I set up an interview with Jiří Janouškovec, hoping he would remember this article and could provide more details about its publication and the context of the times.

Oh yes, I remember it. It was a long process, you know?... I worked in the department of letters so all the letters came to my desk. It was my daily bread. When the letter [of Petr P.] came, I decided that I want to write about it. My boss [editor-in-chief of *Rudé právo* Zdeněk Hoření] was generous and he trusted me. I could write whatever I wanted. But I wanted to prepare. So I went to Sexological Institute to ask more [about homosexuality]. Procházka — he is a really nice guy, you know — invited me to come to the homosexual club they had. So I went there several times to absorb the atmosphere (*nasával jsem atmosféru*). I was going there for a whole year before I felt I knew enough and the article could be published.[429]

Janouškovec repeatedly insisted in the interview that his work in *Haló na sobotu* was not subject to any censorship: "No one told me what I can or cannot do." According to him, there were no objections in the leadership of the paper to the article on homosexuality before its publication; at the same

---

429 Interview with Jiří Janouškovec, Dec. 17, 2020.

time, "The whole editorial board was surprised that nothing happened afterwards."[430] Janouškovec shared that not only was he preparing the article
for a full year, but he even cooperated closely with Procházka on the design,
structure, and argumentation of the article. The context of this article reveals once again how important and positive a role Czechoslovak sexologists
played in the emancipatory efforts. It is also quite telling about the dispersed
nature of power in Socialist Czechoslovakia. While both Janouškovec and
Procházka represented the institutional side of the state, one as an editor in
the main Communist daily and the other as a medical doctor in the Sexological Institute, they cooperated together to liberalize state attitudes towards
homosexuality and on the behalf of queer people. In his own words, the only
problem Janouškovec encountered while working on this article were the
pejorative remarks of his colleagues, who made fun of him, belittled him and
harrassed him for writing about homosexuality. "But it was all in good spirit,
just for fun," he assured.[431]

Janouškovec considered himsef to be a professional and took an ideologically detached pride in the fact that his piece objectively reflected the
situation of homosexuals in the country, as well as critically described the
inadequate and disinterested approach of the state. Janouškovec exhibited
the same attitude towards his work with the readers' letters. He recalled that
he felt a "professional obligation to report thruthfully" on the responses to
the article that arrived on his desk.

> I was surprised how many letters came. That was very uncommon. Usually, a maxi-
> mum of about ten letters arrived [in response to an article]. But this time, it was really
> a lot. I read them all — it was my job. And I answered them all. A lot of them were very
> long, I remember... It did not surprise me that most of them were positive. I expected
> that... I sent them to Procházka because we agreed that I would do that.[432]

There is an interesting discrepancy between Janouškovec's own experience of homophobic teasing at his work, the seriousness with which he
approached the letter of Petr P., his knowledge of the difficult conditions of
homosexual lives he learned about during the club sessions in the Sexological
Institute, his declared expectations of overwhelmingly positive responses to

---

430 Janouškovec's comment on the generosity and autonomy given to him by editor-in-chief Zdeněk
Hořeni was interesting because in recollections by other *Rudé právo* journalists, Hořeni was described as a loyal Communist Party member, who led *Rudé právo* with a strong hand, applied
detailed censorship to the content of the paper, and strictly upheld the directives from the Central Committee. He was also responsible for *Rudé Právo* staunchly denying any police violence
during the student protests in Prague on Nov. 17, 1989. See, for example, Zdeněk Porybný, "Můj
Listopad v *Rudém právu*" ("My November in *Rudé právo*"), *Právo*, Dec. 30, 2009.
431 Interview with Jiří Janouškovec, Dec. 17, 2020.
432 Interview with Jiří Janouškovec, Dec. 17, 2020.

the article, and yet his dismissal of all of this context as unrevealing . Nonetheless, the autonomy and objectivity with which Janouškovec was able to work in the main Communist daily newspaper is perhaps surprising. At the same time, it reveals once again that in certain contexts and times the most important element governing the 'state approach to homosexuality' was low-level state officials, who had the discursive freedom to interpret and act as they saw fit.

In their responses, the readers mostly expressed strong disagreements with the presented opinions of the lawyer, Vítězslav Květenský, who dismissed discrimination against homosexuals in Socialist Czechoslovakia as non-existent, offering instead their own experiences with homophobic hostility and obstacles in their lives. Overwhelmingly, however, homosexual people writing to *Rudé právo* were not complaining about repression enacted by the Communist state but about its passivity and lack of interest in creating conditions for homosexuals to meet each other and spend a shared communal time in some organizations. Most writers sharply criticized the discriminatory legal code, which set different ages for homosexual and heterosexual consensual sex, but instead of characterizing the state and its institutions as homophobic, writers complained about latent homophobia present in society and expressed by their neighbors, co-workers, and families. They also praised *Rudé právo* and Janouškovec himself, thanking them for breaking the taboo on homosexuality, taking additional critical stabs at state media and institutions.

The matter-of-factness, with which the lawyer Květenský swept the whole problem off the table, was incredible and at the same time typical of the attitude of some institutions towards homosexuality... Our legal system discriminates a lot between heterosexuals and homosexuals." (Zdeněk)[433]

I was provoked to write by the presented opinions of JUDr. Květenský. When I compare his expertise with reality, I have to conclude that he either does not understand the issue at all... or he purposefully distorts and obfuscates the topic. (Milan)[434]

I think that officially homosexuals are not discriminated against, but unofficially they most likely are. They are harassed and rejected by their closest surroundings. (Mojmír)[435]

---

433 SfQM Archive, Fond č. 16, karton 15. "Jiří Hromada." Letter from Zdeněk (Brno), Sept. 20, 1989.
434 SfQM Archive, Fond č. 16, karton 15. "Jiří Hromada." Letter from Milan (Český Krumlov), Sept. 21, 1989.
435 SfQM Archive, Fond č. 16, karton 15. "Jiří Hromada." Letter from Mojmír (Frýdek-Místek), Sept. 10, 1989.

I was pleased to read the article about homosexuality. Not because I am a homosexual myself but because *Rudé právo* pays attention to taboo topics... It's nice to see that *Rudé právo* started to use a more factual tone than it had in the past, when it functioned as a megaphone for a senile and morose part of the population. (anonymous)[436]

Dear Editorial Office, I have to inform you that the extensive article... which you published on Sept. 9, was a total bombshell for many people (*byl pro mnoho lidí úplnou bombou*). At least in my circles it caused a huge debate. At the same time, it also became clear that the article caught most people completely unready. So far, homosexuality has never been discussed in the public, nor explained scientifically. That's why people have a lot of stereotypes about it. (Milena)[437]

According to estimates, there are more of us than ethnic Hungarians living in Czecho-slovakia but what was ever done for us? Besides a few articles in the papers. (Milan)[438]

Significantly, many writers agreed that the only professionals, who were "on their side" and did anything positive for them, were sexologists.

Clearly, we don't have to look too far for a helping hand. It was already offered to us by the [doctors from] the Sexological Institute in Prague. Such an organization [the homosexual club] could not be created without the help of experts. We have to solve our problems ourselves but we do need professional help. (Radomír)[439]

I don't agree with removing homosexuality from the list of illnesses. If we couldn't use the help of psychiatrists, we would have no one on our side. Homosexuality is a strictly social issue but other institutions [besides the medical ones] are absolutely not ready to deal with it. (Miroslav)[440]

At the same time, most writers utilized in their letters medical terms and definitions, which they adopted from the sexological and media discourse and which pathologized homosexuality as a disorder and handicap. Such formulations were most striking, when used in the descriptions of their own subjectivity by the self-identified homosexuals. On the one hand, those self-identified homosexuals clearly were not passive and had the courage and

---

436 SfQM Archive, Fond č. 16, karton 15. "Jiří Hromada." Anonymous letter, Sept. 21, 1989.
437 SfQM Archive, Fond č. 16, karton 15. "Jiří Hromada." Letter from Milena (Lysá nad Labem), Sept. 15, 1989.
438 SfQM Archive, Fond č. 16, karton 15. "Jiří Hromada." Letter from Milan (Praha), Sept. 23, 1989.
439 SfQM Archive, Fond č. 16, karton 15. "Jiří Hromada." Letter from Radomír (Ostrava), Sept. 10, 1989.
440 SfQM Archive, Fond č. 16, karton 15. "Jiří Hromada." Letter from Miroslav (Přerov), Sept. 9, 1989.

agency to step out and share their lives. On ther other hand, they internalized the only labeling, which was available to them in the surrounding discourse.

I am twenty years old and I am also handicapped by this sexual disorder (*jsem postižená touto sexuální poruchou*). (Světlana)[441]

Unfortunately, I am also one of the handicapped ones (*Jsem, bohužel, také jedním z postižených*). (Karel)[442]

I plead for all of us handicapped in this way (*přimlouvám se za nás všechny takto postižené*). (Mojmír)[443]

Instead of using the medical terminology but essentially making the same point, Karel ended his letter with a poetic metaphor: "When I'm hosting at my table a friend who is limping, I will ask him to sit down and not to dance."[444]

Both the original article and the expert discussion, as well as the letters from readers were also symptomatic of the gender blindness and male perspective of the Socialist discourse on homosexuality. Homosexuality was framed as a 'men's world'; no one pointed out the absence of attention to women and female homosexuality or the lack of women's voices. At the same time, only six out of 39 letters addressed to the paper were written by women and only one of the twenty self-identified homosexual writers was a woman. In this sense, the readers' reactions to the article perpetuated the stereotypes articulated by Petr P. and the sexologists in their initial pieces that homosexuality is a "male matter."

The collection of readers' letters is remarkable in many respects. It is surprising how open and frank the writers of the letters were, especially the self-identified homosexual men (and one woman), who shared quite intimate details and experiences from their lives. The level of revelation, intimacy, and trust expressed in the letters were extraordinary, given the fact that the letters were addressed to the main Communist daily newspaper and that most of the writers shared their full names and home addresses. This suggests that the writers were not afraid the 'regime' would come after them to destroy their lives because of their revealed sexual orientation. To the contrary, like Petr P. before them, they turned directly to the state with their frustrations

---

441 SfQM Archive, Fond č. 16, karton 15. "Jiří Hromada." Letter from Světlana (Olomouc), undated.
442 SfQM Archive, Fond č. 16, karton 15. "Jiří Hromada." Letter from Karel (České Budějovice), Sept. 12, 1989.
443 SfQM Archive, Fond č. 16, karton 15. "Jiří Hromada." Letter from Mojmír (Frýdek-Místek), Sept. 10, 1989.
444 SfQM Archive, Fond č. 16, karton 15. "Jiří Hromada." Letter from Karel (unidentified), Sept. 9, 1989.

and complaints about the state's inadequate attention and care, demanding improvements. The institutional approach to homosexuality was identified by the writers as yet another failure of the Socialist state. There was even a shared sense of communal undertaking, a collective interest in improving the lives of homosexual people together, along with the state.

In *Mladý svět* 38 I read of the current negotiations about the possibility to start a social organization for homosexuals. I am definitely in favor of it! I assume that it will be publishing its own magazine, which would contain same-sex personal ads. This way, we would create better conditions for homosexual people to meet each other. (Jana)[445]

Every person with average intelligence has already met a homosexual person in their life. For the others, TV should occasionally show movies in which homosexuals play positive roles so that people would understand that homosexuality is an integral part of their lives and would not feel insulted or offended when they'll see a same-sex ad in a newspaper or two guys kissing on the street. (Dalibor)[446]

Most of the letters were written in a deeply conversational way, as if the addressee (*Rudé právo*) was a serious discussion partner. The letters contained suggestions for concrete steps to take, analyzed point by point arguments they disagreed with in the initial article, shared intimate details from their personal lives, complained about work conditions, neihgbors, family members, and asked for help and contacts. Josef even included a sealed letter for Petr P., asking the editorial office to "please pass it on to him because I don't know his address," or return it unopened back to Josef, ideally "with the home address of Petr P. so that I could send it to him myself."[447] In another letter, Alois wrote to Janouškovec, "Dear Comrade, I chose you. I don't even know why but I trust that my letter will get to the right hands... I am 66 years old. I remember a lot and that's why I would like to share with you something."[448] The sense of familiarity and belief in actually "talking to the state" — personified by the main Communist newspaper and editor Janouškovec — permeating through the letters further elucidates how problematic it would be to analyze queer encounters with power under state socialism in simple or clearly dichotomous ways.

This article, published on the brink of the Communist regime's collapse, and the ensuing flood of letters sent to *Rudé právo*, together embody a fitting end to this book. They do not provide any closure; they bring more questions

---

445 SfQM Archive, Fond č. 16, karton 15. "Jiří Hromada." Letter from Jana (Pardubice), Sept. 20, 1989.
446 SfQM Archive, Fond č. 16, karton 15. "Jiří Hromada." Letter from Dalibor (Ostrava), Sept. 19, 1989.
447 SfQM Archive, Fond č. 16, karton 15. "Jiří Hromada." Letter from Josef (Děčín), Sept. 17, 1989.
448 SfQM Archive, Fond č. 16, karton 15. "Jiří Hromada." Letter from Alois (Hlučín), Sept. 10, 1989.

than they offer answers; they only further complicate the relationship between queer individuals and the Socialist state. But in many ways, in the
small space of one concrete moment they also encapsulate the larger story
that this book has been narrating. Queer people did not have easy lives during
the Communist era: they could not live their lives openly; their gender and
sexual identities were not recognized as healthy and legitimate. Despite this,
the Communist state did not actively hunt queer people down for their sexuality. People's sexuality mattered only when it could be used for political
purposes. The realm of sexuality was left in the hands of medical professionals, who by and large supported queer people's ability to live dignified lives
and participated in trying to improve the structural conditions. Queer people themselves were not passive, invisible, tortured, and depressed. Some,
of course, had extremely difficult lives, but others remembered their lives
in Socialist Czechoslovakia with joy and positive nostalgia. It is not possible
to homogenize their lives and put some simple label on them. Queer people
lived their lives in very diverse ways, having radically different relationships
to their own subjectivies, bodies and sexualities, as well as to Communist
power and the Socialist state.

* * *

A narrative of the history of queer sexuality during state socialism in
Czechoslovakia is a challenging undertaking. Combining the methods of
oral history with discursive analysis of institutional materials (mainly sexological medical scholarship) and correspondence between queer individuals
and the state from the Socialist era, the book analyzed the ways in which
state approaches to non-heterosexual sexuality in Communist Czechoslovakia intersected with the actually lived lives and experiences of ordinary
people who identified (mainly retroactively) as homosexual, lesbian, gay,
transsexual, transgender, or queer. The confrontations of the institutional
frameworks and state attitudes towards homosexuality and transsexuality
with individual queer lives in Socialist Czechoslovakia has brought several
new and important insights.

First, the analysis revealed the multilayered and complicated role of
Czechoslovak sexology, which is not possible to interpret simply, and only,
as a heteronormative arm of the Socialist state. This part of the book was
based on the comprehensive research of more than 120 sexological articles
and books, published between 1947 and 1989, collected in the *Bibliographia
medica Čechoslovaca* database of the National Medical Library in Prague,
which collects all scholarship written by Czech and Slovak medical doctors,
published both in Czechoslovakia (or Czech Republic and Slovakia respectively) and abroad, continuously since its foundation in 1947 to the present.

This research and subsequent analysis showed that Czechoslovak sexology diligently fulfilled the role of the 'expert voice' and in its publications was loyal to the ideological claims of the normative ideal of heterosexuality as the only 'healthy' sexual identity, which helped to maintain the social order and Communist monopoly on power. At the same time, Socialist sexology was by no means static and its arguments about homosexuality and transsexuality, as well as its attitudes towards them, developed from the early 1950s to the late 1980s in emancipatory ways.

Contrary to current dominant historical and sociological perceptions of Czechoslovak sexology as essentially uniform, regulatory, and repressive which homogenously defined homosexuality and transsexuality as 'disorderly' and 'deviant' and disciplined the objects of its definitions, this book argues that sexological discourse in Socialist Czechoslovakia was first and foremost internally diverse, and often surprisingly empathetic and liberal. The published arguments and clinical case studies, as well as the personal attitudes and therapeutic practice of some Czech and Slovak sexologists, indicated that at times they also crossed the borders of officially sanctioned definitions of sexualities and actively sought not only to improve the lives of homosexual and transsexual people, but also to change the overall societal perception of non-heterosexuality. The queer oral history interviews, as well as personal letters of self-identified homosexual people in the last decade of the Communist regime, revealed that queer people in Czechoslovakia were well aware of this situation and appreciatively regarded sexologists as the only representatives of the Communist state 'on their side.'

The book also shows that it was sexologists, who initiated the changes in the legal approach of Socialist Czechoslovakia to homosexuality and helped to enact its decriminalization in the late 1950s. During the 1960s, based on several major studies, many sexologists changed their belief that homosexuality could be cured and transformed their attitudes from curing the 'poor deviants' to a reconceptualization of sexology as a socio-therapeutic support for the processes of coming out and the formation of a healthy, strong, and positive 'homosexual' identity. Sexological discourse in Socialist Czechoslovakia was also at the vanguard of therapeutic approaches to transsexuality. In both contexts, however, Socialist sexological writings and approaches reflected a strong gender bias and essentialist binary understanding of the biological body. While sexologists specializing in transsexuality supported, perhaps surprisingly, 'heterosexual' marriages and the rasing of children by transsexual women and men who underwent full sex-reassignment surgery, they still understood transsexuality and transsexual people within the confines of the heteronormative gender order and a dual concept of sexual orientation. Official sexological discourse was part of the 'regime,' on which other experts and Communist ideologues relied, at the same time, the analyzed sexological writings also showed that its arguments and attitudes were complex and diplomatic, and that since the late 1970s, sexological offices in Socialist Czechoslovakia basically functioned as the first gay clubs in the country.

Second, the queer oral history project offered a valuable window into the lives of queer people in the period of state socialism, about which we still know very little. This part of the book was based on 54 biographical narratives and written autobiographical accounts with queer people, especially women, born between 1929 and 1952, which were collected from 2008 through 2018. The memories and recollections of the narrators brought new insights about growing up, youth, and family constellations of queer people during socialism. They challenged myths about passive female sexuality, as well as myths of homogeneity among "homosexuals" before 1989. To the contrary, the narratives provided evidence of the immense diversity of queer people, their life situations, strategies, choices, and attitudes toward the state and Communist power, which were often more important and had more severe consequences for their lives than their sexuality. People, who during the period of state socialism had little (often almost no) terminological and political tools to define themselves openly as lesbians, gays, or transsexuals, with their stories brought evidence that despite the legal invisibility, they lived these identities, and not only in stress and fear, but also with courage, passion and cunning.

By primarily focusing on the memories and experiences of state socialism by queer women, this project has sought to incorporate new historical voices into the considerations of our recent past. By shifting the focus of attention, as well as by asking different questions, the queer oral history project inevitably invited new ways of looking at dominant mainstream, and male-oriented, historical narratives of both the history of homosexuality and the history of Czechoslovakia during the Socialist period. Emancipatory narratives of gay and lesbian movements in the "West" were built around and based on oral history projects and self-reflections of gay and lesbian identity formations experienced in the past. Such oral history projects often served as entry points into the study of the social history of homosexuality and the study of legal and political conditions of queer people. This has not been the case in post-Communist Eastern Europe in general, or the Czech Republic in particular. Even though in the legal sense the 'Communist regime' in Socialist Czechoslovakia might have been arguably less restrictive of homosexuality than many other countries in the democratic 'West', for almost twenty years after the collapse of Communism (until the recent efforts of the Society for Queer Memory), a systematic gay and lesbian oral history project was not a part of the Czech or Slovak LGBT movement and activities. Similarly, while oral history has been a common methodological approach in research projects studying diverse aspects of socialism and coming to terms with the

Communist past, attention to non-heterosexuality and the lives of queer people has not been a part of the mainstream oral history efforts.

An important question is why it has taken so long and why it has been so difficult to incorporate queer perspectives into the mainstream historical accounts of the Czechoslovak Communist past. A simple answer would be because queer people do not want to talk about their lives during socialism or because there is not an interested audience, which would actively encourage them to share their life stories. It is likely a combination of both but the context is more complicated. Often, even when approached, lesbian women, gay men, and transsexual and transgender people have not been particularly eager to talk about their past during the Communist regime. While working on this book, I repeatedly came across an evident reluctance to opening up with life stories and personal information commonly shared by queer people. Even though the oral history biographical narratives were anonymized or worked with changed names, narrators voiced concerns of not wanting to expose their personal information in the fear of hurting their past or current partners, parents, relatives or children. Almost all my narrators repeatedly sought to make sure that their real names would not appear anywhere in the text and that I would change the topography of their lives. Quite a few narrators were relieved when they learned that I plan to publish the book in English because they felt it would be harder for others to identify them. Even though all the narrators were open about their homosexuality, bisexuality, or transsexuality at the times of their interviews, many of them also still had people in their lives who did not know about their queerness and the narrators wished to keep it that way.

Arguably, this hesitation is connected to persistent latent homophobia and a stigma attached to homosexuality, and especially transsexuality, in the mainstream public and media discourses. The current Czech societal attitudes towards queer identities can be more fittingly described as conditional tolerance rather than full acceptance and respect. There is still social stigma attached to being lesbian, gay or transgender so, logically, some queer people have continuous concerns with openness and visibility. Such an atmosphere no doubt influences queer seniors, who are in especially vulnerable positions. Many of them have internalized shame, stigma or even self-hatred over the decades of their lives and see no benefit in opening themselves up to heteronormative judgments late in their lives. It does make a difference whether one is asked to participate in an oral history project because one is 'a' woman, presumably a heterosexual one, or if a person is being asked to participate in an explicitly queer oral history project because one is a 'lesbian' woman. Consequently, the position of narrating one's life during the Communist period as a 'homosexual' might seem equally stigmatizing.

Closely connected to the previous point was also the lack of 'homosexual' subjectivity during state socialism. Since being a homosexual was only a medical diagnosis, not a category of identity, many older gay and lesbian people simply lived with, or loved, same-sex partners, but did not *feel* and *identify as* homosexual, lesbian, or gay. Even though narrators did share similar experiences as well as a shared queer commonality and solidarity, even across gender lines, such perceptions and feelings were mostly unarticulated and unnamed. It is also possible that the feelings of shared queer commonality some narrators applied only retrospectively, to function as a retroactive empowerment for the times of their lives when they did not feel they had control over their sexual subjectivities. Many narrators, when approached to participate in this project, initially stated that their "sexuality is not an important topic" or that they are "not into categories and labels." From their point of view then, there was nothing interesting or special to share about their lives, which they "lived like everybody else." Moreover, dissident and subversive accounts of ordinary lives under communism have often been told through the prism of heroism or victimization, which the narrators also did not perceive as relevant for their lives, and thus they felt that they had "nothing to say." But as German historian Dorothee Wierling shrewdly pointed out, the narrators who tell you they have nothing important to say, usually have very relevant and interesting stories to share.[449]

Moreover, the concept of living a 'double life' gets a distinct meaning when applied to 'homosexuals' during state socialism. This concept has been quite commonly used to describe social reality of the people in the 'gray zone' during the Communist period, when people would say one thing publicly and think something else in the privacy of their homes. While Václav Havel criticized double morality as destructive hypocrisy, for the majority of ordinary people it was a way to maintain their dignity on the one hand, and to keep a job that will feed their families and send their children to school on the other.[450] Living a 'double life' by homosexual people, either in heterosexual marriage or hiding their sexual orientation, has been interpreted as a sign of weakness, hypocrisy, repression and lack of choice. Not surprisingly, there has been little interest on the part of queer people themselves to dispel such stereotypes, even though, as was clear from the shared stories, some queer people lived their 'double lives' in consciously creative and subversive ways. While for some narrators, the thought of having children never really crossed their minds, others lived with children in same-sex relationships and argued that it was "not a big deal" or even actively stood up to their hostile neighbors

---

449 Dorothee Wierling, "The East as the Past: Problems with Memory and Identity," *German Politics and Society* 15/2 (1997): 53–71.
450 Havel 1991; Šiklová 1990; Salecl 1994; Bren 2010.

or suspicious institutions. Narratives of queer family constellations during the Communist period shared in this book thus added an important emancipatory dimension to the concept of 'double lives' during state socialism in Czechoslovakia.

It is crucial to keep collecting and documenting queer voices and memories of the Socialist past. For one, such narratives bring invaluable and irreplaceable individual experiences, which cannot be transmitted by anybody else. They bring an authenticity of experience, which cannot be told *about* queer people, either by written documents or by other people, and which would otherwise stay hidden and forgotten. Also, such memories are important in order to expose how social discrimination and latent homophobia worked under communism, which cannot be gleaned only from laws and policies. There are major gaps between official laws and attitudes and the actual ways in which people lived their lives. The institutional levels and approaches of the Socialist state to homosexuality are well documented but so far we have only fragmented knowledge of how ordinary queer people found their own ways and meanings within those structures. And three, perhaps most importantly, these differing narratives also help break down the false uniformity and homogeneity of 'homosexual' lives, demonstrating that 'homosexual' people viewed their bodies and identities in vastly diverse ways, reacted differently to similar situations, made different choices about their lives, and experienced events in very individualized ways — and not always did their sexual identity even play an important role. In other words, while there is a unitary legal framework and certain structural patterns of discrimination, which can prove that a certain group of people is being treated a certain way because of a common characteristic (such as sexual orientation, for example), oral history provides the evidence that people are primarily and foremost individuals.

While recognizing and naming the social, political, and medical stigma that was placed on various queer identities before 1989, the narratives revealed that the lives of queer people during state socialism were filled with a surprisingly large amount of self-identified freedom, consciousness, and love. The most important contribution of the queer narratives is in exposing how complex the social context of the "Communist era" was. They show that within mainstream heterosexual society it was possible to live diverse sexual lives. Each narrative also demonstrates that all queer people had their own unique (and not necessarily commonly shared) stories of defiance, subversion, conformity, and submission to the 'order of things' during state socialism, which every individual person experienced, and also retrospectively narrated, differently. Together, more than any definite answer or collective historical narrative about 'homosexuals during socialism,' these biographical stories present a small window into the past, challenge many myths and stereotypes about gender and sexuality during the Communist period in Czechoslovakia, and invite further exploration. As a whole, the shared queer encounters with Communist power contribute to a multilayered and complicated reading of the borders between normality and deviance, the public and the private, and submission and resistance in state Socialist regimes. Last, but not least, they demonstrate how valuable the history of sexuality and oral history are for the study of our recent past.

ACKNOWLEDGEMENTS

In researching and writing this book I benefited from the help and support of many people and institutions. First and foremost, I would like to thank the narrators who shared their life stories with me. Without their interest in the project and willingness to share their personal experiences, there would be no book to write. I am grateful to every single one of them for their courage, honesty, and enthusiasm, with which they met with me, allowed me to enter the world of their memories and patiently walked me through their lives.

Research for this project could not have been carried out without the generous institutional and financial support of the Academy of Sciences of the Czech Republic, Association of Women in Slavic Studies, British Association of Slavonic and East European Studies, Czech Oral History Association, Faculty of Humanities of Charles University, Czech Science Foundation, National Library of the Czech Republic, National Medical Library, Society for Queer Memory, University of Pardubice, University of Washington, and the Wilson Center.

Many colleagues and friends at the Faculty of Humanities of Charles University (FHS UK) have either participated in reading and discussing various aspects of this book or have helped and supported me in other important ways. I would like to acknowledge the intellectual influence of the late Hana Havelková, who has been my academic mentor and dear friend for almost three decades. I owe so much of my own critical and analytical skills to our deep, challenging discussions we had for so many years. I would not have been able to finish this book without the ongoing encouragement, support and positive feedback from my colleagues at my institutional home in the graduate program in Gender Studies at FHS UK: Tatiana Chavalková Badurová, Jana Dvořáčková, Petra Ezzeddine, Ivy Helman, Tereza Jiroutová Kynčlová, Blanka Knotková Čapková, Lubica Kobová, Kateřina Kolářová, Dagmar Lorenz-Meyer, and Petr Pavlík, who together have helped me tremendously by creating a friendly and stimulating professional environment to work in. Equally importantly, I would like to thank the students of the Gender Studies graduate program at FHS UK, both past and current, who over the years have provided meaning to my academic work, pushed my horizons, enriched my passion, and never let me stagnate.

Over the years, I have been very fortunate to be surrounded by many supportive and inspirational friends and colleagues, who have made my professional journey an intellectually stimulating and personally exciting endeavor. I would like to thank in particular Nicolaas P. Barr, Kate Brown, Celina Bukowy, Hana Fifková, Magda Górska, Lenka Grünbergová, Miloš Havelka, Barbara Havelková, Patricia Hill Collins, Jitka Malečková, Milena Lenderová, Libora Oates-Indruchová, Annalisa Oboe, Martina Pachmanová, Tereza Pospíšilová, Miroslav Prokeš, Michal Pullmann, Jan Seidl, Marek Skovajsa, Anu Taranath, Kari Tupper, and Dorothee Wierling.

On a personal level, I am grateful to my entire family, which has tirelessly supported me in everything I do. My deepest appreciation goes to Sebastian, Toby and Kaisa, and especially Michael L. Smith, without whose presence, intellect, and generosity this project could not have been completed.

Last, but not least, I would like to thank Martin Janeček and *Karolinum* for their interest in my work, the book reviewers for their critical comments and suggestions, which doubtlessly and significantly improved the final version of the manuscript, and finally, to Robert Michael Baugh for his dedication, energy, and meticulous editing of this book. All responsibility for the arguments and conclusions presented here is, of course, solely my own.

BIBLIOGRAPHY

ORAL HISTORY / BIOGRAPHICAL INTERVIEWS (2009–2018)

AB (born 1938) — 13. 8. 2015 and 15. 10. 2015 (SfQM, M-019-112, M-019-122) *
Antonín (born 1932) — (SfQM, M-030-112, M-030-122) *
Dana (born 1938) — 13. 10. 2010 and 21. 10. 2010 (VS)
Eva (born 1952) — 5. 2. 2008, 4. 3. 2008 and 10. 5. 2009 (VS)
František (born 1941) — 15. 3. 2011 and 6. 4. 2011(VS)
Heda (born 1929) — 2. 2. 2010 and 10. 2. 2010 (VS)
Ivan (born 1941) — 26. 11. 2015 and 22. 6. 2016 (SfQM, M-022-112, M-022-122) *
Ivo (born 1958) — 18. 7. 2018 and 15. 8. 2018 (SfQM, M-033-112, M-033-122) *
Jana (born 1948) — 9. 6. 2015 and 3. 8. 2015 (SfQM, M-016-112, M-016-122) *
Josef (born 1947) — 23. 10. 2010 and 23. 11. 2010 (VS)
Kamila (born 1948) — 28. 12. 2010 and 6. 1. 2011(VS)
Karla (born 1941) — 15. 4. 2008 and 7. 5. 2008 (VS)
Ludmila (born 1946) — 12. 6. 2009 and 29. 6. 2009 (VS)
Marcela (born 1945) — 29. 10. 2014 and 26 .11. 2014 (SfQM, M-012-112, M-012-122) *
Marie (born 1948) — 10. 11. 2009 and 15. 11. 2009 (VS)
Miloš (born 1942) — 24. 6. 2014 and 20. 8. 2014 (SfQM, M-004-112, M-004-122) *
Miriam (born 1945) — 16. 12. 2009 and 5. 1. 2010 (VS)
MM (born 1937) — 3. 10. 2014 and 19. 12. 2014 (SfQM, M-010-112, M-010-122) *
Olina (born 1946) — 21. 12. 2010 and 29. 12. 2010 (VS)
Ota (born 1921) — 2009 (SfQM, M-029-112, M-029-122) *
Pavel (born 1938) — 6. 1. 2014 and 20. 1. 2014 (SfQM, M-001–112, M-001-122) *
Petr (born 1930) — 31. 3. 2014 and 28. 4. 2014 (SfQM, M-003-112, M-003-122) *
Petra (born 1952) — 3. 12. 2010 and 10. 12. 2010 (VS)
Soňa (born 1942) — 8. 1. 2014 and 6. 2. 2014 (SfQM, M-002-112, M-002-122) *
Standa (born 1937) — 13. 2. 2008 and 22. 3. 2008 (VS)
Tamara (born 1950) — 1. 3. 2008 and 16. 3. 2008 (VS)
Vili (born 1942) — 8. 4. 2014 and 30. 4. 2014 (SfQM) *
Vlasta (born 1949) — 11. 1. 2011 and 28. 1. 2011 (VS)
Zuzana (born 1935) — 15. 8. 2010 and 1. 10. 2010 (VS)

* Interviews conducted by other historians and archived in the Oral History Subcollection of the Archive of the Society for Queer Memory in Prague (SfQM).

ARCHIVES, LIBRARIES, AND DATABASE COLLECTIONS

AMPSV — Archiv Ministerstva práce a sociálních věcí, Praha
ANLK — Archiv Národní lékařské knihovny (Archive of the National Medical Library, Prague)

AÚSD — Archiv Ústavu pro soudobé dějiny AV ČR (Archive of the Institute of Contemporary History, Prague)

BMČ — *Bibliographia medica Čechoslovaca*, comprehensive medical database, 1947–present

KAV — Knihovna Akademie Věd ČR (Library of the Academy of Sciences of the Czech Republic)

KSÚ — Knihovna Sexuologického ústavu v Praze (Library of the Sexological Institute, Prague)

NAČR — Národní archiv České republiky (National Archive of the Czech Republic), fonds of the Central Committee of the Communist Party 1945–1989.

NKP — Národní knihovna České republiky v Praze, Klementinum (National Library in Prague)

NPMK — Národní pedagogické muzeum a knihovna J. A. Komenského (State Pedagogical Archive), Praha

PAHF — Personal Archive of sexologist Hana Fifková, transsexual autobiographies

PAJF — Personal Archive of Josef F., correspondence with ČÚTI and FÚTI

SfQM — Archiv Společnosti pro Queer Paměť (Society for Queer Memory), Oral History Subcollection; collection "Jiří Hromada"

ÚČL — Ústav pro českou literaturu AV ČR, v.v.i. (The Institute for Czech Literature), digitalizovaný archiv časopisů

ÚSTR — Ústav pro studium totalitních režimů, Knihovna Jána Langoše (The Institute for the Study of Totalitarian Regimes, Ján Langoš Library)

PRINTED MEDIA FROM THE SOCIALIST ERA

Activitas nervosa superior
Ahoj na Sobotu
Časopis lékařů českých
Československá dermatologie
Československá pediatrie
Československá psychiatrie
Československý psychiatr
Lidová demokracie
Mladá fronta
Mladý Svět
Moravskoslezský Referátový Sborník
Neurologie a psychiatrie československá
Práce
Praktický lékař
Protialkoholický obzor
Review of Czechoslovak medicine
Rozhledy v chirurgii
Rudé právo
Sborník lékařský
Soudní lékařství
Svobodné slovo
Tvorba
Vesmír
Vlasta
Vojenské zdravotnické listy
Zdraví

PRIMARY SOURCES

Bártová, Dagmar. "Skupinová psychoterapie pacientů s poruchami psychosexuální identifikace." *Moravskoslezský Referátový Sborník* 11 (1979): 92–94.

Bártová, Dagmar, and Vlastimil Škoda. "Příspěvek k psychiatrickým aspektům homosexuality." *Časopis lékařů českých* 116/33 (1977): 1029–1030.

Bouchal, Milan, and Dagmar Bártová. "The Attitude of Homosexuals after the Change in the Criminal Code." *Activitas nervosa superior* 6/1 (1964): 100–101.

Brauerová, Eva, Viera Satková, and Antonín Topiař. "K otázce transvestitických projevů v dětském věku," *Československá pediatrie* 31:1 (1976): 20–21.

Brzek, Antonín. "Muž nebo žena?" *Zdraví* 27/2 (1979): 18.

———. "Manželství a homosexualita." *Zdraví* 29/7 (1981): 18.

———. "Láska k témuž pohlaví." *Zdraví* 34/5 (1986): 19.

———. "Ještě o homosexualitě." *Zdraví* 35/8 (1987): 19.

Brzek, Antonín, and Petr Krekule. "Posuzování schopnosti k vojenské službě u transsexuálů po změně pohlaví." *Vojenské zdravotnické listy* 49:3 (1980): 114–116.

Brzek, Antonín, and Slavomil Hubálek. "Homosexuals in Eastern Europe: Mental Health and Psychotherapy Issues." *Journal of Homosexuality* 15/1–2 (1988): 153–162.

Brzek, Antonín, and Iva Šípová. "Dnešní možnost změny pohlaví u transsexualismu." *Praktický lékař* 59:19/20 (1979): 752–756.

Charvát, František. *Sociální Struktura Socialistické společnosti a její vývoj v Československu — srovnávací analýza, reprodukce, perspektivy.* Praha: Academia, 1980.

Charvát, Josef. "Josef Hynie, zakladatel československé sexuologie." *Časopis lékařů českých* 109 (1970): 631.

Čížková-Písařovicová, Jiřina. "Několik poznámek k homosexualitě u dorostu." *Praktický lékař* 56/7 (1976): 260–262.

Důvěrné hovory: rozhlasové besedy o problémech sexuálního života. Praha, Státní zdravotnické nakladatelství, 1968.

Freund, Kurt. *Homosexualita u muže.* Praha: Avicenum, 1962.

———. "Otázka pohlavní úchylnosti z hlediska sociálního," *Problémy psychiatrie v praxi a ve výzkumu.* Praha: Státní zdravotnické nakladatelství, 1957).

———. "Diagnostika homosexuality u mužů." *Československá psychiatrie* 53 (1957): 382–394.

———. "Tři úvahy o práci psychopatologa." *Československá psychiatrie* 54 (1958): 177–183.

Freund, Kurt, and Karel Nedoma. "Otázka příčetnosti a nápravných opatření u sexuálních delikventů." *Československá psychiatrie* 55 (1959): 264–269.

Freund, Kurt, and Václav Pinkava. "K otázce věkové preference u homosexuálních mužů." *Československá psychiatrie* 55 (1959): 362–367.

———. "K otázce souvislosti mezi homosexualitou a nepřítomností rodičů." *Československá psychiatrie* 55 (1959): 334–336.

———. "Homosexuality in man and its association with parental relationships." *Review of Czechoslovak medicine* 7/1 (1961): 32–40.

Freund, Kurt, and Jan Srnec. "K otázce mužské homosexuality: Analysa změn sexuální appetence během pokusné léčby podmiňováním." *Sborník lékařský* 55 (1953): 125–164.

Ginsberg, Allen. *Kvílení* (Praha: Světová literatura, 1959, translated by Jan Zábrana).

Günther, Erwin. "Homosexualita a společnost." *Zdraví* 34/12 (1986): 19.

Hall, Radclyffe. *Studna osamění: připsáno našich třem já.* (Praha: Symposion, Rudolf Škeřík, 1931. Reprinted 1933, 1938, 1948, 1969, 1992, 2002. Translated by Vladimír Vendyš). From English original *The Well of Loneliness* (New York: Covici-Friede-Publishers, 1928). The publisher in 1969 was the official Communist publishing house Práce a ROH.

Havelka, Jiří. *Populační politika v Československu.* Praha: Orbis, 1978.

Himal, Juraj. "Mládež a společnost." *Sociologický Časopis / Czech Sociological Review* 10:4 (1974): 339–343.

Holda, Dalibor. "Čtyřicet let společenského rozvoje mládeže." *Sociologický Časopis / Czech Sociological Review* 21:5 (1985): 452–469.

Hubálek, Slavomil. "Skupinová psychoterapie homosexuálních pacientů." *Praktický lékař* 68/5 (1988): 187–188.

_____. "Výskyt různých forem sexuálních kontaktů u homosexuálních mužů." *Časopis lékařů českých* 126/31 (1987): 979–980.

Hynie, Josef. *Úvod do lékařské sexuologie.* Praha: Josef Svoboda, 1940.

_____. "Několik poznámek k podstatě a therapii homosexuality." *Neurologie a psychiatrie československá* 13 (1950): 327.

_____. *Lékařská sexuologie.* Praha: Universita Karlova, 1967.

_____. "Principy sexuálního chování a sexuální morálky." *Časopis lékařů českých* 108/19 (1969): 553–556.

_____. "Lékařská opatření při transsexualismu." *Československá psychiatrie* 65:5 (1969): 295–299.

_____. *Sexuální život a jeho nedostatky.* Praha: nakladatelství Josef Svoboda, 1937, 1939, 1941, 1942, 1946, 1948.

_____. *Sexuológia pre každého.* Bratislava: Osvěta, 1970.

_____. *Základy sexuologie.* Praha: Universita Karlova, 1974.

_____. *Dospíváte v muže.* Praha: Avicenum, 1976.

Hynie, Josef, and Karel Nedoma. "Homosexualita v sexuologické praksi." *Neurologie a psychiatrie československá* 13 (1950): 328.

Hynie, Josef, and Iva Šípová. "Transsexuálky." *Československá psychiatrie* 71:1 (1975): 48–52.

Janula, Jan. "Sociologický a venerologický průzkum podílu homosexuálně založených jedinců na šíření pohlavních nemocí." *Československá dermatologie* 59/3 (1984): 168–177.

Jenerál, Jaroslav. "Mládež a společnost." *Sociologický Časopis / Czech Sociological Review* 21:5 (1985): 446–451.

Kluzák, Richard. "Chirurgická transformace pohlaví u ženského transsexualismu." *Rozhledy v chirurgii* 47:4 (1968): 253–261.

Kole, Oswalt. *Kouzlo lásky.* Praha, Avicenum, 1970.

Masters, William and Virginia Johnson, *Lidská sexuální aktivita (Human Sexual Response).* Praha, nakladatelství Horizont, 1970.

Medvecký, Jozef. "Prípad transsexualizmu." *Československá psychiatrie* 69:4 (1973): 236–240.

Myšková, Jana, and Martin Mocek. "K osobnostem partnerů transsexuálů." *Praktický lékař* 60:15/16 (1980): 548–550.

Nedoma, Karel. "Homosexuální prostituce u mladistvých." *Československý psychiatr* 58/5 (1962): 312–314.

_____. "Nový trestní zákon a trestné činy lidí s odchylnými sexuálními tendencemi." *Praktický lékař* 33 (1953): 316–319.

_____. "Homosexualita v sexuologické praksi," *Neurologie a psychiatrie československá* 13 (1950): 328.

Nedoma, Karel and Jiří Mellan. "Syndrom transsexualismu." *Československá psychiatrie* 1 (1966): 42–47.

Neoral, Lubomír. "K soudní lékařské problematice kastrace při transsexualismu." *Soudní lékařství* 14:3 (1969): 33–36.

Neumann, S.K. *Zlatý oblak.* Praha: František Borový, 1932.

Plzák, Miroslav. *Manželské judo.* Praha: Avicenum, 1970.

_____. *Taktika a strategie v lásce.* Praha: Mladá fronta, 1970.

Podmele, Ladislav. *Komunistická morálka a výchova nového člověka.* Praha: SPN, 1971.

_____. *Učení o společnosti a státu.* Praha: SPN, 1972.

Pondělíček, Ivo, and Jaroslava Pondělíčková-Mašlová. *Lidská sexualita jako projev přirozenosti a kultury.* Praha: Avicenum, 1971.

_____. *Sexuální zrání mladého muže.* Praha: Avicenum, 1977.

Private correspondence of JF with ČÚTI and FÚTI. 1986. Private archive of JF.

Procházka, Ivo. "Hovoříme o zdravém manželství. Part VIII: Žijí mezi námi." *Svobodné slovo*, August 9, 1987: 4.

Raboch, Jan. "K sedmdesátinám prof. MUDr. Josefa Hynieho, DrSc." *Časopis lékařů českých* 109 (1970): 632.

————. *Očima sexuologa*. Praha, Avicenum, 1977.

Resch, Radomil. "Jde jen o lásku k témuž pohlaví?" *Zdraví* 35/4 (1987): 19.

Roubíček, Jiří. "Ze života Čs. psychiatrické společnosti. Zpráva o odborné činnosti, sjezdech a pracovních schůzích v roce 1960." *Československá psychiatrie* 57 (1961): 133-139.

Správná Dívka. Zábavní pořad ČST (1972-1973).

Syřišťová, Eva a kol. *Normalita osobnosti*. Praha: Avicenum, 1972.

Šípová, Iva. "Terapie LSD u homosexuálů a transsexuálek." *Časopis lékařů českých* 113:48 (1974): 1491-1493.

————. "Intelektová úroveň u transsexuálů." *Československá psychiatrie* 71: 2-3 (1975): 131-136.

————. "Dětství intersexuálních osob." *Československá pediatrie* 31:8 (1976): 450-453.

————. "Rodinné prostředí u intersexuálních lidí." *Československá pediatrie* 31:11 (1976): 629-631.

————. "Interpersonální vztahy transsexuálních žen." *Časopis lékařů českých* 119:17/18 (1980): 509-511.

Topiař, Antonín, Vilč, M. and E. Gladr, "Homosexuální agresivní počínání v alkoholovém opojení," *Protialkoholický obzor* 21/2 (1986): 73-75.

Van de Velde, Theodor Hendrik. *Dokonalé manželství: Studies o jeho fyziologii a technice*. Praha: Avicenum 1968 and 1972.

Věstník ministerstva zdravotnictví 28:1-2, 1980.

Výborný, František. *O výchově dětí ke kázni*. Praha: SPN, 1958.

Zákon č. 94/1963 Sb. "O rodině." Ústava ČSSR.

Zákon č. 140/1961 Sb. Ústava ČSSR.

Zemek, Pavel. "Žijí mezi námi." *Mladý svět* 15/4 (1973): 20.

Zvěřina, Jaroslav. "Homosexuální chování v dětství a dospělosti." *Zdraví* 29/9 (1981): 18.

————. "Sexuální deviace: kvalitativní odchylka struktury sexuální motivace." *Českoslovenký psychiatr* 78/5 (1982): 303-307.

————. "Fakta a emoce v sexuální výchově." *Praktický lékař* 68/6 (1988): 216-218.

SECONDARY SOURCES

Abrams, Bradley. *The Struggle for the Soul of the Nation: Czech Culture and the Rise of Communism*. Lanham, MD: Rowman & Littlefield Publishers, Inc., 2005.

Analýza situace LGBT menšin v ČR. Praha: Úřad vlády, 2007.

Anzaldúa, Gloria. *Borderlands: The New Mestiza: 25th Anniversary*. San Francisco: Aunt Lute Books, 2012.

Argent, Angie. "Post-communism and 'Women's Experience'?," in Robin Teske and Mary Ann Tetreault, eds., *Feminist Approaches to Social Movements, Communism and Power*. Columbus: University of South Carolina Press, 2000.

Barany, Zoltan D. *The East European Gypsies: Regime Change, Marginality, and Ethnopolitics*. Cambridge: Cambridge University Press, 2002.

Basiuk, Tomasz, and Jedrzej Burszta, *Queers in State Socialism: Cruising 1970s Poland*. London: Routledge, 2020.

Besemeres, John. *Socialist Population Policy: The Political Implications of Demographic Trends in the USSR and Eastern Europe*. New York: M.E. Sharpe, 1980.

Better, Allison and Brandy Simula. "How and for Whom Does Gender Matter? Rethinking the Concept of Sexual Orientation." *Sexualities*. 2015: 18(5-6), 665-680.

Biebuyck, Erin K., "The Collectivisation of Pleasure: Normative Sexuality in Post-1966 Romania," *Aspasia* 4 (2010): 49-70.

Blažek, Petr, "Vyhoštění krále majálesu. Allen Ginsberg a Státní bezpečnost," *Paměť a dějiny* 5:2(2011): 28–43.

Boswell, John. *Christianity, Social Tolerance and Homosexuality*. Chicago, London: University of Chicago Press, 1980.

Bourdieu, Pierre. *Language & Symbolic Power*. Cambridge, MA: Harvard University Press, 1991.

Boym, Svetlana. *Common Places: Mythologies of Everyday Life In Russia*. Cambridge, MA: Harvard University Press, 1994.

Bren, Paulina. *The Greengrocer and His TV: The Culture of Communism after the 1968 Prague Spring*. Ithaca and London: Cornell University Press, 2010.

_____."Weekend Getaways: The *Chata*, the *Tramp* and the Politics of Private Life in Post-1968 Czechoslovakia" in *Socialist Spaces: Sites of Everyday Life in the Eastern Bloc*, David Crowley and Susan E. Reid, eds. Oxford and New York: Berg 2002.

Brown, Kate. *A Biography of No Place: From Ethnic Borderland to Soviet Heartland*. Cambridge, MA: Harvard University Press, 2005.

Brown, Kathleen. *Good Wives, Nasty Wenches & Anxious Patriarchs: Gender, Race, and Power in Colonial Virginia*. Chapel Hill: University of North Carolina Press, 1996.

Bryant, Dara. 2009. Queering the Antifascist State: Ravensbruck as a site of Lesbian Resistance. In Philpotts, Matthew, a Sabine Rolle, eds. *Edinburgh German Yearbook, Volume 3: Contested Legacies: Constructions of Cultural Heritage in the GDR*. Rochester, NY: Camden House.

Brzek, Antonín, a Jaroslava Pondělíčková-Mašlová. 1992. *Třetí pohlaví*. Praha: Scientia medica.

Butler, Judith, *Gender Trouble: Feminism and the Subversion of Identity*. New York: Routledge, 1990.

Čadková, Kateřina, Milena Lenderová, and Jana Stráníková, eds. *Dějiny žen aneb Evropská žena od středověku do poloviny 20. století v zajetí historiografie*. Pardubice: Univerzita Pardubice, 2006.

Calhoun, Greg, ed. *Social Theory and the Politics of Identity*. Cambridge: Blackwell, 1994.

Califia, Pat. *Speaking Sex to Power: The Politics of Queer Sex*. San Francisco: Cleis Press, 2002.

Canaday, Margot. *The Straight State: Sexuality and Citizenship in Twentieth-Century America*. Princeton: Princeton University Press, 2011.

Carragher, Daniel. "Trying to Hide: A Cross-National Study of Growing up Non-Heterosexual for Non-Identified Gay and Bisexual Male Youth," *Clinical Child Psychology and Psychiatry* 7:3 (2002): 457–474.

Carruthers, Charlene. *Unapologetic: A Black, Queer, and Feminist Mandate for Radical movements*. Boston: Beacon Press, 2018.

Chamberlayne, Prue, Michael Rustin, and Tom Wengraf, eds., *Biography and social exclusion in Europe: Experience and Life Journeys*. Bristol: The Policy Press, 2002.

Chamberlayne, Prue, Joanna Bornat, and Tom Wengraf, eds., *The Turn to Biographical Methods in Social Science: Comparative Issues and Examples*. New York and London: Routledge, 2000.

Chauncey, George Jr. 1994. *Gay New York: Gender, Urban Culture, and the Making of the Gay Male World, 1890–1940*. New York: Basic Books.

Chelstowska, Agáta. "Stigmatisation and Commercialisation of Abortion Services in Poland: turning sin into gold," in *Reproductive Health Matters* 2011, Vol. 19/37: 98–106.

Chou, Rosalind and Joe Feagin. *The Myth of the Model Minority*. 2nd edition. Boulder, CO: Paradigm Publishers, 2015.

Cohen, Stephen. *Rethinking the Soviet Experience: Politics & History Since 1917*. Oxford: Oxford University Press, 1985.

_____. *Black Feminist Thought: Knowledge, Consciousness, and the Politics of Empowerment*. Boston: Unwin Hyman, 1990.

Craft, Christopher. *Another Kind of Love: Male Homosexual Desire in English Discourse, 1850–1920*. Cambridge: University of California Press, 1994.

Crenshaw, Kimberlé. "Mapping the Margins: Intersectionality, Identity Politics, and Violence against Women of Color." *Stanford Law Review*, (1991): 43/6.

————. "Demarginalizing the Intersection of Race and Sex: A Black Feminist Critique of Antidiscrimination Doctrine, Feminist Theory and Antiracist Politics." *The University of Chicago Legal Forum*, (1989): 139–67.

Crowley, David, and Susan E. Reid, eds. *Socialist Spaces: Sites of Everyday Life in the Eastern Bloc.* Oxford and New York: Berg 2002.

Danielová, Helena, Dana Zajoncová, a Jana Haragaľová, eds. 2001. *Paměti romských žen: Kořeny I.* Brno: Muzeum romské kultury.

Darwin, Helana. "Doing Gender Beyond the Binary." *Symbolic Interaction* 2017, 2–18.

David, Henry, and Robert McIntyre. *Reproductive Behavior: Central and Eastern European Experience.* New York: Springer Publ. Co., 1981.

D'Emilio, John, and Estelle B. Freedman. *Intimate Matters: A History of Sexuality in America.* New York: Harper and Row, 1988.

Dijk van, Teun A. "Multidisciplinary CDA: A Plea for Diversity." In Ruth Wodak and Michael Meyer, eds., *Methods of Critical Discourse Analysis.* London: Sage Publications, 2001.

Duberman, Martin Bauml, Martha Vicinius, a George Chauncey, Jr. 1989. *Hidden from History: Reclaiming the Gay and Lesbian Past.* New York: New American Library.

Dudová, Radka. *Interrupce v České republice: Zápas o ženská těla.* Praha: Sociologický ústav, 2012.

Duggan, Lisa. "Queering the State." *Social Text* 38/1994: 1–14.

Einhorn, Barbara. *Cinderella Goes to Market: Citizenship, Gender and Women's Movements in East Central Europe.* London and New York: Verso, 1993.

Ellis, Havelock, *Sexual Inversion.* London: F.A. Davis, 1901.

Essig, Laurie. 1999. *Queer in Russia: A Story of Sex, Self and the Other.* Durham: Duke University Press.

Faderman, Lillian. *Surpassing the Love of Men: Romantic Friendship and Love Between Women from the Renaissance to the Present.* London: HarperCollins, 1998.

Fairclough, Norman. "Critical Discourse Analysis as a Method in Social Scientific Research." In Ruth Wodak and Michael Meyer, eds., *Methods of Critical Discourse Analysis*, 121–138. London: Sage Publications, 2001.

Fanel, Jiří. *Gay historie.* Praha: Dauphin, 1999.

Faust, Drew Gilpin. 1996. *Mothers of Invention: Women of the Slaveholding South in the American Civil War.* Chapel Hill: University of North Carolina Press.

Fausto-Sterling, Ann. *Sexing the Body: Gender Politics and the Construction of Sexuality.* New York: Basic Books, 2000.

Feagin, Joe. *The White Racial Frame: Centuries of Racial Framing and Counter-Framing.* 2nd edition. New York: Routledge, 2013.

Fejes, Nárcisz, and Andrea P. Balogh. *Queer Visibility in Post-Socialist Cultures.* London: Intellect Books, 2013.

Fifková, Hana, Petr Weiss, Ivo Procházka, Ladislav Jarolín, Jiří Veselý, and Vladimír Weiss. *Transsexualita: diagnostika a léčba.* Praha: Grada, 2002.

Fifková, Hanka, Petr Weiss, Ivo Procházka, Peggy T. Cohen-Kettenis, Friedemann Pfäfflin, Ladislav Jarolín, Jiří Veselý, and Vladimír Weiss. *Transsexualita a jiné poruchy pohlavní identity.* Praha: Grada, 2008.

Fischer, Mary Ellen. "Women in Romanian Politics: Elena Ceausescu, Pronatalism, and the Promotion of Women," in Sharon Wolchik and Alfred Meyer, eds., *Women, State, and Party in Eastern Europe*, 121–137. Durham: Duke University Press, 1985.

Foucault, Michel. *Birth of the Clinic: An Archeology of Medical Perception.* New York: Vintage, 1973.

————. *Discipline and Punish: The Birth of the Prison.* New York: Vintage Books, 1979.

————. *History of Sexuality: An Introduction.* New York: Vintage, 1980.

————. *The Order of Things: An Archeology of the Human Sciences.* London: Tavistock, 1970.

————. "The Subject and Power," in Hubert Dreyfus and Paul Rabinow, *Michel Foucault: Beyond Structuralism and Hermeneutics.* Chicago: University of Chicago Press, 1983.

Frančíková, Dáša. "Female Friends in Nineteenth-Century Bohemia: Troubles with Affectionate Writing and "Patriotic Relationships." *Journal of Women's History* 12/3 (2000): 23–28.

Freedman, Estelle B., "Sexuality in Nineteenth-Century America: Behavior, Ideology, and Politics," *Review in American History* 10/4 (1982): 196–215.

Freud, Sigmund. *Three Essays on the Theory of Sexuality*. London: Imago Publishing, 1949, first published 1905.

Frýdlová, Pavla. 1998a. *Všechny naše včerejšky: Paměť žen*. Praha: Gender Studies.

————. 1998b. *Všechny naše včerejšky II.: Paměť žen*. Praha: Gender Studies.

————. 2006. *Ženská vydrží víc než člověk*. Praha: Nakladatelství Lidové noviny a Gender Studies.

Frýdlová, Pavla, ed. 2007. *Ženám patří půlka nebe*. Praha: Nakladatelství Lidové noviny a Gender Studies.

Fulbrook, Mary. *The Anatomy of a Dictatorship: Inside the GDR, 1949–1989*. New York: Oxford University Press, 1995.

Funk, Nannette, and Magda Mueller, eds. *Gender Politics and Post-communism: Reflections from Eastern Europe and the Former Soviet Union*. New York: Routledge, 1993.

Fuss, Dianne, ed. *Inside/Out: Lesbian Theories, Gay Theories*. New York: Routledge, 1991.

Ghodsee, Kristen. *Why Women Have Better Sex Under Socialism and Other Argument for Economic Independence*. New York: Nation Books, 2018.

Ghodsee, Kristen and Julia Mead, "What Has Socialism Ever Done for Women?" *Catalyst* 2018, Vol. 2/2: 101–133.

Gilman, Sander. *Difference and Pathology: Stereotypes of Sexuality, Race, and Madness*. Ithaca and London: Cornell University Press, 1985.

Glassheim, Eagle. "Ethnic Cleansing, Communism, and Environmental Devastation in Czechoslovakia's Borderlands, 1945–1989." *The Journal of Modern History*, 78:1 (2006): 65–92.

Gluck, Sherna Berger and Daphne Patai, eds. *Women's Voices: The Feminist Practice of Oral History*. New York and London: Routledge, 1991.

Goffman, Erwin. 2003. *Stigma. Poznámky o způsobech zvládání narušené identity*. Praha: SLON.

Gramsci, Antonio. *Selections from the Prison Notebooks of Antonio Gramsci*. New York: International Publishers, 1972.

Halberstam, J. Jack. *Gaga Feminism: Sex, Gender and The End of Normal*. Boston: Beacon Press, 2012.

Halberstam, Judith. *Female Masculinity*. Durham: Duke University Press, 1998.

————. *In a Queer Time and Place*. = New York: University Press, 2005.

Hall, Timothy McCajor and Rosie Read, eds. *Changes in the Heart of Europe: Recent Ethnographies of Czechs, Slovaks, Roma and Sorbs*. Stuttgart: ibidem-Verlag, 2006.

Hamplová, Dana. "Stručné poznámky o ideových přístupech k rodině v období socialismu." In *Cahiers du CeFReS No 22, Česko-francouzský dialog o dějinách evropské rodiny*, edited by Mares, Antoine, and Pavla Horská. Praha, CeFReS, 2010.

Harding, Sandra. *The Science Question in Feminism*. Ithaca: Cornell University Press, 1986.

————. *Is Science Multicultural? Postcolonialisms, Feminisms, and Epistemologies*. Bloomington: Indiana University Press, 1998.

Hauer Gudrun, Doris Hauberger, Helga Pankratz, and Hans Vonk. *Rosa Liebe unterm roten Stern. Zur Lage der Lesben und Schwulen in Osteuropa*. Vienna: HOSI Wien and Christiane Gemballa Verlag, 1986.

Havel, Václav. "The Power of the Powerless," in *Open Letters*. London: Faber and Faber, 1991.

Havelková, Hana. "Abstract Citizenship? Women and Power in the Czech Republic," *Social Politics: International Studies in Gender, State and Society*, 3:2–3 (Summer/Fall 1996): 243–260.

————. "Women in and after a 'classless' society," in Christine Zmroczek and Pat Mahony, eds., *Women and Social Class — International Feminist Perspectives*, 69–84. London: Taylor and Francis Group, 1999.

Havelková, Hana. Ed., *Existuje středoevropský model manželství a rodiny? Sborník z mezinárodního sympozia*. Praha: Divadelní ústav, 1995.

Havelková, Hana, and Libora Oates-Indruchová, eds. *The Politics of Gender Culture under State Socialism: An Expropriated Voice*. London and New York: Routledge, 2014.

Healey, Dan. *Homosexual Desire in Revolutionary Russia: The Regulation of Sexual and Gender Dissent*. Chicago: University of Chicago Press, 2001.

Heimann, Mary. *Czechoslovakia: The State that Failed*. New Haven and London: Yale University Press, 2011.

Heitlinger, Alena. *Reproduction, Medicine and the Socialist State*. London: The Macmillan Press, 1987.

_____. *Women and State Socialism: Sex Inequality in the Soviet Union and Czechoslovakia*. Montreal: McGill-Queen's University Press, 1979.

Hekma, Gert. 2007. Foreword. In Kuhar, Roman, a Judit Takács, eds. *Beyond the Pink Curtain: Everyday Life of LGBT People in Eastern Europe*. Ljubljana: Mirovni Inštitut.

Herza, Filip. 2018. *Imaginations of "Otherness" and Freak Show Culture in the 19th and 20th century Prague*. Unpublished Ph.D. Dissertation, Charles University.

Herzog, Dagmar. *Sexuality in Europe: A Twentieth-Century History*. New York: Cambridge University Press, 2011.

_____. *Sex after Fascism: Memory and Morality in Twentieth-Century Germany*. Princeton: Princeton University Press, 2005.

Highleyman, Liz. "Politics of Identity." In *Bisexual Politics: Theories, Queries and Visions*, edited by Naomi. Binghamton: Harrington Park Press, 1995.

Hill Collins, Patricia. *Black Feminist Thought: Knowledge, Consciousness, and the Politics of Empowerment*. Revised tenth anniversary edition. London: Routledge, 2000.

Himl, Pavel, *Zrození vagabunda: neusedlí lidé v Čechách 17. a 18. století*. Praha, Argo, 2007.

Himl, Pavel, Jan Seidl, and Franz Schindler, eds. *"Miluji tvory svého pohlaví': Homosexualita v dějinách a společnosti českých zemí*. Praha: Argo, 2013.

Hirschfeld, Magnus. *Homosexuality of Men and Women as Biological Phenomenon*. 1914 in German, Prometheus Books, 1922 in English.

Hodos, George. *Show Trials: Stalinist Purges in Eastern Europe, 1948–1954*. New York: Greenwood Publishing Group, 1987.

Hoffmannová, Jana. "Seznamovací inzeráty mladých lidí." *Naše řeč* 68/1985: 113–124.

Holý, Ladislav. *The Little Czech and the Great Czech Nation: National Identity and the Post-communist Social Transformation*. Cambridge: Cambridge University Press, 1996.

Homophobic Bullying. Safe to Learn: Embedding Anti-bullying Work in Schools. Nottingham: DCSF Publications, 2007.

Honneth, Axel. *The Critique of Power*. Cambridge, MIT Press, 1991.

Hroch, Miroslav. *Social Preconditions for National Revival in Europe: A Comparative Analysis of the Social Composition of Patriotic Groups Among Smaller European Nations*. New York: Columbia University Press, 2000.

Hromada, Jiří. 2000. Zakladatelé: Cesta za rovnoprávností českých gayů a lesbiček. http://gay .iniciativa.cz/www/index.php?page=clanek&id=266.

Jäger, Siegfried. "Discourse and Knowledge: Theoretical and Methodological Aspects of a Critical Discourse and Dispositive Analysis." In *Methods of Critical Discourse Analysis* edited by Ruth Wodak and Michael Meyer, 31–62. London: Sage Publications, 2001.

Jagose, Anamarie. "Limity Identity," in *Lesby-by-by: Aspekty polititiky identít*, edited by Hanna Hacker. Bratislava: Aspekt, 2004.

Jancar, Barbara. *Czechoslovakia and the Absolute Monopoly of Power: A Study of Political Power in a Communist System*. New York: Praeger Publishers, 1971.

Janošová, Pavlína. *Homosexualita v názorech současné společnosti*. Praha: Karolinum, 2000.

Jensen, Erik N. 2002. "The Pink Triangle and Political Consciousness: Gays, Lesbians, and the Memory of Nazi Persecution." *Journal of the History of Sexuality* 11/1,2: 319–349.

Johnson, Lonnie. *Central Europe: Enemies, Neighbors, Friends*. Oxford: Oxford University Press, 1997.

Jörgens, Frédéric. 2007. "East" Berlin: Lesbian and Gay Narratives on Everyday Life, Social Acceptance, and Past and Present. In Kuhar, Roman, a Judit Takács, eds. *Beyond the Pink Curtain: Everyday Life of LGBT People in Eastern Europe*. Ljubljana: Mirovni Inštitut.

Kaiser, Charles. *The Gay Metropolis: The Landmark History of Gay Life in America*. New York: Grove Press, 2007.

Kaplan, Karel. *The Communist Party in Power: A Profile of Party Politics in Czechoslovakia.* Boulder and London: Westview Press, 1987.

———. *O cenzuře v Československu v letech 1945-1956.* Praha: Ústav soudobých dějin, 1994.

Katz, Jonathan. 1990. The Invention of Heterosexuality. *Socialist Review* 20: 6-30.

———. 1995. *The Invention of Heterosexuality.* New York: Dutton Books.

Kenawi, Samirah, 1995. *Frauengruppen in der DDR der 80er Jahre. Eine Dokumentation.* Berlin: GrauZone.

Kennedy, Elizabeth Lapovsky and Madeleine D. Davis. *Boots of Leather, Slippers of Gold: The History of a Lesbian Community. 20th Anniversary Edition.* New York and London: Routledge, 2014.

Kershaw, Ian. "Totalitarianism Revisited: Nazism and Stalinism in Comparative Perspective," in Ian Kershaw, ed., *The Nazi Dictatorship: Problems and Perspectives of Interpretation.* London, Baltimore: Edward Arnold, 1985 and 2000.

Kevill-Davies, Harriette. "Children Crusading against Communism: Mobilizing Boys as Citizen Soldiers in the Early Cold War State." *Rhetoric and Public Affairs* 21/2 (2018): 235-78.

Kinsey, Alfred. *The Sexual Behavior in the Human Male.* Philadelphia: W.B. Saunders Company, 1948.

———. *The Sexual Behavior in the Human Female.* Philadelphia: W.B. Saunders Company, 1953.

Kiczková, Zuzana, and kol. *Pamäť žien. O skúsenosti sebautvárania v biografických rozhovorech.* Bratislava: Iris, 2006.

Kligman, Gail. *The Politics of Duplicity: Controlling Reproduction in Ceaucescu's Romania.* Berkeley: University of California Press, 1998.

Kligman, Gail, and Susan Gal, eds. *Reproducing Gender: Politics, Publics, and the Everyday Life after Socialism.* Princeton: Princeton University Press, 2000.

Klímová, Barbora. 2006. *Replaced* (Kat.) Brno: autorská edice.

Kolář, Michal. *Skrytý svět šikanování ve školách.* Praha, Portál, 1997.

———. *Bolest šikanování.* Praha, Portál, 2001.

Kolářová, Kateřina. "AIDS sem, AIDS tam aneb: Hroutíme se z tempa doby. Role genderového diskurzu ve vyjednávání ideologického konsenzu v pozdně socialistickém Československu," in *Proměny genderové kultury v české společnosti, 1948-1989,* edited by Hana Havelková and Libora Oates-Indruchová. Praha: SLON, 2013.

———. "Homosexuální asociál a jeho zavirované tělo: vir HIV a nemoc AIDS v socialistickém diskurzu (Československo 1983-89," in *'Miluji tvory svého pohlaví': Homosexualita v dějinách a společnosti českých zemí,* edited by Pavel Himl, Jan Seidl and Franz Schindler. Praha: Academia, 2013.

———. "Já a moje Láska." Nad deníky Michaela Fielda Works and Days," in *Vztahy, jazyky, těla,* edited by Libuše Heczková, 405-424. Praha: FHS, 2007.

Kolářová, Kateřina, and Věra Sokolová, eds. *Gender and Generation: Interdisciplinary Intersections and Approaches.* Praha: Litteraria Pragensia, 2007.

Konrad, Geörgy. *Antipolitics: An Essay.* Longon: Quartet, 1984.

Košela, Josef. 1981. *Homosexualita a její trestnost.* Diplomová práce. Brno: Univerzita Jana Evangelisty Purkyně, Právnická fakulta.

Koukal, Luboš. "S negativními reakcemi jsem se nesetkala. Rozhovor s 'mámou homosexuálů' — MUDr. Dagmar Bártovou." *Lambda* 1/9 (1990): 3.

Kovály, Heda Margolius. *Under a Cruel Star: A Life in Prague, 1941-1968.* New York: Holmes and Meier, 1986.

Krafft-Ebing, Richard von, *Psychopatia Sexualis.* Stutgart: F. Enke, 1886.

Kramářová, Jana, a kol. 2005. *(Ne)bolí: Vzpomínky Romů na válku a život po válce.* Praha: Člověk v tísni.

Kubiš, Karel, ed. *Obrazy druhého v historické perspektivě: Identity a stereotypy při formování moderní společnosti.* Praha: Univerzita Karlova, 2003.

Kučera, Milan. "Rodinná politika a její demografické důsledky v Socialistickém Československu." In *Cahiers du CeFReS No 22, Česko-francouzský dialog o dějinách evropské rodiny,* edited by Mares, Antoine, and Pavla Horská. Praha, CeFReS, 2010.

Kubik, Jan. *The Power of Symbols Against the Symbols of Power*. University Park: Pennsylvania State University Press, 1994.

Kuhar, Roman. *Media Representations of Homosexuality: An Analysis of the Print Media in Slovenia, 1970-2000*. Ljublana: Mirovni inštitut, 2003.

Kuhar, Roman, and Judit Takács, eds. *Beyond the Pink Curtain: Everyday Life of LGBT People in Eastern Europe*. Ljubljana: Mirovni Inštitut, 2007.

Kulpa, Robert and Joanna Mizielinska, eds. *De-centring Western Sexualities: Central and Eastern European Perspectives*. London: Routledge, 2016.

Lacqueur, Thomas. *Making Sex: Body and Gender from the Greeks to Freud*. Cambridge: Harvard University Press, 1990.

Lebsock, Suzanne. *The Free Women of Petersburg: Status and Culture in a Southern Town 1784-1860*. Chapel Hill: University of North Carolina Press, 1984.

Leff, Caroll S. *National Conflict in Czechoslovakia: The Making and Remaking of a State, 1918-1987*. Princeton: Princeton University Press, 1988.

Leiner, Marvin. *Sexual Politics in Cuba: Machismo, Homosexuality and AIDS*. Boulder: Westview Press, 1994.

Lemke, Jürgen. *Gay voices from East Germany*. Bloomington: Indiana University Press, 1991.

Lenderová, Milena. *K hříchu i k modlitbě: Žena v minulém století*. Praha: Mladá Fronta, 1999.

————.*Chytila Patrola aneb Prostituce za Rakouska a I. republiky*. Praha: Karolinum, 2002.

————. "Zpovědní zrcadla jako pramen k sexualitě druhé polovině 19. století." In *Sex a tabu v české kultuře 19. století*, 94-103. Praha: Academia, 1999.

Lenderová, Milena, Božena Kopičková, and Eduard Maur, *Žena v českých zemích od středověku do 20. století*. Praha: Nakladatelství Lidové noviny, 2009.

Lišková, Kateřina. *Sexual Liberation, Socialist Style: Communist Czechoslovakia and the Science of Desire, 1945-1989*. Cambridge: Cambridge University Press, 2018.

————. "Perverzní sex a normální gender. Normalizační sexuologie promlouvá o sexu a gender," *Gender, rovné příležitosti, výzkum* 13/2 (2012): 40-49.

Ludvíková, Alena. *Až budu velká, napíšu román. Deník matky a dcery z doby protektorátu*. Praha: GplusG, 2006.

Maleck-Lewy, Ewa, and Myra Marx Ferree. "Talking about Women and Wombs: The Discourse of Abortion and Reproductive Rights in the G.D.R. during and after the *Wende*." In *Reproducing Gender: Politics, Publics, and Everyday Life after Socialism*, edited by Susan Gal and Gail Kligman. Princeton, N.J.: Princeton University Press, 2000.

Malečková, Jitka. *Úrodná půda: žena ve službách národa*. Praha: ISV nakladatelství, 2002.

————. "Nation and Scholarship: Reflections on Gender/Women's Studies in the Czech Republic." In *New Frontiers in Women's Studies: Knowledge, Identity and Nationalism*, edited by Mary Maynard and June Purvis. London: Taylor and Francis, 1995.

Malínská, Jana. *Do politiky prý žena nesmí — proč? Vzdělávání a postavení žen v české společnosti v 19. a na počátku 20. Století*. Praha: SLON, 2005.

Malý, Karel, and Ladislav Soukup, eds. *Vývoj práva v Československu v letech 1945-1989*. Praha: Karolinum, 2004.

Malý, Karel. "Vývoj práva v Československu v letech 1989-2004 jako předmět vědeckého zkoumání. Úvodní slovo při zahájení conference." In *Vývoj práva v Československu v letech 1945-1989*, edited by Karel Malý and Ladislav Soukup. Praha: Karolinum, 2004.

Mares, Antoine, and Pavla Horská, eds. *Cahiers du CeFReS No 22, Česko-francouzský dialog o dějinách evropské rodiny*. Praha, CeFReS, 2010.

Mazierska, Ewa. 2008. *Masculinities in Polish, Czech and Slovak Cinema: Black Peters and Men of Marble*. New York and Oxford: Berghahn Books.

McLellan, Josie. "State Socialist Bodies: East German Nudism from Ban to Boom," *The Journal of Modern History* 79/1 (2007): 48-79.

Michnik, Adam. *Letters from Prison and Other Essays*. Berkeley: University of California Press, 1986.

Miller, Neil. *Out of the Past: Gay and Lesbian History from 1869 to the Present*. New York: Alyson Books, 2006.

Miller, Patrick R., Andrew R. Flores, Donald P. Haider-Markel, Daniel C. Lewis, Barry L. Tadlock and Jami K. Taylor. "Transgender Politics as Body Politics: Effects of Disgust Sensitivity and Authoritarianism on Transgender Rights Attitudes," *Politics, Groups, and Identities*, 5:1, 4–24.

Miřácký, Radek. *Proces coming-outu u homosexuálních mužů v Československu před rokem 1989*. Bakalářská práce. Praha: Fakulta humanitních studií, 2009.

Mikats, Jana, Susanne Kink-Hampersberger and Libora Oates-Indruchova, eds. *Creative Families: Gender and Technologies of Everyday Life*. London: Palgrave Macmillan, 2021.

Mlynář, Zdeněk. *Československý pokus o reformu 1968: Analýza jeho teorie a praxe*. Cologne: Index, 1985.

Móda: Z dějin odívání 18., 19. a 20. století. Praha: Slovart, 2011.

Money, John. *The Psychological Study of Man*. Chicago: Thomas, 1957.

Moraga, Cherríe, and Gloria Anzaldúa. *This Bridge Called My Back: Writings by Radical Women of Color*. Fourth edition. Albany: SUNY Press, 2015.

Moyano, Nieves, Maria del Mar Sánchez-Fuentes, " Homophobic Bullying at Schools: A systematic Review of Research, Prevalence, School-related Predictors and Consequences," *Aggression and Violent Behavior* 2020, Vol. 53. Article 101441.

Musilová, Dana. *Z ženského pohledu. Poslankyně a senátorky Národního shromáždění Československé republiky*. Hradec Králové: Univerzita Hradec Králové, 2007.

Nash, Rebecca. "Exhaustion from Explanation: Reading Czech Gender Studies in the 1990s," *The European Journal of Women's Studies* 9/3 (2002): 291–309.

Nečasová, Denisa. *Buduj vlast, posílíš mír: ženské hnutí v českých zemích, 1945-1955*. Brno: Matice Moravská, 2011.

_____. "Dějiny žen či gender history? Možnosti, limity, východiska." *Dějiny-teorie-kritika* 1 (2008): 81–102.

Nedbálková, Kateřina. *Matky kuráže: lesbické rodiny v pozdně moderní společnosti*. Praha: SLON, 2012.

_____. "The Changing Space of the Gay and Lesbian Community in the Czech Republic." In *Beyond the Pink Curtain: Everyday Life of LGBT People in Eastern Europe*, edited by Roman Kuhar and Judit Takács, 67–80. Ljubljana: Mirovni Inštitut, 2007.

_____. *Spoutaná Rozkoš: (re) produkce genderu a sexuality v ženské věznici. (Praha: SLON, 2006).*

Neudorflová, Marie. *České ženy v 19. století. Úsilí a sny, úspěchy i zklamání na cestě k emancipaci*. Praha: Janua, 1999.

Oakley, Ann. *Sex, Gender and Society*. New York: Maurice Temple Smith, Ltd, 1972.

Oates-Indruchová, Libora. *Censorship in Czech and Hungarian Academic Publishing, 1969-1989: Snakes and Ladders*. London and New York: Bloomsbury Academic, 2020.

_____."The Beauty and the Loser: Cultural Representations of Gender in Late State Socialism," *Signs* 37/2. (2012): 357–383.

_____. "The Limits of Thought?: Regulatory Framework of Social Sciences and Humanities in Czechoslovakia (1968-1989)," *Europe-Asia Studies*, 60/10 (2008): 1767–1782.

_____. *Discourses of Gender in Pre- and Post-1989 Czech Culture*. Pardubice: Univerzita Pardubice, 2002.

_____. "Gender v médiích: nástin sire problematiky." In *Společnost žen a mužů z aspektu gender*, edited by Eva Věšínová-Kalivodová, 131–152. Praha: Open Society Fund, 1999.

Otáhal, Milan, and Miroslav Vaněk. *Sto studentských revolucí*. Praha: Nakladatelství Lidové noviny, 1999.

Padgug, Robert. "Sexual Matters: On Conceptualizing Sexuality in History," *Radical History Review* 20:2/1979, 3–23.

Parry, Jean, and Gillian. Carrington. *Čelíme šikanování. Metodický materiál*. Praha: IPPP ČR, 1995.

Parsons, Talcott, and Robert Bales. *Family, Socialisation and Interaction Process*. London: Glencoe Press, 1955.

Pechová, Olga, "Diskriminace na základě sexuální orientace." *E-psychologie* 3:3 (2009): 1–16.

Pence, Katherine, and Paul Betts, eds. *Socialist Modern: East German Everyday Culture and Politics*. Ann Arbor: University of Michigan Press, 2008.

Pharr, Suzanne, *Homophobia: A Weapon of Sexism*. New York: Chardonne Press, 1997.

Phillips, Nelson, and Cynthia Hardy. *Discourse Analysis: Investigating Processes of Social Construction*. London: Sage Publications, 2002.

Pisankaneva, Monika. 2005. "The Forbidden Fruit: Sexuality in Communist Bulgaria." *E-magazine LiterNet* 68/7: 1–10.

Podmore, Julie A. "Gone 'Underground'? Lesbian Visibility and the Consolidation of Queer Space in Montréal," *Social & Cultural Geography*, 2006: 7/4, 595–625.

Polášková, Eva. *Plánovaná lesbická rodina: klíčové aspekty přechodu k rodičovství*. Brno: Masaryk University Press, 2009.

Porybný, Zdeněk. "Můj Listopad v *Rudém právu*". ("My November in *Rudé právo*"), *Právo*, Dec. 30, 2009.

Pošová, Kateřina. *Jsem, protože musím… napsala jsem si ve čtrnácti do lágrového deníku*. Praha: Prostor, 2003.

Postavení lesbické ženy v České společnosti. Praha: Alia, 1997.

Prajerová, Andrea. *Za hranicemi: Analýza potratových diskurzů v (ne)demokratickém Československu*. M.A. Thesis. Prague: FHS UK, 2012.

Procházka, Ivo. "Czech and Slovak Republics." In *Sociolegal Control of Homosexuality: A Multi-nation Comparison*, edited by Donald James West and Richard Green, 243–254. New York: Plenum Press, 1997.

Procházka, Ivo, David Janík, and Jiří Hromada. *Společenská diskriminace lesbických žen, gay mužů a bisexuálů v ČR*. Praha: Gay iniciativa, 2003.

Prosser, Jay. *Second Skins: The Body Narratives of Transsexuality*. New York: Columbia University Press, 1998.

Průcha, Jan. *Multikulturní výchova: Teorie, praxe, výzkum*. Praha: nakladatelství ISV, 2001.

Pullmann, Michal. *Konec experimentu. Přestavba a pád komunismu v Československu*. Praha: Scriptorium, 2011.

Putna, Martin, and Milena Bartlová, eds. *Homosexualita v dějinách české kultury*. Praha: Academia, 2011.

Raková, Svatava. *Víra, rasa a etnicita v koloniální Americe*. Praha: Nakladatelství Lidové noviny, 2005.

Ratajová, Jana."Dějiny ženy a koncept genderu v české historiografii," *Kuděj* 1/2 (2005): 159–174.

Rauvolf, Josef. "Viděl jsem nejlepší hlavy…," *Lidové noviny* 8.1. 2011: 28.

Renzetti, Claire and Daniel Curran. *Women, Men, and Society*. Boston: Allyn and Bacon, 2012.

Renzetti, Claire, and Charles Harvey Miley, eds. *Violence in Gay and Lesbian Domestic Partnerships*. New York: Harrington Park Press, 1996.

Říčan, Pavel. *Agresivita a šikana mezi dětmi*. Praha: Portál, 1995.

Řídký, Josef. "'Neexistuje dobře přizpůsobený a šťastný homosexuál.' Pozice homosexuality v českých populárně sexuologických příručkách 30.-90. let 20. století." In *"Miluji tvory svého pohlaví': Homosexualita v dějinách a společnosti českých zemí*, edited by Pavel Himl, Jan Seidl, and Franz Schindler. Praha: Argo, 2013.

Ristock, Janice. *No More Secrets: Violence in Lesbian Relationships*. New York: Routledge Press, 2002.

Roberts, Dorothy. *Killing the Black Body: Race, Reproduction and the Meaning of Liberty*. New York: Vintage, 1999.

Rodríguez, Irina. *My Soviet Youth: A Memoir of Ukrainian Life in the Final Years of Communism*. Jefferson, North Carolina: McFarland & Co., 2019.

Roubal, Petr. *Spartakiads: The Politics of Physical Culture in Communist Czechoslovakia*. Prague: Karolinum, 2019.

Rupnik, Jacques. *Dějiny komunistické strany Československa: od počátků do převzetí moci*. Praha: Academia, 2002.

Rupp, Leila. *A Desired Past: A Short History of Same-Sex Sexuality in America*. Chicago: University of Chicago Press, 1999.

_____. "Thinking About "Lesbian History" *Feminist Studies* 39/2, 2013: 357-36.

Russell, Stephen T. and Stacey S. Horn, eds. *Sexual Orientation, Gender Identity, and Schooling: the Nexus of Research, Practice, and Policy*. Oxford Univresity Press, 2017.

Ryan, Caitlin, and Ian Rivers. "Lesbian, Gay, Bisexual and Transgender Youth: Victimization and its Correlates in the USA and UK." *Culture, health and sexuality* 5:2 (2003): 103-119.

Rychlíková, Monika. 2002... *to jsou těžké vzpomínky (Holocaust Romů)*. DVD. Brno a Praha: Muzeum romské kultury a Asociace Film a sociologie.

Salas, Luis. *Social Control and Deviance in Cuba*. Westport, Praeger Publishers, 1979.

Salecl, Renata. *The Spoils of Freedom: Psychoanalysis and Feminism after the fall of Socialism*. New York: Routledge, 1994.

Sangster, Joan. "Telling Our Stories: Feminist Debates and the Use of Oral History," *Women's History Review* 3/1, 1994: 5-28.

Schindler, Franz. "Život gayů za socialismu." In "'*Miluji tvory svého pohlaví': Homosexualita v dějinách a společnosti českých zemí*, edited by Pavel Himl, Jan Seidl, and Franz Schindler. Praha: Argo, 2013.

Scott, Joan Wallach. *Gender and the Politics of History*. New York: Columbia University Press, 1988.

_____. "Gender: A Useful Category of Historical Analysis, *The American Historical Review* 91/5 (1986): 1053-1075.

_____. "The Evidence of Experience." *Critical Inquiry* 17/4 (1991): 773-797.

Sedgwick, Eve Kosofsky, *Epistemology of the Closet*. Berkeley: University of California Press, 1990.

Seidl, Jan, a kol. *Od žaláře k oltáři: Emancipace homosexuality v českých zemích od roku 1867 do současnosti*. Brno: Host, 2012.

Seidl, Jan, ed. *Teplá Praha: průvodce po queer historii hlavního města 1380-2000*. Brno: Černé pole, 2014.

Seidman, Steven. "Identity and Politics in a Postmodern Gay Culture: Some Historical and Conceptual Notes." In *Fear of a Queer Planet: Queer Politics and Social Theory*, edited by Michael Warner. Minneapolis: University of Minnesota Press, 1993.

Sex a tabu v české kultuře 19. století. Praha: Academia, 1999.

Snitow, Ann, Christine Stansell, a Sharon Thompson, eds. 1983. *Powers of Desire: The Politics of Sexuality*. New York: Monthly Review Press.

Scott, Hilda. *Does Socialism Liberate Women? Experiences from Eastern Europe*. Boston: Bacon Press, 1974.

Scott, Joan Wallach. "The Evidence of Experience," *Critical Inquiry* 17/4 (1991): 773-797.

_____. "Gender: A Useful Category of Historical Analysis," *The American Historical Review* 91/5 (1986): 1053-1075.

Stacey, Judith and Timothy J. Biblarz. "(How) Does the Sexual Orientation of Parents Matter?," *American Sociological Review*, 2001: 66/2, 159-83.

Staar, Richard. *Communist Regimes in Eastern Europe*. Stanford: Stanford University Press, 1982.

Sibalis, Michael. "Urban Space and Homosexuality: The Example of the Marais, Paris' "Gay Ghetto"', *Urban Studies* 2004: 41/9, 1739-1758.

Šiklová, Jiřina. "The Grey Zone and the Future of Dissent in Czechoslovakia." *Social Research* 57/1990: 347-363.

Šimáčková, Kateřina, Barbora Havelková, Pavla Špondrová, eds. *Mužské právo: jsou právní pravidla neutrální?* Prague: Wolters Cluwer, 2020.

Šimečka, Milan. *The Restoration of Order: The Normalization of Czechoslovakia, 1969-1976*. New York: Verso, 1984.

Šmausová, Gerlinda. "Proti tvrdošíjné představě o ontické povaze gender a pohlaví." *Politika rodu a sexuální identity*. Sociální studia 7 (2000): 15-27.

————. "Rasa jako rasistická konstrukce," *Sociologický časopis*, 35/4 (1999): 433–446.

Šmejkalová, Jiřina. "Gender as an Analytical Category of Post-Communist Studies," in G. Jahnert, J. Gohrisch, D. Hahn, H. M. Nickel, I. Peinl a K. Schafgen, eds., *Gender in Transition in Eastern and Central Europe Proceedings*. Berlin: Trafo Verlag, 2001.

————. "Zpráva o knihách zapomnění, " *Aspekt* 1/1999, 193.

Smetáčková, Irena, and Richard Braun. *Homofobie v žákovských kolektivech: homofobní obtěžování a šikana na základních a středních školách*. Praha, Úřad vlády ČR, 2009.

Šmausová, Gerlinda. „Rasa jako rasistická konstrukce," *Sociologický časopis* 1999, 35/4: 433–446.

Šmídová, Olga. "Vlastnictví a kvazi-vlastnictví bytů za socialismu a jejich postsocialistická mutace." In *Původní a noví vlastníci*, edited by Anne Olivier. Praha: Cahiers du CEFRES. N° 11, 2012.

Smith-Rosenberg, Carroll. "The Female World of Love and Ritual: Relations between Women in Nineteenth-Century America." *Signs* 1/1 (1975): 1–29.

Sokolova, Vera. *The cultural politics of ethnicity: discourses on Roma in Communist Czechoslovakia*. Stuttgart: ibidem-Verlag, 2008.

————. "Identity Politics and the (B)Orders of Heterosexism: Gays, Lesbians and Feminists in the Czech Media after 1989." In *Mediale Welten in Tschechien nach 1989: Genderprojektionen & Codes des Plebejismus*, edited by Jirina van Leeuwen-Turnovcová and Nicole Richter, 29–44. München: Kubon und Sagner, 2006.

————. "'Don't Get Pricked!': Representation and the Politics of Sexuality in the Czech Republic." In *Over the Wall/After the Fall: Post-Communist Cultures Through an East-West Gaze*, edited by Sibelan Forrester, Magdalena Zaborowska, and Elena Gapova. Bloomington, Indiana: Indiana University Press, 2004.

————. "Representations of Homosexuality and the Separation of Gender and Sexuality in the Czech Republic before and after 1989," in in *Political Systems and Definitions of Gender Roles*, edited by Katherine Isaacs, 273–290. Pisa, Italy: Edizione Plus, Universita di Pisa, 2001.

Sokolová, Věra, and Simona Fojtová. "Strategies of Inclusion and Shifting Attitudes torwards Visibility in the Gay, Lesbian, and Queer Discourse in the Czech Republic after 1989." In *Queer Visibility in Post-Socialist Cultures*, eds. by Narcisz Fejes and Andrea P. Balogh, pp. 105–129. Chicago and Bristol: Intellect Books, 2013.

Sokolová, Věra, and Lubica Kobová, eds. *The Courage to Disagree: Feminist Thought of Hana Havelková and its Reflections,*. Prague, FHS UK: 2019.

Sokolová, Věra, and Kateřina Kolářová. "Gender and Generation in Mutual Perspective." In *Gender and Generation: Interdisciplinary Intersections and Approaches*, edited by Kateřina Kolářová and Věra Sokolová, 1–20. Praha: Litteraria Pragensia, 2007.

Staněk, Josef. Zn. *"Jen Upřímně a vážně." Hierarchie hodnot v seznamovacím inzerátu*. Praha: Mladá fronta, 1977.

Stárek, František Čuňás, and Jiří Kostúr. *Baráky - souostroví svobody*. Praha: Pulchra, 2011.

Stehlíková, Džamila, Ivo Procházka, and Jiří Hromada. *AIDS, homosexualita a společnost*. Praha: Orbis, 1995.

Strayer, Robert. *Why Did the Soviet Union Collapse?: Understanding Historical Change*. New York: M.E. Sharpe, 1998.

Strnadová, Tereza. 2009. Zemřela „matka brněnských gayů," sexuoložka Dagmar Bártová. *www.brnoidnes.cz*, 17. dubna: 1–2.

Stulhofer, Aleksandar, and Theo Sandfort. *Sexuality and Gender in Postcommunist Eastern Europe and Russia*. New York: Haworth Press, 2005.

Talandová, Jaroslava. *Sociální postavení lesbických žen a alternativní modely v kontextu heterosexuální společnosti*. Praha: L-klub, 1997.

Taylor, Charles. *Sources of the Self: the Making of the Modern Identity*. Cambridge, MA: Harvard University Press, 1989.

Thompson, Paul, with Joanna Bornat, The Voice of the Past: Oral History, 4th edition. Oxford: Oxford University Press, 2017.

Tinková, Daniela. *Hřích, zločin, šílenství v čase odkouzlování světa.* Praha: Argo, 2004;

_____. *Tělo, věda, stát. Zrození porodnice v osvícenecké Evropě.* Praha: Argo, 2010.

_____. "Žena" – prázdná kategorie? Od (wo)men's history k gender history v západoevropské historiografii posledních desetiletí 20. století," In *Dějiny žen aneb Evropská žena od středověku do poloviny 20. století v zajetí historiografie,* edited by Kateřina Čadková, Milena Lenderová, and Jana Stráníková, 19–32. Pardubice: Univerzita Pardubice, 2006.

Toomey, Russell B., Caitlin Ryan, Rafael Diaz, Noel Card, and Stephen Rusell. "Gender-Nonconforming Lesbian, Gay, Bisexual, and Transgender Youth: School Victimization and Young Adult Psychosocial Adjustment," *Developmental Psychology* (Advance online publication. doi: 10.1037/a0020705, 2010: 1–11.

Trestní právo České republiky. Praha: Fakulta Právní Univerzity Karlovy, 1995.

Turcescu, Lucian, and Lavinia Stan, "Religion, Sexuality and Politics in Romania," in *Europe-Asia Studies* 57:2 (3005): 291–310.

Urbášek, Pavel, a Miroslav Vaněk. 2005. *Vítězové? Poražení? Životopisná interview. Dissent a politické elity v období tzv. normalizace.* Praha: Prostor.

Valenta, Zdeněk, and Vladimír Zápotočný, "Martina Navrátilová Američankou," *Radio Praha, Český rozhlas 7,* January 27, 2001.

Vaněk, Miroslav. 2009. *Obyčejní lidé.* Praha: Academia.

_____. *Orální historie ve výzkumu soudobých dějin.* Praha: Ústav pro soudobé dějiny AV ČR, 2004.

Vaněk, Miroslav and Pavel Mücke, *Velvet Revolutions: An Oral History of Czech Society.* Oxford: Oxford University Press, 2016.

Vaněk, Miroslav, Pavel Mücke, a Hana Pelikánová. 2007. *Naslouchat hlasům paměti: Teoretické a praktické aspekty orální historie.* Praha: Ústav pro soudobé dějiny AV ČR.

Vévoda, Rudolf. "Státní bezpečnost a perzekuce homosexuálů v 70. a 80. Letech minulého století." Lecture presented during the *Queer History Month* at Society for Queer Memory, April 1, 2016.

Vodochodský, Ivan, and Petra Klvačová. "Obraz manželství v předlistopadové populárně naučné literatuře." In *Proměny genderové kultury v české společnosti, 1948-1989,* edited by Hana Havelková and Libora Oates-Indruchová. Praha: SLON, 2013.

Vittvarová, Zuzana. *Osudová kaňka: Příběhy dcer politických vězňů Československa.* Praha: Pavel Mervart, 2011.

Wagnerová, Alena, *Die Frau im Sozialismus, Beispiel ČSSR.* Hamburg: Hoffmann und Campe, 1974.

Warner, Michael. *The Trouble with Normal: Sex, Politics, and the Ethics of Queer Life.* Cambridge, MA: Harvard University Press, 1999.

Warner, Michael, ed. *Fear of a Queer Planet: Queer Politics and Social Theory.* Minneapolis: University of Minnesota Press, 1993.

Weeks, Jeffrey. *Coming Out: Homosexual Politics in Britain from the Nineteenth Century to the Present.* London: Quartet Books, 1977.

Weinerman, Richard. *Social Medicine in Eastern Europe: The Organization of Health Services and the Education of Medical Personnel in Czechoslovakia, Hungary and Poland.* Cambridge, MA: Harvard University Press, 1969.

Weiss, Petr, et al. *Sexuologie.* Praha: Grada, 2010.

West, Donald James, and Richard Green, eds. *Sociolegal Control of Homosexuality: A Multi-nation Comparison.* New York: Plenum Press, 1997.

Wierling, Dorothee. "Youth as Internal Enemy: Conflicts in Education Dictatorship in the 1960s," in *Socialist Modern: East German Everyday Culture and Politics,* edited by Katherine Pence and Paul Betts, 157–182. Ann Arbor: University of Michigan Press, 2008, 157–182.

_____. "The East as the Past: Problems with Memory and Identity," *German Politics and Society* 15/2 (1997): 53 – 71.

Williams, Kieran. *The Prague Spring and Its Aftermath: Czechoslovak Politics, 1968-1970*. New York: Cambridge University Press, 1997.

Wing, Sue. *Microaggressions in Everyday Life: Race, Gender, and Sexual Orientation*. Hoboken, New Jersey: Wiley, 2010.

Wolchik, Sharon, and Alfred Meyer, eds. *Women, State and Party in Eastern Europe*. Durham: Duke University Press, 1985.

Zábrodská, Kateřina, "Between Femininity and Feminism: Negotiating the Identity of a 'Czech Socialist Woman' in Biographical Interviews." In *Proměny genderové kultury v české společnosti, 1948-1989*, edited by Hana Havelková and Libora Oates-Indruchová. Praha: SLON, 2013.

Zvěřina, Jaroslav, "Historie sexuologie." In *Sexuologie*, edited by Petr Weiss et al., 1-10. Praha: Grada, 2010.

Žižek, Slavoj. *The Sublime Object of Ideology*. New York: Verso, 1989.

INDEX